Counterpoints

Counterpoints:

Selected Essays on Authoritarianism and Democratization

Guillermo O'Donnell

UNIVERSITY OF NOTRE DAME PRESS

NOTRE DAME, INDIANA

Manufactured in the United States of America

The author and publisher are grateful for permission to reprint material from the following sources:

"State and Alliances in Argentina, 1956–1976" first appeared in the *Journal of Development Studies*, vol. 15, no. 1, 1979.

"Tensions in the Bureaucratic-Authoritarian State and the Question of Democracy" appeared in David Collier, ed., *The New Authoritarianism in Latin America.* Copyright © 1979 by Princeton University Press. Reprinted by permission of Princeton University Press.

"Democracy in Argentina: Macro and Micro" appeared in *El "Proceso" crisis y transción democrática*, ed. Oscar Oszlak, published by Centro Editor de América Latina, SA.

"On the Fruitful Convergences of Hirschman's *Exit, Voice, and Loyalty* and *Shifting Involvements*" appeared in *Development, Democracy, and the Art of Trespassing*, ed. Alejandro Foxley, Michael S. McPherson, and Guillermo O'Donnell. Copyright © 1986 by University of Notre Dame Press.

"Notes for the Study of Processes on Political Democratization in the Wake of the Bureaucratic-Authoritarian State" appeared as working paper 2, no. 9, 1979, C.E.D.E.S.

"On the State, Democratization, and Some Conceptual Problems" is reprinted from *World Development*, vol. 21, no. 8, 1993, with permission from *Elsevier Science*.

"Delegative Democracy" and "Illusions about Consolidation" appeared in the *Journal of Democracy*, vol. 5, no. 1, 1994, and vol. 7, no. 2, 1996, respectively.

"Poverty and Inequality in Latin America: Some Political Reflections" appeared in *Poverty and Inequality in Latin America,* ed. Víctor E. Tokman and Guillermo O'Donnell. Copyright © 1998 by the University of Notre Dame Press.

Library of Congress Cataloging-in-Publication Data

O'Donnell, Guillermo A.
    Counterpoints : selected essays on authoritarianism and
democratization / Guillermo O'Donnell.
        p.   cm.—(A title from the Helen Kellogg Institute for
International Studies)
    Includes bibliographical references.
    ISBN 0-268-00837-X (cloth : alk. paper).—ISBN 0-268-00838-8
(pbk. : alk. paper)
        1. Authoritarianism—Argentina.   2. Democratization—Argentina.
3. Argentina—Politics and government—1955–1983.   4. Argentina—
Social conditions—1945–1983.   I. Title.   II. Series.
    HM271.032   1999
    320.53'0982—dc21   98-48107

For David Apter, my principal mentor at Yale, in thankful remembrance of his intellectual stimulation and gratitude for the generosity with which he dedicated many hours to helping me improve the original version of my first book

Contents

PART III
Transitions

PART IV
Perspectives

APPENDIX

Preface*

I

The texts selected for this book—written over the past two decades—are part of an intellectual trajectory that is still open. The central, almost obsessive, theme is democracy, its vicissitudes and its possibilities in Latin America. Very early I discovered that having a passionate interest in politics did not guarantee that I would be a good politician. During the agitated years of the early 1960s in Argentina (which included the overthrow of President Arturo Frondizi, battles between the "red" and "blue" factions of the armed forces, the provisional government of José María Guido, and the confused transition that in 1963 brought Arturo Illia to the presidency), I participated in processes that increased the political irrationality and the resentments that had long eroded the ability to resolve the problems of our country in a civilized manner. The resulting self-critical appraisal dissuaded me from direct participation in politics and propelled me into full-time dedication to intellectual life.

* The origin of this book lies in the prodding by friends that I put together a selection of my essays, some of which are not easily available. The book finally took shape thanks to the generous efforts of a young Argentine colleague, Sebastián Mazzuca, who made the translations and editing necessary for its publication in Spanish, *Contrapuntos. Ensayos escogidos sobre autoritarismo y democratización* (Buenos Aires: Editorial Paidós, 1997). For the present English version, Carol D. Stuart has performed, with no less dedication and skill, a similar task, translating the preface, chapter 3, and chapter 5, and editing the volume. In both cases we resisted the temptation to introduce substantial modifications in the texts; we made changes only in order to clarify a few points or avoid unnecessary repetitions. Stuart introduced several "Notes from the Editor" for the same purpose.

The translation of chapter 6 was revised and edited by John Rieger.

In 1968, during the military government of General Juan Carlos Onganía, I left for Yale University to pursue graduate studies in political science. In 1971 I returned to my country, carrying what should have been my doctoral thesis (why it was not is a long story not worth the telling). This book, *Modernization and Bureaucratic-Authoritarianism: Studies in Latin American Politics,* was published in 1973 by the Institute of International Studies of the University of California (Berkeley) and in Argentina by Editorial Paidós (its title in Spanish, *Modernización y Autoritarismo*). To my luck, this book had quite an impact.[1] It gave rise to numerous studies and discussions on "bureaucratic authoritarianism," a type of authoritarian rule that I analyzed therein (and that, from here on, I will refer to, as I did in my subsequent writings, as "BA"). In Argentina it was not this exercise that was the most influential but chapter 4 of the same book, in which I discuss the "impossible game" that the electoral proscription of peronism implied for the workings and ultimately for the survival of democracy in Argentina.

Although the title of this book refers to authoritarianism, its true theme is its opposite, democracy. This is so in a triple sense. First, in my attempts to explain the repeated misadventures of democracy in Argentina. Second, in my argument, influenced by my own experiences in politics, about the need to fully commit ourselves to democracy if we really wanted it. And, finally, in the concern expressed throughout the book for what I perceived as the high probability that BA rule would continue to spread in Latin America. Remember that in the early 1970s the apparently triumphant march of the Brazilian BA was underway, while in Argentina General Alejandro Lanusse's efforts to lead the transition after the collapse of Onganía's attempts to establish a corporatist state ended in defeat at the hand of Perón's cunning tactics. This was a period not only of growing violence but also of its almost unanimous idolization, when the animosities that had been brewing for decades erupted almost without limits. Apparent in this book, then, is my concern that the transition from the Argentine BA inaugurated in 1966 would lead to anything except democracy. The book expresses similar concerns regarding two rather old democracies, Chile and Uruguay, both also subject to acute polarization and violence. In 1973, shortly after my book was published, these countries fell prey to a long night of brutal authoritarian domination. In 1976 Argentina fell into a similar night, culminating a paroxysm of violence that evolved, after the 1976 coup, into the monstrous case of a terrorist state that for several years hid its own repression in a cloak of clandestinity.

It is difficult to depict what it was like to live in Argentina during those years of state terrorism. I will not do so now, though chapters 3, 4, and 5 of this volume are a partial attempt at this. Immediately after I published my first book, I embarked, with a group of students from the University of El Salvador, on an extensive investigation that culminated in *Bureaucratic*

Authoritarianism: Argentina, 1966–1973, in Comparative Perspective. This book, which seemed to me a natural continuation of my first one, included a detailed examination of the origins of the Argentine BA inaugurated in 1966, its internal functioning and tensions, its main economic and social impacts, and, finally, its collapse and the subsequent launching of a particularly uncertain transition that ended in 1973 with the overwhelming electoral victory of peronism. This book again expressed my concern for the cruel denouement that I was convinced would result from the extreme violence that punctuated this transition.[2] This concern led us to include in our research a detailed count of the acts of violence that were being committed during this period.[3] The violence that pervaded this transition and the resulting (1973–76) peronist governments, the numerous discourses that justified violence from almost every angle of the ideological spectrum, the fearful silence of those who disagreed with it, the lack of response to the few who dared to condemn it, and the generalized depreciation of democracy made it nearly inevitable that the transition from the relative moderation of the 1966 BA would not be to democracy but, in 1976, toward a much more cruel and exacerbated version of this same kind of authoritarian rule. The final two chapters of *Bureaucratic-Authoritarianism,* written before the coup of 1976 but when already anyone who wanted to see could have predicted it, elicit my painful and impotent vision of these processes and their likely consequences.

In the Introduction of this same book I tell the story, as melancholic as it is emblematic, of what, in one way or another, occurred to many Argentines during those fateful years. We completed our research in 1974 and I finished the book, except for a few details, shortly before the 1976 coup. After the coup, for obvious reasons, I could not publish the book in Argentina and had to bury the manuscript in a drawer. In 1979 I went to Brazil, partly for personal reasons and partly because I could not continue to endure the silences and the fear imposed by the repression then prevailing. Despite the fact that my writings attracted international attention, I decided that I would not publish this book until I could do so in my own country. This only became possible in 1982, when Editorial de Belgrano finally felt it could dare to publish it (but not to publicize it; this is surely one of the few books ever that the publisher took pains to see that it not become widely known . . .).[4]

II

I have told this story because it helps put into context the chapters that follow, all of them closely linked to the books mentioned above and to the four volumes that I later coedited with Philippe Schmitter and Laurence Whitehead. Chapter 1 of the book you now hold in your hands was originally intended to give a historical perspective to *Bureaucratic-Authoritarianism.* After the coup of 1976 I reformulated this article as an autonomous piece. It presents a long-term view of the pattern of political and social alliances that have shaped Argentina's agitated history. This text also served to ask if, and to what extent, the BA inaugurated in 1976 would succeed in destroying the strong defensive power that the Argentine popular sector had exhibited for decades. Even then, during the first couple of years of this BA and at the peak of its terrorism, it seemed to me that beyond the repression, and supported by it, was a scheme (of which Finance Minister José Martínez de Hoz and his team were emblem and executors) to vindictively dismantle the plebeian, popular, and rebellious Argentina that for decades had thwarted the oligarchic designs of this group and their supporters. My fear is that in spite of their extraordinary incompetence as economists, the goal of this group was largely met, and that it has been reinforced by the devastating economic crisis that this BA bequeathed to its successors and by the no less devastating social consequences of recent economic policies.

If chapter 1 looks primarily toward the past, the text that follows is directed toward the future. Also written during the first two years (1976–78) of the second Argentine BA, chapter 2 of the current book unites two themes. One is that of the tensions and intrinsic weaknesses of BA rule, especially in its most repressive guises. This argument (which develops ideas contained in my already published books, as well as in the as-yet-unpublished one) seemed to me particularly important during a period in which the BA projected itself, and was believed by many—not only in Argentina—to be an enduring, efficient, and potentially legitimate form of political authority.

The other theme, anticipated in the title of chapter 2, is that of democracy. What I present here is not just an exhortation but an argument regarding why the struggle for democracy (political democracy *tout court,* without adjectives) was the most appropriate way, both morally and strategically, to take advantage of the fissures and tensions that a close examination discovered behind the imposing facade of the BA. This work, like the previous ones but in a more explicit form, made even more clear in the article included here as chapter 6, has a subtext that is worth explicating. In those years, writing about the weaknesses of the BA and prospects for democracy sounded, to put it mildly, rather esoteric. The chapters contained in this section were originally mimeographed as working papers of the Centro de Estudios del Estado y la Sociedad (CEDES), a catacombs of sorts that Marcelo Cavarozzi, Elisabeth Jelin, Oscar Oszlak, and I founded shortly before the coup of 1976. This Center attracted other intellectuals who, like us, had decided to remain in Argentina as long as it was not too risky—a situation that soon ceased to exist for several of them. Our works, which we mimeographed and others photocopied, circulated in a semi-clandestinity that did not save us from visits by heavily moustached men donning the stereotypical trenchcoats of God-knows which "security" service, nor did it save us from threatening visits and telephone calls. The chapters presented here (and others found in the bibliography of the Appendix) were formally published abroad, from where, in various languages, they made a circuitous return to Argentina. That the content of these texts is strenuously critical of the domestic situation is obvious, yet some exiled Argentines accused us of being complicitous legitimators of the BA, solely because we had remained in the country.

But there was another flank. My argument that these were not fascist states but bureaucratic-authoritarian ones, and that the appropriate way to oppose them was through an unconditional commitment to democracy, sharply contradicted the positions of the revolutionary left. Its members asserted the fascist character of these systems of power—at times adding the qualifier "colonial"—and, therefore, by means of a convoluted argument that does not merit repetition here, advocated armed struggle and, through it, a leap toward some kind of revolutionary socialism. The achievement of "formal democracy" was viewed by these actors as no more than an eventual imposition of the existing "relation of forces," to be surpassed once these relations were transformed in their favor. These were tough debates, carried out in the shadow of the repression imposed by the BA, in which our opponents did have the stronger voice,[5] at least in the sense of persuading many young people to immolate themselves for the sake of their revolutionary dreams.

To live in Buenos Aires during this epoch . . . One thing I then learned was that to understand authoritarian domination it was not enough to concentrate on macro political processes, as I had done up until then. Especially under acutely repressive circumstances, in which fears are fed by constant uncertainty regarding who would be the next victim and why, one learns that the wolves are loosed: the small despots who exist among us and who, in less brutal social conditions, are forced to conceal their pathos to repress others, obtain from the state ideological support and broad permission to exercise their microdespotisms. This took place in workplaces, in schools, in the streets, and in other places where, according to the rulers and the micro-despots, many individuals had been so "infected by subversion" that they had to be eliminated or, at least, as it was repeated *ad nauseam* in the media, be "put in their place once and for all." These grim situations led me to reflect on the need to recognize, in addition to the horrors perpetrated by the macro and micro despots, certain characteristics of Argentine and Brazilian societies that in the future could weigh on the type of democracy we might achieve. Chapters 3, 4, and 5 of the present book are the result of these observations. The latter has the touch of humor made possible by the fact that I wrote it after leaving the cold night of repression in Buenos Aires and while living in the marvelous city that Rio de Janeiro, despite its many problems, continues to be.[6]

Perhaps it is not immediately evident, but these microlevel texts have continued to echo in my recent work, although now *a contrario sensu.* Although I argued—and continue to argue—for the intrinsic value of political democracy (that is, democracy quite narrowly defined according to political criteria) a definition that is limited to these factors does not seem sufficient to me. The spectacular denial of citizenship implied by state terrorism and its promotion of microdespotisms highlights the need to include in the definition of citizenship, and therefore in the definition of democracy, legal and social factors that go beyond a purely political or, to be more precise, politicist definition. This argument, however, opens up complex problems of which the texts presented in the final part of this book only scratch the surface.

III

Continuing with democracy. In part because, as we said in those times, it provided an umbrella to counter some of the winds of repression, and in part for the vanity of being recognized and discussed by my colleagues abroad, especially after the 1976 coup I cultivated diverse international contacts and activities. One of the activities that sounded most useful to me as an umbrella and, at the same time, most intellectually stimulating, was to be a member of the Advisory Board of the Latin American Program of the Woodrow Wilson Center for International Scholars, in Washington, D.C. The chair of this Board was Albert Hirschman, and the director of the program was Abraham Lowenthal. In 1978, while traveling to a meeting at the Center with another board member, Fernando Henrique Cardoso, inspired by the transitions recently initiated in Southern Europe, we told ourselves that we should propose a comparative study of transitions from different types of authoritarian regimes that would, of course, include "our" Latin American BAs. This project could be based on work that each of us had already done criticizing the authoritarianism of our respective countries and arguing for democracy as the desirable way out. As soon as we arrived in Washington we spoke with Phillippe Schmitter, our friend and fellow board member, who had been engaged in the defense of human rights during the most repressive period of the Brazilian BA and whose works pointed in a convergent direction to ours. Schmitter agreed and the three of us presented our proposal to the Board which, with decisive support from Hirschman and Lowenthal, approved it.

From today's perspective, it may seem obvious that a virtual industry on the study of transition and democratization processes would have arisen. At the time of proposing our project, however, as some people told us, proposing to study these topics from the perpetual breeding ground of authoritarianism that Latin America seemed to be was an idle dream of intellectuals who were totally marginalized in their own countries. Despite the inconveniences that this type of objection provoked (including within the Wilson Center),[7] Lowenthal's efforts secured the institutional and financial support needed to launch the project.[8] Immediately I threw myself into writing chapter 6 of the present volume. I did it with enthusiasm; after having dedicated myself for years to a theme that I detested—authoritarianism and its correlates—now I could at least speculate about a theme that gave me great pleasure, the termination of authoritarian rule and the eventual inauguration of democracy. I wrote this text in late 1978, and although it was printed in 1979 as a working paper of CEDES and served as one of the basic background documents of the Wilson Center project, for obvious reasons—given its subject matter and orientation—it could not be published in Argentina until 1982. Later we incorporated many of the ideas contained in this text, along with important contributions by Schmitter, into the book that we wrote together.[9]

This book has been criticized for its emphasis on strategic decisions, political alliances, and the great uncertainty that surrounds transitions from authoritarian rule, to the neglect of more long-term and structural factors. This debate is still open and I am not going to enter into it here.[10] Yet at that time the attainment of political democracy seemed—and indeed it was—so immensely important that we wanted to concentrate on the political processes and factors that could lead to it as quickly as possible, without having to wait the long time that changes in the structural factors tied to the emergence of the BA would have presumably required.[11] The horror of the repression suffered at both the macro and the micro levels, as well as the memory of the huge mistake committed by those who scorned democracy because they wanted to jump immediately into a revolutionary system, seemed to all of the authors during that first wave of writings on transitions to be reason enough to give a process-oriented focus to our studies.[12] The first and most important problem was getting rid of authoritarian rule and arriving at political democracy understood in terms similar to Robert Dahl's polyarchy;[13] that is, clean and competitive elections along with certain basic liberties: freedom of opinion and movement; freedom to form and belong to associations including political parties; and access to information that is not monopolized by the state. These liberties, once obtained, seem, for good reason, insufficient; but from the perspective of Latin America and many other parts of the world during the 1970s, just postulating them sounded almost ridiculously unrealistic.

IV

And so, later on (but in most cases sooner than we could have imagined) we shared with many others the immense victories implied by the termination of various authoritarian monsters. No one who participated in these great events will ever forget the joy and hope felt when finally, after the social atomization imposed by repression, we were together and could tell each other that the emperor had no clothes. But from that point on, issues that had been morally quite simple since they involved sharing an unconditional opposition to authoritarian rule became more complicated, ethically and politically.

Truly it was and continues to be important to remember that the inauguration of political democracy is an immense advance with respect to the authoritarian past. But at this point the waters begin to divide. On one side, of course, are the politically overthrown but still socially and economically powerful supporters of authoritarian rule. On the other side are, among others, those who landed in high offices in the new governments, not a few of whom have shown that their merits as opponents of authoritarianism were no guarantee that they would be good governors or advisors. They are joined by others, old or newly converted conservatives, in claiming that it is imprudent to criticize the failings of the new democracies because this plays into the hands of the unrepentant authoritarians or may disturb the "social peace" that technocratic styles of decision-making demand. There are also others, initially few but increasing in number as disillusionment has spread,[14] who are returning to old themes, condemning these democracies as "purely formal" mechanisms inherently antagonistic to aspirations of social justice.

V

When, from the depths of authoritarian rule, we dreamed of democracy we wanted one that would endure, not like the ones that had appeared and disappeared during the agitated interludes that preceded the authoritarian periods. We imagined a democracy that would be firm and strong, something "consolidated" that our children could inherit and perfect. Many antiauthoritarian struggles in the South and in the East were nourished by the dream that once the tyrants were eliminated, these countries would rather quickly generate democracies that looked similar to those found in the Northwest. This naive belief was very useful for encouraging the struggles against authoritarian regimes. But later it was at the origin of the deep disenchantment that was felt by many when a series of grim realities became evident: serious economic crises, along with technocratic and socially insensitive responses to them; the weakening of social actors who were historically important supporters of democratic advancements; the parallel weakening, if not the destruction, of a good part of the state apparatus that accompanied the crises and neoconservative policies; the persistence, and often the accentuation, of great inequalities and of social relations with a distinct authoritarian content;

and, indeed, the sad discovery that, like their authoritarian predecessors, more than a few of the democratically elected leaders had serious difficulty in distinguishing the public good from their private interests.

These problems have deep historical roots; their continuity under democratic as well as authoritarian political forms should not really surprise us. The difficulty is that we know little about how to conceptualize these problems in terms of their relationship to, and implications for, the theory and practice of democracy. In some important matters, contemporary democratic theory, which is basically a product of the historical experience of advanced capitalist countries, gives us little assistance. In particular, most of these theories have taken for granted some crucial issues, such as the effectiveness of the rule of law and of civil citizenship.[15] This I believe is a consequence of the fact that, at least for the adult male population, in the advanced capitalist countries, such issues had been largely resolved before the advent of full political democratization. Therefore, these theories do not deem it necessary to analyze the implications of the absence or severe curtailment of the rule of law and civil citizenship. In other words, such questions have remained largely exogenous to the theory of polyarchy, or political democracy. But many new polyarchies, in Latin America and elsewhere, show that the lack or the intermittent effectiveness of the social and legal conditions of citizenship are extremely important. The omission of this consideration, combined with the frequent idealization of the central countries which (explicitly or not) are held as the norm toward which new polyarchies should reach, underlies a good part of the current torrent of works on the "consolidation of democracy." This seems to me, as I argue in chapter 9, an erroneous vision, teleological and arguably even ethnocentric.

Of course, one way of freeing oneself from the questions raised by what ultimately amounts to the incompleteness of citizenship, as well as by related problems such as the pervasive weight of particularism and the frequent refusal of those in office to submit themselves to the control of citizens and diverse public institutions, is simply to ignore them: i.e., to decide by definitional fiat that democracy is "only" a political regime, that as such it should be defined strictly in terms of political variables, and that these, in turn, should be limited to those that revolve around electoral competition for governmental positions. This is a rigorously politicist vision: it permits very useful studies of some formal institutions of the new polyarchies,[16] but it obscures the need to also investigate two fundamental themes, by declaring them external to the proper realm of democratic theory.

One of these themes is that of social citizenship—or rather, as noted, of its absence or incompleteness in many of the new polyarchies, and of the role that the state plays, or fails to play, in guaranteeing and enforcing this aspect of citizenship. My first explorations of this theme are contained in chapter 7 of the present book. The other theme, which I begin to discuss in chapter 8 and continue in chapter 9, is the impact that the informal but highly influential institution of particularism (including phenomena such as familism, clientelism, and corruption), jointly with delegative patterns of political authority, have on the functioning not only of the regime but also of the state.

One conclusion of these explorations, spelled out in chapter 9, is that a premise of much of the current literature—that the new democracies are somehow programmed to convert themselves into some sort of mirror image of the old democracies—leads us to characterize the new polyarchies not on the basis of positively described traits but on what they lack relative to these normative images. It seems to me that this focus obscures realities that may be unpleasant but do not for this reason cease to merit description and analysis through a positive description of their features. It is important to note, first, that nowadays many countries in Latin America (and elsewhere) satisfy all of the attributes of polyarchy, but they have little or none of the formal institutionalization and the accountability that the old democracies share to a significant extent. Second, these curious (that is to say, little theorized) Latin American polyarchies do not seem to be in the process of acquiring these characteristics. Intending to avoid teleologies and definitions based on negatively defined attributes, in chapter 8 I label these regimes "delegative democracies," to differentiate them from the representative and formally institutionalized democracies of highly developed countries.

Nevertheless, these texts fall short of analyzing another extremely important matter: the close relationship that I believe exists, on one hand, between delegative, plebiscitarian, poorly representative, scarcely accountable, and informally institutionalized types of polyarchy[17] and, on the other hand, the profound (and, in most cases, increasing) inequalities of all sorts that most Latin American countries exhibit. As a step in the analysis of this theme I wrote the text contained in chapter 10, which addresses a problem that is part, but only part, of the question of inequality: the crushing poverty suffered by a large part of the Latin American population.

VI

This completes the overview I wanted to share on the texts that follow. As I said in the beginning, this book is part of a trajectory that is still full of unanswered questions. If the reader has the patience to reach the final chapter, he or she will understand the reason for this statement. The work outlined in the present volume remains open; to continue it seems to me to require at least the following: (1) to achieve a satisfactory conceptualization of democracy, one that is not restricted to exclusively political factors nor expanded to the point that it becomes synonymous with social justice or economic equality, and which establishes reasonably clear analytical and empirical criteria for the inclusion of specific cases in each category; (2) a focus on the *problématique* of citizenship in its diverse (not merely political) aspects as the cornerstone of this conceptualization; and (3) along with these elements, to continue tenaciously to make a democratic critique of our current polyarchies.

Notes

1. See, especially, the influential volume edited by David Collier, *The New Authoritarianism in Latin America* (Princeton: Princeton University Press, 1979).

2. For another expression of these concerns and an argument in favor of peaceful forms of social and political change, see Guillermo O'Donnell and Delfina Linck, *Dependencia y Autonomía* (Buenos Aires: Amorrortu Editores, 1973).

3. This we did primarily through a painstaking compilation of events from journalistic sources. The results are deposited in machine-readable form in the University of Michigan, Ann Arbor.

4. The English language version of this book was published by the University of California Press in 1988, under the title *Bureaucratic Authoritarianism: Argentina, 1966–1973, in Comparative Perspective.*

5. At times, this voice was a menacing one. I remember one particularly surreal day in which, along with the horrible reports of deaths and disappearances that reached us almost daily, a young man appeared in the CEDES office. He claimed to be a member of a guerrilla organization and informed me that since we were obviously agents of imperialism (at this time CEDES was supported by donations from SAREC of Sweden and the Ford Foundation) we should pay his organization a "tax" whose value far exceeded the total we received from both organizations. Since my negative response led to some nasty threats which converged with the ones we received from the other side of the spectrum, I found myself making a grim joke: that the list of human rights should be amended to include the right to know who killed you!

6. In the current volume I use the title that I originally gave to this text, "And Why Should I Give a Shit? Notes on Sociability and Politics in Argentina and Brazil" ("*¿Y a mi qué Mierda me Importa? Notas sobre Sociabilidad y Política en Argentina y Brasil*"). Apparently the vulgar word in the title was considered inappropriate by the original publishers in three languages of this text (Spanish, English, and Portuguese) who unanimously decided to delete this word without consulting me. The fact remains, however, that this phrase, *mierda* included, is frequently repeated in Argentina on occasions like the ones that I discuss in this text.

7. On the other hand, it did help that at this time President Carter had launched a policy of promoting human rights and was trying to apply it with particular force in Latin America.

8. Shortly thereafter, the progress of the transition in Brazil and the important role that Cardoso took on when he became a senator from the state of São Paulo meant that

he had to leave the co-coordination of this project. At that point Schmitter and I invited Laurence Whitehead to take Cardoso's place, and we were fortunate that he accepted.

9. *Tentative Conclusions about Uncertain Democracies,* volume IV of *Transitions from Authoritarian Rule* (Baltimore: Johns Hopkins University Press, 1986).

10. I do not resist the temptation, however, to comment that it seems to me unjust the criticism sometimes made that we failed to consider the contributions that the popular sector made to many of these transitions. The role of this sector, by itself and as part of the "resurrection of civil society," is discussed in my joint text with Schmitter with no less detail and causal emphasis than is the role of other social sectors. [This topic is also addressed in chapter 6 of the present volume.—*Ed.*]

11. This focus, centered on the political strategies that could launch the transition and bring it to the inauguration of political democracy, was shared at that time by our colleagues in Southern Europe and, later, in other Latin American countries, as well as in the Philippines, Korea, Taiwan, South Africa, and several postcommunist countries. One result was the translation of the text by Schmitter and myself into several languages, including clandestine translations that, to our great satisfaction, were circulated in countries still subject to severe repression.

12. Beginning with the inspiration provided by the brilliant seminal article of Dankwart Rustow, "Transitions to Democracy: Toward a Dynamic Model" (*Comparative Politics* 2 [no. 3, 1970]: 337–63) and continuing with the text included here as chapter 6, and with a paper that Schmitter wrote, intended like mine to help guide the launching of our project. In his text, Schmitter imaginatively speculated on the advice that Machiavelli would give to the democratic opposition ("Speculations about the Prospective Demise of Authoritarian Regimes and Its Possible Consequences," Working Paper no. 60, Wilson Center, Washington, D.C., 1980). From then on, a series of texts that were part of, or were partly motivated by, our project made important contributions to the study of these processes. Among the authors of studies published in our edited volumes are Spaniards (José Maria Maravall and Juan R. Santamaría), Italians (Gianfranco Pasquino), and Greeks (Nikifouros Diamandouros) who could in part reflect on what had already occurred in their region; Chileans (Manuel Antonio Garretón) and Poles (Adam Przeworski) for whom the hope of democratization in their respective countries seemed even further away than it was for the rest of us; Argentines (Marcelo Cavarozzi), Brazilians (Luciano Martins and the previously mentioned Cardoso) who were in the beginning of their protracted transitions; and Peruvians (Julio Cotler) who came from authoritarian experiences that were less repressive and socially vengeful than the BAs; as well as colleagues from Europe (Charles Gillespie, Alain Rouquié, and Whitehead) and the United States (Robert Kaufman, Lowenthal, Terry L. Karl, Kevin Middlebrook, John Sheahan, and Alfred Stepan) who had been sharing our dreams and aspirations, both with moving personal solidarity and with important intellectual contributions of their own.

13. See especially Robert Dahl, *Democracy and Its Critics* (New Haven: Yale University Press, 1989).

14. Or, what Schmitter and I, adopting a term coined, of all places, in that most successful of transitions, Spain, called *desencanto*.

15. I refer to the extent to which there effectively exists a rule of law *(estado de dere-cho)* and with it the generalized enforcement of basic civil rights such as inviolability of the domicile, reasonably fair access to the judiciary power, humane treatment by the police and other state agents, and others that I discuss in chapter 7 of this book. More detailed analysis of these matters may be found in my "Polyarchies and the (Un)Rule of Law in Latin America," in Juan Méndez, Guillermo O'Donnell, and Paulo Sérgio Pinheiro, eds., *The (Un)Rule of Law and the Underprivileged in Latin America* (Notre Dame, Ind.,: University of Notre Dame Press, 1999).

16. Especially parties, party systems, electoral laws, and presidential vs. parliamentary systems. See, among others, Scott Mainwaring and Timothy Scully, C.S.C., eds., *Building Democratic Institutions: Party Systems in Latin America* (Stanford: Stanford University Press, 1995); Matthew Shugart and John Carey, *Presidents and Assemblies: Constitutional Design and Electoral Dynamics* (Cambridge: Cambridge University Press, 1992); Juan Linz and Arturo Valenzuela, eds., *The Failures of Presidentialism* (Baltimore: Johns Hopkins University Press, 1994); and Arendt Lijphart and Carlos Waisman, eds., *Institutional Design and New Democracies: Eastern Europe and Latin America* (Boulder: Westview Press, 1996).

17. This is so much the case that we do not have a word in Spanish or Portuguese (and, for that matter, in many other languages) for "accountability," the idea that political leaders are subject to the obligation to render accounts of, and to be legally and politically responsible for, their conduct before various social and public organizations, not only at the moment of elections but during their incumbency. I discuss this topic in "Horizontal Accountability in New Polyarchies," in Andreas Schedler, Larry Diamond, and Mark Plattner, eds., *The Self-Restraining State: Power and Accountability in New Democracies* (Boulder and London: Lynne Rienner Publishers, 1999).

PART I
Misadventures

1

State and Alliances in Argentina, 1956–1976

This paper pursues the historical perspective which I have employed in a re-cently completed book.* In that book I study the attempt, begun in 1966, to implant and consolidate in Argentina what I have called a "bureaucratic-au-thoritarian" (BA) state.[1] I have compared the modalities of its alliance with the large bourgeoisie and with international capital, its social impact and, fi-nally, its collapse, with those of Brazil since 1964 and Chile after 1973. Rather than pointing out similarities between the Argentine case and the others, I shall stress here some differences, for these offer a basis for understanding why, in recent decades, attempts to establish any type of political domination have failed in Argentina.[2]

The following pages contain no analysis of specific conjunctures. This work places itself at the level of the long-term tendencies which link the said conjunctures with the historical process in which they have emerged and dis-solved. In the book already mentioned I indicate some specific differences be-tween the 1966–73 Argentine case of "bureaucratic-authoritarianism" and other Latin American cases. Briefly, the principle differences were: (1) the smaller threat level before the implantation of the BA state;[3] (2) the less severe

This work was first presented at the Symposium on the State and Development in Latin America, held at the University of Cambridge, December 12–16, 1976. It was later published in English in the *Journal of Development Studies* 15 (no. 1, 1979).

* O'Donnell refers to *Bureaucratic Authoritarianism: Argentina, 1966–1973, in Comparative Perspective* (Berkeley: University of California Press, 1988), a book that was completed shortly be-fore this article but was not published until much later, for reasons that the author presents in the preface to this book.—*Ed.*

repression imposed on the popular sector and its political allies; (3) the greater autonomy of the popular sector (and, within it, of the working class) and of the trade unions, with respect to the state and the dominant classes; (4) the moderate fall of industrial wages and the more pronounced decline in the incomes of a sizable proportion of the employed middle sectors; (5) the rapid formation of an alliance of the popular sector and the unions with the domestic bourgeoisie,[4] against the new state and, particularly, against its "efficientist" and internationalizing policies; (6) the conflict between the government—and, with it, the large bourgeoisie—and the pampa bourgeoisie; and (7) the decisive role of peronism as the expression and mobilization channel of a heterogeneous constellation of forces in opposition to the BA state. These elements are fundamental in an explanation of the unusual conflicts which arose within the state's institutions and, also, of the social explosions which provoked a collapse unparalleled so far in the other Latin American BA states.[5] These factors account for the short-term differences between the fate of the BA state in Argentina in the period 1966–73 and other comparable experiences. But these, in turn, call for an explanation, which requires a longer historical perspective.

I. Historical Background

In this section I shall point out certain features of Argentina's incorporation into the world capitalist system which gave rise to the country's peculiarity in comparison with the rest of Latin America.[6] These differences continue to bear upon certain characteristics of Argentine capitalism and class structure and also—centrally for our subject—on the power resources and on the political alliances available to the popular sectors.

The following are the most crucial features for our analysis:

1. As in the rest of Latin America, the pace and characteristics of Argentine capitalist expansion were fundamentally determined by the incorporation of some of its regions as exporters of primary products. This allows us to make an initial distinction between those vast regions of Latin America with no direct linkage to the world market[7] (such as the Andean *hacienda*) and those which were directly linked to such a market as exporters of primary products. Among these the *estancia* of the Argentine pampas and Uruguay differed substantially from the enclaves and plantations which were the principal form of incorporation elsewhere in the continent. The *estancia* was less labor intensive than the plantation and the *hacienda,* and it was also less capital and technology intensive than the plantation and the enclave. Largely because of the latter, the control of the principal productive resource (land) was left, in the Argentine pampas and in Uruguay, in the hands of an early domestic agrar-

ian bourgeoisie, while the enclave and the plantation were usually directly owned by international capital, and the *hacienda* was left in the hands of an oligarchy with hardly any capitalist traits. This pattern, combined with a high differential rent, endowed the pampean and the Uruguayan bourgeoisie with an important capital accumulation base of their own. This bourgeoisie did not escape dependence on European capital via the transport, finance, and international marketing of its products, but its base of capital accumulation did foment a significantly wealthier and more diversified urban, commercial, and incipient industrial sector than was to be found in those economies which revolved around the *hacienda*, the enclave, and the plantation. These characteristics are well known[8] but others, to which less attention has been given, stem from them.

2. The cereal, wool, and later also beef exporting economy covered a relatively larger portion of the national territory than the exporting sectors of other countries. Above all, in Argentina the areas not directly incorporated with the world market carried much less economic and demographic weight than in the rest of Latin America. Furthermore, in Argentina and Uruguay there was only a very small peasantry subject to precapitalist relations of production compared with much of the continent. The insertion of a much larger proportion of the population into the export economy meant that, from the end of the nineteenth century, Argentina exhibited a significantly greater homogeneity than the rest of Latin America,[9] which, in spite of later mishaps, continues to be noticeable.[10]

3. Besides the sizable base of local accumulation due to direct control of land, the high productivity of land in international terms until approximately 1930[11] and the low labor requirements of "extensive" farming contributed decisively to the greater diversification and prosperity of the pampa region and its urban centers—compared to the regions dominated by the enclave, the plantations, and the *hacienda*. Suffice it to say that wages in the pampa region and the Argentine urban centers, until approximately the Second World War, were higher than in many European countries,[12] whilst those of the rest of Latin America—if and when wage relationships were established—were much lower. Thus, not only was intranational homogeneity higher, but also the region of Argentina which was directly incorporated into the world economy was more diversified and generated a significantly higher income for its popular sector than in the other Latin American countries. This, in turn, had other consequences: in Argentina, both industrialization and the formation of a working class occurred prior to the world crisis of 1930 and proceeded faster than in the rest of Latin America.[13] Around the beginning of the twentieth century, the existence of a fully capitalist and relatively wealthy urban (and, largely, also pampean) consumer market in Argentina induced an industrialization which received further stimulus from the import restrictions

resulting from the First World War. An early working class therefore also emerged, which developed organizational patterns autonomous both of the state and of the incipient industrial bourgeoisie, although it entered the political arena only later.[14] In the absence of a large peasantry providing cheap labor, the strong demand for labor could only favor such an outcome. Because of the specific characteristics of Argentina's insertion in the world capitalist system, its economic growth was powered fundamentally by its civil society and its relationships with the international market. The dynamizing impulse did not depend on the state, as generally tended to happen—with many difficulties—in the other Latin American economies. This point must be developed in greater detail.

In the period between roughly 1870 and 1930,[15] the Argentine state had certain features in common with the liberal states of the great world centers: although a more ostensibly fraudulent political democracy, the level of electoral participation was not lower,[16] and the state machine did not go beyond providing crucial, though limited, general conditions for the functioning of the economy.[17] But this state was the creation of the pampa bourgeoisie and its financial and commercial appendages, by means of a process which also entailed the making of the bourgeoisie, and of the system it dominated, in a marginal yet integral corner of the world capitalist market. To clarify this statement we must resort to some comparisons.

The pampa bourgeoisie and its urban branches directly constituted a national state, not the regional state[18] which was the main political power base of the dominant classes in so many Latin American countries. The Argentine national state also eliminated—earlier, and with greater ease and completeness—the autonomy of the regions not directly linked to the world market, largely because those regions carried much less weight in the country as a whole than in most other Latin American cases.[19] This implied that the state was an expression of changing power relationships between regions directly incorporated in the world market and others marginal to it to a much smaller extent than in the rest of Latin America.

Thus the pampa bourgeoisie and its urban tentacles held both a central economic position and, through the national state, a central political position as an internally dominant class burdened by other regions. Furthermore, the shifts in the relative importance of export products took place within the pampean zone and its bourgeoisie[20] and not, as in most other cases, by means of the incorporation of new products from new regions leading to shifting alliances with existing locally dominant classes and established segments of the international capital.

Nevertheless, the pampa bourgeoisie and the national state became the principal channels of the internationalization of both society and economy, because of the nature of their insertion in the world market. The "liberal" characteristics of the Argentine state and the strong relative weight of its civil society can only be understood as consequences of the position of the state at the intersection of the pampa bourgeoisie with international capital—which had deeply penetrated the economy through its control of the financing, transportation, and external marketing of pampa production. Paradoxically therefore, this original internationalization of an economically dynamic and internally homogeneous region, including a decisive part of the country with barely any peasants, through the local retention of capital accumulation shares, enabled a highly internationalized state to become devastatingly national with respect to the regions marginalized from the pampean system. In contrast, the Andean oligarchy or that of Brazil's northeast could directly and diaphanously control "their" regional state apparatus, while international capital, based on enclaves and plantations, controlled a state which was less an emanation from than a graft imposed upon a society which lacked a local bourgeoisie endowed with its own accumulation base. Instead, in Argentina, the existence of such a bourgeoisie arising from the very process of incorporation into the international market generated a situation in which the regional states were of little weight; furthermore, the national state was one of the crucial channels of the rapid and early internationalization, which, due to the weight of the pampa economy, covered much more of the country than in other Latin America cases. That is why—not in spite of, but as a very condition of, its centrality—the relationship between the pampa bourgeoisie and the state did not exhibit the transparency and immediacy which the regional oligarchies and international capital imposed in a large portion of Latin America's regional and (for a long time, mostly nominal) national states.[21]

Although the liberal Argentine state did not survive the crisis of the thirties, the factors summarized above allowed it to recover from the economic impact of the world crisis more quickly and easily than most other Latin American countries. The crisis induced a new wave of industrialization through import substitution (helped by a comparatively broad internal market)[22] and the absorption of a large part of the still available work force from the nonpampa regions, thus reducing their relative weight even further. However, this is not the place to analyze how this affected the emergence of peronism; instead, we turn to the central theme of the paper.

II. Dilemmas

I have already mentioned the emergence in Argentina of a popular sector, which included a politically significant working class, with larger economic and organizational resources than those of the rest of Latin America.[23] This in turn resulted from the combination of large available economic surpluses and the negligible pressure exerted on the urban labor market by an almost nonexistent peasantry. If this was an advantage for Argentina's capitalist development, it also strengthened its popular sector. When the bonanza disappeared and the economic conditions approached zero sum, there was no sizable peasantry to bear a substantial part of the costs of agreements negotiated between the classes located within the fully capitalist region.

The second point to be singled out arises from another peculiarity of this economy: its main export products—cereals and beef—are wage goods, foodstuffs which constitute the main consumption item of the popular sector. Let us initially note some general consequences of this peculiarity. Other Latin American primary export products have less influence on the consumption of the popular sector and therefore, on the relative prices of their consumption baskets. Furthermore, the way in which their price changes influence popular consumption is, in most cases, indirect, generated by mechanisms which are difficult to apprehend; in this situation in contrast, a change in the relative prices of foodstuffs is immediately perceivable. In addition, this perception arises in a popular sector with a significantly higher level of income (and, presumably, of expectations) and organizational autonomy (and therefore greater capacity for resistance) than in the other Latin American cases. We are now in a position to analyze more concrete processes.

The world crisis of the 1930s depressed the prices of pampean goods. Subsequently the peronist government (1946–55) offered a foretaste of the problems which would explode later. First (1946–50) the state appropriated a substantial part of the proceeds of pampean exports, kept internal foodstuff prices depressed, and thus increased the income of the popular sector and provoked an expanding demand for other goods, especially industrial ones. But this was to generate a balance-of-payments squeeze, due to the "discouragement" effect of low prices on pampa production and to increasing internal consumption of exportable foodstuffs. Subsequently (1952–55) agricultural prices improved, whereupon—because of the operation of the inverse joint effect—the balance-of-payments situation improved. But this in turn generated political troubles, due to the regressive redistribution of income it entailed and to the reduction of the domestic demand on which the urban bourgeoisie depended.

Following this, around 1960, a wave of direct foreign investment in industry and services provoked a rapid internationalization of the urban productive structure[24] (by means of capital and activities different from those involved in export activities). Contrary to the "developmentalist" hopes, this new stage resulted in a marked increase in demand for imports, which outran the growth rate of GNP, exports, and pampa production.[25] Faced with this situation the only economically "evident" solution—repeatedly expounded—lay in a large increase of exports, which would have provided the urban pro-

creased the exportable surplus, especially of foodstuffs. But this generated resistance among the many penalized by these policies, while the resulting easing of the balance-of-payments made possible economic reactivation policies. Consequently, the liquidity increase, the relaxing of controls on the fiscal deficit, the availability of foreign exchange, the growth in employment, and the salary increases ended the downward phase of the cycle and inaugurated the upward phase. But the latter led into a new balance-of-payments crisis,[38] after which further devaluation, and the consequent stabilization program, opened up another downward phase. . . .[39]

IV. Pendulums

In each phase of the cycle, the large bourgeoisie has played on the winner's side. I have already pointed out that the recessions provoked by stabilization programs have, at the very least, not damaged that fraction. At the same time, as a direct appendage of (or intimately linked to) international capital, it is the large bourgeoisie which best perceives—and most fears—the costs of international insolvency.[40] It has the most direct nterest in an improvement of the balance-of-payments.[41] Furthermore, the free international movement of capital enhances the privileged position, in an ever narrower domestic credit market, of this most internationalized (and therefore internally dominant) fraction, while at the same time reopening the "normal" channels for the transfer of capital accumulation towards the center of the system,[42] of which it is the most intrinsic part. In the final stretch of the upward phase of the cycle, these factors turn the large bourgeoisie into an ally of the pampa bourgeoisie (and of the whole of the exporting sector) in the clamor for the devaluation and deflationary policies which launch the downward phase. Thus, faced with the onset of the balance-of-payments crisis, the large bourgeoisie swings towards the objective interests of the pampa bourgeoisie, favoring and supporting stabilization programs which transfer a mass of resources toward the latter, mostly at the expense of the urban sector.

But the regressive and recessionary impact of these measures generated a reaction among the weaker fractions of the urban bourgeoisie and of the popular sector[43] at the same time as the improvement in the foreign exchange position made feasible the economic and reactivation measures for which they were clamoring. Faced with this, the large bourgeoisie did repeatedly what all bourgeoisies do in the absence of a tutelary state to induce them to adopt longer-term strategies: they looked to their short-term economic interests, supported the economic reactivation policies, and thus rode the crest of the wave of economic recovery—from which, we may safely assume, they were able to profit in a privileged manner.[44] In this it covered a full swing of the pendulum, joining the rest of the urban sector and abandoning the pampa bourgeoisie to a solitary lament for the deterioration of its relative prices;[45] all of which produced the great fluctuations of relative prices observable in Figure 1.

Although this describes the recurrent pendulation of the large bourgeoisie, I have still to explain it. However, it must be added that, apart from their economic consequences, these displacements had political implications of the greatest importance: they repeatedly broke up that intrabourgeois cohesion essential for its stable political domination. More precisely, they broke the cohesion of its two superior fractions (the urban oligopolistic and the pampa bourgeoisie), whose respective capital accumulation base made them potentially capable of "modernizing" Argentine capitalism. Another aspect, no less important and to which I shall shortly turn, is that such swings not only generated the political space for, but also were to a large extent the consequence of, an alternative alliance which encompassed the weaker fractions of the bourgeoisie and the popular sector.

Let me insist on a crucial point. The alliance of the dominant fractions of the bourgeoisie could have borne fruit if it had lasted long enough to bring about significant productivity increases in the pampa region. This was prevented by the large fluctuations in relative prices. But in their political demands the pampean bourgeoisie concentrated on the level and not the stability of their prices, thus contributing to the pendulations I have already mentioned. The productivity increases could have taken place with relatively depressed but stable pampean prices (thus meeting the necessary condition of stability stated above), combined with public policies which would have forced them through by more structural measures. This was the motivation behind the various projects designed to tax the difference between the potential and the actual productivity of pampa land.

Such an alternative, obviously conflicting with the short-term interests of the pampa bourgeoisie in its present composition, is not against those of the urban sector as a whole (since it does not presuppose a fall in their relative prices), and in the medium term it could have achieved the sought-after increase in pampa production and productivity. However, the attempts to impose such a tax on the "potential rent of the land" repeatedly failed. This must be contrasted with what has happened in many other Latin American countries, where the state—impelled by and allied with the large bourgeoisie—has usually been able to force through the "modernization" of agrarian regions and their dominant classes.[46] But those agrarian classes were fundamentally regional ones[47] and, although their production might temporarily fall, their contribution to total exports was not comparable to that of the pampa bourgeoisie. That is why other Latin American states have been able to subordinate those classes, and the regional states which they controlled, without simultaneously worsening their balance-of-payments problems.

The case of the pampa bourgeoisie has been very different. I have pointed out its early position as a national class, even with respect to its linkage with a national state. This meant that intrabourgeois struggles usually occurred, in contrast with other Latin American cases, at the very heart of a national state which was continually fractured by them. Besides, the "discouragement" of the pampa bourgeoisie[48] caused by the fall in its prices and attempts to "restructure it" by means of tax mechanisms had strong immediate repercussions on the balance-of-payments—at the same time that, in the upward phase of the economic cycle, the increase in domestic consumption of exportables further diminished the potentially available exports, before pampean productivity had undergone any substantial improvement. Thus a balance-of-payments crisis ensued, and its alleviation by means of devaluations not only turned relative prices against the urban sector but also entailed the expulsion from the governing alliances of the sectors which had impelled the reactivation of the cycle.

As long as the stabilization programs lasted, the immediate interests of the pampa bourgeoisie weighed heavily in the institutional system of the state. Naturally enough, it opposed any prospect of its own "restructuring," centering the issue on a sharp increase in its prices and thus creating the conditions for a renewal of the cycle. . . . In other words, although it has long lost its position as the dynamic vanguard of Argentine capitalism, the pampa bourgeoisie, compared with other Latin American agrarian classes, has retained an unusually central economic and political position. This position was sufficient both to block any attempt to "restructure" it and to use periodic balance-of-payments crises to bring about massive income transfers for its benefit. Meanwhile, and as a consequence, channels for capital accumulation in Argentina were repeatedly short circuited and the state danced to the pendular tune of civil society.

This accounts for some of the characteristics of the period beginning in 1966, especially the economic policies followed between March 1967 and May 1969. The Economics Minister, Krieger Vasena, transparently carried out the policies of the large bourgeoisie. This entailed, among other things, a large devaluation which for the first time did not benefit the pampa and exporting sector. On the contrary, the March 1967 devaluation (40%) was wholly appropriated by the state, which withheld a percentage of the value of pampa exports equivalent to the devaluation. This fiscal revenue was used in a substantial program of investment in physical infrastructure and communications. A fixed *peso* price of pampean production depressed the internal price of pampean foodstuffs, as can be seen in Figure 1. It also allowed a rapid reduction of inflation and—in contrast with other cases of bureaucratic-authoritarianism—only a moderate fall in industrial wages (see Figures 2 and 3).

Even so, this situation could not be maintained and, as can be seen in

Figure 1, after 1970 pampean prices (especially those of beef) rebounded until
they reached a very high level in 1971–72. Krieger Vasena's was the only clear
and sustained attempt by the large bourgeoisie unilaterally to subordinate the
pampa bourgeoisie[49] to its own accumulation needs. But the result was an internal rupture in the cohesion of the BA state and a political and economic
collapse impelled from outside by other social actors. While this attempt
marked the limits of a unilateral enforcement of supremacy by the large bourgeoisie, the history of previous devaluations, by pushing the upper bourgeoisie into alliances with the urban sector, had shown that it was impossible
to return to the good old times of pampean supremacy.[50]

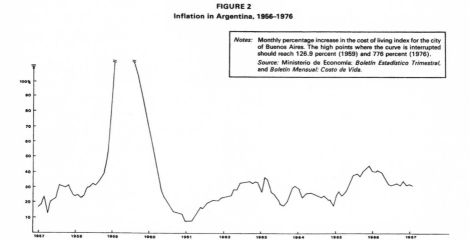

FIGURE 2
Inflation in Argentina, 1956–1976

Notes: Monthly percentage increase in the cost of living index for the city
of Buenos Aires. The high points where the curve is interrupted
should reach 126.9 percent (1959) and 776 percent (1976).

Source: Ministerio de Economía: *Boletín Estadístico Trimestral,*
and *Boletín Mensual: Costo de Vida.*

FIGURE 2 continued

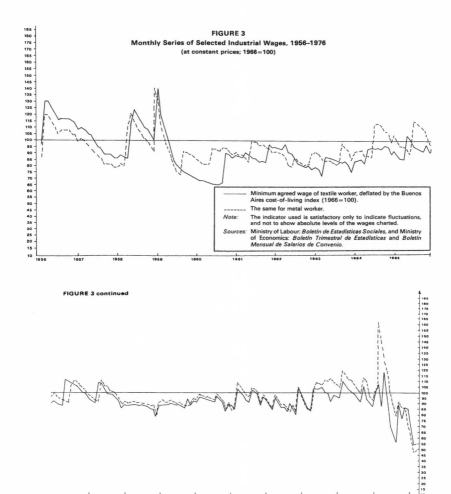

FIGURE 3
Monthly Series of Selected Industrial Wages, 1956–1976
(at constant prices; 1966=100)

———————— Minimum agreed wage of textile worker, deflated by the Buenos Aires cost-of-living index (1966=100).

- - - - - - The same for metal worker.

Note: The indicator used is satisfactory only to indicate fluctuations, and not to show absolute levels of the wages charted.

Sources: Ministry of Labour: *Boletín de Estadísticas Sociales*, and Ministry of Economics: *Boletín Trimestral de Estadísticas* and *Boletín Mensual de Salarios de Convenio*.

FIGURE 3 continued

V. The Defensive Alliance

If the political and economic centrality of the pampa bourgeoisie marks an important difference with respect to other Latin American countries and their agrarian classes, a no less important difference stems from the greater political vulnerability of the weaker (and genuinely national) fractions of the urban bourgeoisie in those countries when faced with the expansion of the large bourgeoisie. The growth of the dominant productive structure, oligopolistic and internationalized, has occurred at the expense of many fractions of national capital, weakening its position vis-à-vis international capital and the state. This has caused complaints and strains, but has not, so far, been translated into serious political challenges to such "development" patterns. No such development has taken place in Argentina. The reason for the local bourgeoisie's comparatively greater political capacity is to be found not so much in itself as in the characteristics of the popular sector and in the country's relative national homogeneity. Elsewhere, a weaker urban sector, less organized and autonomous, deprives the weaker fractions of the Latin American bourgeoisie of the extremely important ally they had in Argentina. This is a crucial point.

Not only is the Argentine popular sector endowed with greater autonomy and organizational capacity than in most other Latin American countries. It also so happens that the medium- and long-term alliance of the upper fractions of the bourgeoisie depends on the level and stability of the relative prices of the main internal foodstuffs. This gives the popular sector a precise target for its political action, which has interrupted the accumulation circuits of those upper bourgeoisie fractions. These are necessary but not sufficient conditions for the recurrent breakdown of the latter's alliances. To account for the specificity of the phenomena with which we are concerned we must also see how the popular sector associated itself with the objective interests and political action of the weaker fractions of the urban bourgeoisie.

These fractions are usually penalized by devaluations and stabilization programs. Given an alleviation of the balance-of-payments squeeze, their immediate interest lies in economic reactivation policies which increase employment, liquidity, and credit availability, and give the state an expansionary role once again. This is also a direct effect of wage and salary increases; thus, it is not surprising that the bourgeois fraction in control of the most labor intensive enterprises should support these increases, when the even greater costs to them of recession are taken into account. The concurrence with the unions in demanding wage increases is, besides, a token which it offers the popular sector to forge the alliance.[51] Such a bourgeoisie—more or less weak and more or less penalized by the expansion of oligopolistic and internationalized capital—exists in other Latin American countries, but only in Argentina has it found a popular ally whose immediate short-term interests are compatible with its own, and which possesses a significant capacity for political action.[52]

The main organizational supports of this alliance have been the CGE, the CGT, and the national leadership of the main unions. Its first, principal, and possibly last expression has been peronism. It was not the only one, since—above all in the periods in which peronism was proscribed—it was channeled through other parties and within state institutions by diverse "nationalist" military and civilian groups. Their banner has been the defense of the internal market, in the sense both of raising the level of its activity and of limiting the expansion of international capital in it.

The characteristics of this popular sector and of this local bourgeoisie cannot be understood in isolation from each other. It has been their conjunction in the multiplying effect of their alliance which has made it possible to impose, again and again, the satisfaction of their immediate demands. We can now examine the characteristics and principal consequences of this alliance:

1. The alliance was sporadic but recurrent. It appeared only in the downward phases of the cycle, when demands for wage and salary increases and for diverse measures to relieve "the suffocation of the small and medium sized national enterprise"[53] concurred in the reactivation of the internal market at the expense of the pampean exporting sector. Once the cycle revived the alliance dissolved, partly due to the attempts of the local bourgeoisie and the unions to negotiate special agreements individually with the state and with the large bourgeoisie, partly because of the return of more "normal" class cleavages.

2. The alliance was defensive. It arose against the offensives of the upper fractions of the bourgeoisie. Its ideology of "nationalist" and "socially just" development overlooked what it was unable to problematize: the deeply oligopolistic and internationalized structure of the capitalism of which its members were the weakest components. It was defensive because in its victory it could not create an alternative capital accumulation system. All it achieved was the transition from the downward phase to the upward phase in conditions which were doomed to provoke the repetition of the cycle.

3. But despite its defensive nature, and although its victories signified the completion and not a way out of the cycle, this alliance was quite successful. It scored repeated victories in annulling the stabilization programs, limiting the domestic expansion of international capital, and launching economic reactivation policies and new "discouragements" for the pampa bourgeoisie. Thus, it is not surprising that the wage series of Figure 2 should also show erratic behavior; its peaks are the result of victorious struggles which soon led to marked reductions in wages. The upward movements of wages were accompanied by growth of the GNP and, in general, by higher profit rates for the industrial bourgeoisie as a whole—although, being also subject to the overall cycle, profits also seem to have undergone marked fluctuations.[54] The consequence of these processes may be seen in a phenomenon as intrinsically political as it is economic: the inflation which, as can be seen in Figure 3, is even more remarkable for its fluctuations than for its generally high level.

More basically, the defensive alliance was victorious because it managed to destroy the alliance between the two dominant fractions of the bourgeoisie. The large bourgeoisie, when the time came to weigh the immediate benefits from a revival of the economy against the political abyss entailed by aligning with the pampa bourgeoisie and the exporting sector when the remainder of civil society had joined forces against them, opted to support a new upward phase. Repeatedly the defensive alliance politically broke "from below" the cohesion of the dominant fractions and—economically—blocked the only alliance which could implant a new capital accumulation system and move the economy off its cyclical path.

4. The alliance was polyclassist, in the sense that it included the popular sector (with a strong working class component) and various bourgeois fractions. Its repeated successes were based on this conjunction. But, on the other hand, this ensured that its orientations were nationalistic[55] and capitalist. Its polyclass character, based on the achievement of shared tactical goals, offered a popular base for the demands of the weak bourgeoisie. This fraction thus appeared as a "progressive" one which, contrasting with the large bourgeoisie's "efficientist" orientations and the "landholding oligarchy's" archaism, seemed to embody the possibility of a "development with social justice." On the other hand, the popular sector (especially the unions and the working class) gained, through the polyclassist nature of the alliance, access to resources and mass media which it could not otherwise have had.

In particular, the bourgeoisie respectability of the alliance made more difficult the harsh repression which has been directed at the popular sector elsewhere in Latin America when it has acted in isolation and/or in pursuit of more radical goals. The impact of this alliance stemmed from the multiplying effect of the concurrence of social actors who had their own resource base and who could cooperate in very concrete and short-term goals. In other Latin American countries, the absence of these joint conditions has meant that the local bourgeoisie has lacked popular support and that the popular sector (weaker, in any case, because of greater intranational heterogeneity) has not enjoyed the political protection of a bourgeois ally. This, in turn, has made it possible for the large bourgeoisie to advance unhindered, naturally encountering protests and conflicts, but not the limits and oscillations which this peculiar alliance imposed in Argentina.

5. Locked in capitalist parameters, the principal political channel of the defensive alliance, peronism, did not transcend these limits. These limitations also arose from the experience of repeated victories and subsequent defeats. The political activation of the popular sector in pursuit of the goals of the defensive alliance, the protection granted by its bourgeois component, and the changes in public policies which it achieved, led, on the one hand, to a positive reinforcement of that activation and, on the other, to the solidifying of the organizational basis—above all the unions—which articulated the popular sector's action. Let us take a closer look at this.

6. In historical terms, the alliance stemmed from the fresh memory of previous mobilizations which had managed to reverse the downward trend of real wages and of economic activity. It was also a function of the low deterrent effect of a repression which tended to cease the moment the state, indi-

cating a shift in the governing alliances, launched a new upward phase of the cycle. This increased the popular sector's capacity for and disposition to political activation, but it also led to an equally repetitive experience of defeat: periods of low wages and salaries, and of mounting unemployment, during which the spokesmen of the defensive alliance were removed from the governing coalition.

However, in contrast with the transparent stimulus entailed by rising food prices and falling salaries and wages, the reversal of the cycle took place because of problems (such as balance-of-payments crises) and through mechanisms (such as devaluations and restrictions in the money supply) whose functioning and impact were harder to grasp. The benefits derived by the pampa bourgeoisie and the exporting sector, and the initial support lent by the large bourgeoisie to each downward reversal of the cycle, fostered the hostility of the popular sector against both fractions and against the internationalization and big business which they embodied. At the same time, the defensive alliance could not abandon its capitalist ideology and goals.

Thus, the interpretation of the sequences of such successes and defeats became a mythology of conspiracies of "powerful interests" which had a magical ability to defeat the "people" and hinder "development." Failure and tension generated in some cases a fascist ideological syndrome and in others a challenging of the capitalist parameters of the situation. But against these centrifugal tendencies a powerful centripetal force operated: as the CGT, the CGE, and peronism tirelessly repeated, since 1955 they had been prevented from carrying out the kind of "socially just" capitalist development which, "placed on the people's side" and exercising wide control of the state's institutions, the local bourgeoisie and the unions seemed to offer.

The feasibility of uniting the "national and the popular" against the "landholding oligarchy" and the "international monopolies," which the short-term coincidences of the defensive alliance seemed to confirm, were expressed in peronism's unusual appeal and were a decisive element in the great wave which in 1973 returned it to government. A further condition for this was that in the previous period the large bourgeoisie had ignored the limits of its supremacy and had tried to impose it unilaterally, even on the pampa bourgeoisie. The social explosions of 1969 and 1970 sealed the defeat of that attempt and, impelled by a great popular activation, forced the political withdrawal of the large bourgeoisie which, in 1973, lost its place in the governing alliance for the first time. Only then could the alternative which the main spokesmen of the defensive alliance claimed to embody be positively put to the test.

7. Rather than cycles we must now speak of spirals, inasmuch as—politically, above all—each swing of the pendulum, with its succession of temporary victories and defeats, sharpened the conflicts from which they derived.

The actors were not classes, fractions, and organizations which retained their "structural" characteristics unchanged, beyond these struggles. Rather, they were the political, organizational, and ideological expression of classes and fractions created and transformed during and through this pattern of alliances and oppositions. In particular, the popular sector found in the unions and—politically—in peronism, an organizational, ideological, and political expression which corresponded closely to the limits of the situation. The mobilization behind the defensive alliance's demands, with its precise aims and polyclass framework, achieved frequent and spectacular victories. This explains the peculiar combination of impressive popular activation with economistic demands, which emphasized—as a token of its alliance with the local bourgeoisie—its rejection of any leap beyond capitalism. Precisely this militant economism, combined with the weaker fractions of the bourgeoisie, permitted repeated defensive victories and perpetuated the illusion of an alternative path of capitalist development.

On the other hand, the moments of political victory and reversal—at any point in the economic cycle—were those when the temporary victors took the state apparatus by storm, seeking to strengthen institutional positions from which they would fight future battles when the situation was once again reversed—as experience taught them it would be. Of course, the unions were no exception to this: the history of the defensive alliance is also that of the extraction from the state of important institutional concessions. These, in turn, reinforced the possibility of renewing the mobilization of the popular sector. The conquest of institutional positions enabled the unions to cover the popular sector with a fine organizational net, from which they could direct it repeatedly toward a militant economism, towards the polyclass alliance, and towards the mirage of the "other" capitalist path which peronism proclaimed.

8. These multiplying fusions of the defensive alliance forced the large bourgeoisie repeatedly to abandon the pampa bourgeoisie to a solitary lament at the falling prices of their products. Such fusions both impelled economic reactivation and opened up the political abyss of a wide and active "national and popular" mobilization which had somehow to be reabsorbed. By swinging from support of the pampean bourgeoisie to support of a new upward phase of the cycle, the large bourgeoisie closely followed its short-term economic interests and managed to remain the only stable member of the governing alliance. It did not lose its dominant position, but the peculiar conditions outlined meant that its domination had to shift continuously backwards and forwards. At the same time and for the same reasons, the channels of capital accumulation were repeatedly short circuited. These clues enable us to understand Argentine politics as a less surrealistic phenomenon than its "political instability" and erratic "development" might lead one to believe.

As I hope is clear, insofar as this discussion refers to the constitution of the classes, it also refers to the state. It is from this viewpoint—starting from and returning to civil society—that the problem of the state must be approached.

VI. The State

The state is not merely a set of institutions. It also includes—fundamentally— the network of relationships of "political" domination activated and supported by such institutions in a territorially defined society, which supports and contributes to the reproduction of a society's class organization. In the Argentine case the pendular movements of the large bourgeoisie and the difficulties it has faced in subordinating civil society as a whole are a tangible indication of a continued crisis of the state as a system of political domination. So are the defensive alliance's recurrent and partially victorious fusions. Out of this was born a democratization by default, which resulted from the difficulties in imposing the authoritarian "solution" that seemed to offer a chance of extracting Argentine capitalism from its political and economic spirals.

By "governing alliance" I mean an alliance which imposes, through the institutional system of the state, policies conforming to the orientations and demands of its components. The large bourgeoisie was the stable member of the governing alliance, but each phase was marked by a temporary change in its partners and by an alternation of scarcely consistent circuits of capital accumulation. That is why public policies were continually changing and hardly ever implemented, as the state danced to the tune of the dynamics of civil society.

The state was recurrently razed to the ground by civil society's changing coalitions. At the institutional level, the coalitions were like great tides which momentarily covered everything and which, when they ebbed, washed away entire segments of the state—segments which would later serve as bastions for the piecing together of a new offensive against the coalition which had just forced its opponents into retreat. The result was a state apparatus extensively colonized by civil society. The upper fractions of the bourgeoisie were not the only ones to hang on to it. Its weakest fractions and part of the subordinate classes did the same—another fundamental difference from other Latin American examples. Civil society's struggles were internalized in the state's institutional system in a way which expressed not only the weight of the bourgeoisie's upper fractions but also the peculiar characteristics of a defensive alliance endowed with a remarkable capacity for partial victory. As a consequence, this colonized state was extraordinarily fragmented, reproducing in its institutions the complex and rapidly changing relationships of dominant and subordinated classes—classes which could use these institutions to fuel the spiraling movements of civil society.

Such a state could not "keep at a distance" from the governing alliance's immediate demands and interests; it could only reinforce the cycles and swings. It was, quite clearly, a weak state; as a support of social domination, because of the recurrent (and increasing) weakening of such domination implied by the popular sector's mobilizations and the unions' bargaining power; as an institutional sphere, because it was deeply colonized and fractionalized. This meant that one possible way out of the cycles—a shift towards some sort of state capitalism—was blocked; the fairly stable and consolidated bureaucratic apparatus, with non-negligible degrees of freedom vis-à-vis civil society, which would have been a necessary condition for such a solution, was not available.

Another obstacle arose from the fact that at times when the large bourgeoisie was in alliance with the pampa bourgeoisie, the stabilization programs entailed an "antistatist" offensive aimed not only to slash the fiscal deficit but also to dismantle the advances which had taken place in a statist direction during the previous phase, when the defensive alliance had been part of the governing alliance. Those attempts blocked any trend towards state capitalism, by dismantling the institutions which could have encouraged it and by dismissing the "technicians" who could have carried it out, replacing them with others who would issue a string of "antistatist" pronouncements and decisions.

In addition, any movement towards state capitalism by the defensive alliance encountered the ambivalence (and, frequently, the opposition) of the governing alliance's permanent member—the large bourgeoisie. Feasible or not, this possibility was blocked *ab initio* by the dynamic of civil society.[56] It can be said, then, that at all levels the Argentine state of the 1956–76 period was an example of extremely limited autonomy. Its peculiarity was not only that it basically moved in time with the upper fractions of the bourgeoisie, but also that it reflected the fluctuating political strength of the subordinate classes in their alliance with the weaker fractions of the dominant classes. The limit of the alliance—which shows that it must not be mistaken for an equilibrium of forces—arose from the fact that, on the one hand, it had to cooperate in the governing alliance with the large bourgeoisie and, on the other hand, that it could only be a defensive alliance.

Could this defensive alliance constitute an independent governing alliance, excluding the large bourgeoisie (and, of course, the pampa bourgeoisie)? Only a crude mechanism could lead us to believe this to be impossible on the grounds that the defensive alliance contained Argentine capitalism's weakest and least capitalist fractions. In fact, it did happen in 1973, when the defensive alliance achieved an extraordinary but pyrrhic victory.

VII. *Provisional Epilogue*

The experiment initiated in 1966 sought, on the one hand, to rebuild capital accumulation mechanisms which subordinated the whole of society to the large bourgeoisie and, on the other hand, necessarily and correlatively, to introduce a system of political domination which, reversing the preceding situation, would aggressively impose itself on civil society. I have mentioned the collapse of that attempt and how this made possible, for the first time, the conquest of the state's institutional system by the defensive alliance, independent of the large bourgeoisie. Recent history cannot be written here. But it is necessary to point out that this alliance could only briefly ignore the economic supremacy of the large bourgeoisie and the pampa bourgeoisie; a glance at the data already presented demonstrates how, after a brief truce in 1974, the cyclical fluctuations were repeated much more violently. Even before Perón's death, the intrinsically defensive content and limitations of the alliance had been shown beyond question. The old crisis reproduced itself with unusual acuteness and the local bourgeoisie had to abandon ship without even rescuing its organization. On the other hand, the exacerbation of "union power" could not go beyond a repetition, with increased force after the retreat of the local bourgeoisie, of the practices which had made it what it was: an aggressive economism and a search for new institutional advantages—pursued now from the very heart of the state institutional system. This cumbersome heritage of past victories created ominous gaps between the union leaders and their own class. It also generated conservative reactions, which threatened the substantial autonomy which the unions and the popular sector had retained throughout this complex process.

Perón's death, a peculiar "palace" irrationality, and a violence which speedily fed on itself helped to shake the foundations of a society and accelerated the spirals of its crisis; this happened with a state that too obviously failed to guarantee the survival of this capitalism. But beneath those facts was the fact that, when the defensive alliance managed, at least, to become the governing alliance, it ran up against its own limitations; the very reasons which had brought about its extraordinary victory precipitated an unprecedented crisis. The promise of a "nationalist" and "socially just" path of capitalist development was subjected to a positive test and the alliance's centrifugal tensions fired off in their opposing directions.

The great victory of the defensive alliance led to the paroxysm of the political and economic crisis, to the ebbing away of the nationalist ideology, to the implantation of a new bureaucratic-authoritarian state, and to the dissolution or subjection to government control of the main organizations of the popular sector and the local bourgeoisie. As a result, for the first time, the defensive alliance's political, ideological, and organizational supports have been neutralized. This has enabled the dominant fractions of the bourgeoisie to explore the possibilities for a long-term reaccommodation on more egalitarian terms—between themselves—than those prevalent in 1967–69. The implication of and precondition for such a reaccommodation is the dispersal of the defensive alliance. This does not entirely preclude a return of that alliance or of the spirals we have studied. But for such a thing to happen, the local bourgeoisie would have to set itself on a hazardous road to Damascus towards a renewed alliance with the popular sector; and it is not certain that, by then, the popular sector will still be confined within the ideological and political parameters which cemented the defensive alliance before its greatest and most catastrophic victory.

Notes

1. For an already published characterization of this type of state see Guillermo O'Donnell, *Modernization and Bureaucratic-Authoritarianism* (Berkeley: University of California Press, 1972); and Guillermo O'Donnell, "Reflections on the Patterns of Change in the Bureaucratic-Authoritarian State," *Latin American Research Review* 13 (no. 1, 1978).

2. For a conception which considers any kind of political domination preferable to "political instability," this cannot but seem the consequence of an acute pathology. Listing the dysfunctional psychological traits of Argentine "masses and elites" has been one of the favorite occupations of influential currents in the social sciences (see among others, Jean Kirkpatrick, *Leader and Vanguard in Mass Society* [Cambridge, Mass.: MIT Press, 1971]) and of the apocalyptic elements of the Argentine right. Reflections on the "stalemate," or mutual blockings of political and social forces in Argentina, have been more fruitful, above all those which have connected it with the Gramscian view of hegemonic crisis (see Juan Carlos Portantiero, "Clases dominantes y crisis política en la Argentina," in Oscar Braun, ed., *El capitalismo argentina en crisis* [Buenos Aires: Siglo XXI, 1973]). But beyond describing the stalemate and outlining some of its consequences, the question still remains: What are the power relationships which have produced this stalemate?

3. The "threat" concept refers to the degree to which internal and external dominant classes and sectors considered that the breach of the capitalist parameters and of the society's international alignments was imminent and willingly sought by the leadership of the popular sector (Guillermo O'Donnell, "Reflections").

4. I define "domestic bourgeoisie" as the fractions of the urban bourgeoisie which control enterprises mostly or totally owned by nationals. The definition excludes, therefore, the local subsidiaries of transnational firms and the agrarian bourgeoisie. Within the latter, the "pampa bourgeoisie" is that which controls the grain and beef exporting region of the Argentine pampas. The domestic bourgeoisie must in turn be disaggregated, since it ranges from the urban bourgeoisie's fully national and weakest layers to oligopolistic corporations intimately connected—by diverse mechanisms—with international capital. Making a different distinction, I shall also further speak on

the "large (urban) bourgeoisie," when referring to the set formed by the branches of transnational corporations and by the domestic bourgeoisie's oligopolistic action. "Below" the large bourgeoisie, what I shall call the "local"—or simply "weak"—bourgeoisie is left, made up of capitalists controlling nonoligopolistic firms, smaller and usually less capital intensive than the large bourgeoisie's. I shall also refer to the General Economic Confederation (CGE), an organization which throughout invoked the representation of the local bourgeoisie. The "popular sector" means the working class and the employed and unionized middle sectors; the General Confederation of Labor (CGT) is the national organization of the working class and middle sector unions and federations of unions.

5. Such a collapse happened in Greece, a case which has significant similarities with the one we shall examine here, especially the combination of a low threat level, a fairly autonomous popular sector, and a relatively moderate earlier economic crisis.

6. And of Uruguay, to which I shall briefly return.

7. When I speak of direct incorporation or linkage I refer to the role which some regions had as (an exporting) part of the world capitalist system. This of course does not imply that regions not linked to the world capitalist system were not importers of products from the center, nor subject to the effects of world capitalist expansion, often through directly incorporated regions.

8. Above all since Fernando H. Cardoso's and Enzo Faletto's book, *Dependency and Development in Latin America* (Berkeley: University of California Press, 1979) where we find the characterization of the types of exporting economy I have mentioned; an important recent contribution is that of Albert Hirschman, who adapts elements of staple theory to his concept of "linkages," widened to include not strictly economic relationships, and from there explores the consequences of the type of export product through which incorporation into the international market took place; unfortunately this author does not deal with pampean and Uruguayan products. See Albert Hirschman, "A Generalized Linkage Approach to Development, with Special Reference to Staples" (Princeton: Institute of Advanced Study, 1976).

9. With the exception of Uruguay, a case of even greater intranational homogeneity, since practically all its territory and its population were incorporated in the world market in conditions similar to those of the Argentine pampean region. Another exception, though partial and more complicated, is that of Chile; here, in the last third of the nineteenth century, the highly homogeneous agrarian economy of the central valley, partly oriented towards the export of foodstuffs, underwent (in contrast with Argentina and Uruguay) a decline, and the mining enclaves of the north emerged. But in contrast with other cases, those enclaves were inserted in a national market and a national state already constituted around the central agrarian region. Uruguay's greater intranational homogeneity allowed the earlier and fuller development of a "liberal" and "welfare" state. But for this very reason the problems concealed by the initial bonanza exploded earlier than in Argentina. Besides, the smaller absolute size of the Uruguayan internal market was decisive in interrupting its industrialization much earlier and thus, in recent decades, the relative weight of its working class has been significantly less than in Argentina.

10. For data and references on Argentina's greater intranational homogeneity with

respect to most of Latin America, see O'Donnell, *Modernization,* ch. 1. For an analysis of the differences in the distribution of income and of its political correlates in Latin America, see Jorge Graciarena, "Estructura del poder y distribución del ingreso en América Latina," *Revista Latinoamericana de Ciencia Política* 2 (no. 2, August 1971).

11. Since then the increasingly capital intensive modalities of the production of wool, cereals, and beef in the world market implied that agrarian productivity in Uruguay and Argentina rapidly fell behind in comparison with other exporters; see Carlos Díaz Alejandro, *Essays on the Economic History of the Argentine Republic* (New Haven: Yale University Press, 1970).

12. Lucio Geller, "El crecimiento industrial argentino hasta 1914 y la teoría del bien primario exportador," in Marcos Giménez Zapiola, ed., *El régimen oligárquico: Materiales para el estudio de la realidad argentina (hasta 1930)* (Buenos Aires: Amorrortu, 1975).

13. The exception to this generalization is São Paulo. Brazil's industrialization, based on the dynamizing stimulus of the coffee economy, does not correspond to any of the generic types I have employed (see Hirschman, "A Generalized Linkage Approach"). But its original use of slave labor, its labor intensive character compared with the pampa economy and—most important for our argument—its location in a national context in which the slave system weighed overwhelmingly, contributed to the lower degree of autonomous organization and political weight of the Brazilian working class compared with Argentina's.

14. This is related to the Spanish and Italian immigration which nourished that class and the anarchist ideology that prevailed in it until approximately 1920. The main source on this point continues to be Gino Germani, especially *Política y sociedad en una época de transición* (Buenos Aires: Editorial Paidós, 1962).

15. That is, between the strong exogenous impulse of the incorporation of the pampa region in the international market and the world crisis which altered the main basis of the system.

16. See Atilio Borón, "El estudio de la movilización electoral en América Latina: Movilización electoral en Argentina y Chile," *Desarrollo Económico* 12 (no. 48, 1972).

17. Above all the transport and warehouse network necessary for shipping the pampa's production, the capture of which by international capital was generously subsidized by the state. If the small technology requirements of direct exploitation of the pampean region permitted domestic control of the land, the much greater requirements of such a network (and later on, of the meatpacking industry) determined a high and early inflow of international capital.

18. I am not concerned here with the details of the respective historical processes. In particular the imposition of the nationalization of Buenos Aires by a coalition of provinces of the interior against the opposition of a sizable part of the pampa interests was no obstacle, once the vigorous exogenous impulses of the European demand for foodstuffs were felt, to the processes alluded to in the text.

19. Even in a case such as Brazil, characterized by relatively early industrialization and by the great weight of the state bureaucratic apparatus inherited from the imperial period, the subordination of the dominant classes of the northeast and the elimination of the barriers interposed by the regional states to the effective functioning of a national market were only completed after 1930; see CEBRAP, *Estado y sociedad en el*

Brasil: La planificación regional en la época de SUDENE (São Paulo: 1976). It should be borne in mind that I am excluding Chile and Uruguay from these generalizations.

20. Of course economic factors were not the only ones operating in this. Its greater weight, condensed in the national state, with respect to the oligarchies of other regions, allowed the pampean bourgeoisie to "discourage" the emergence of other dynamic exporting industries by means of diverse economic and political mechanisms.

21. Of course, if instead of making these comparisons with other Latin American cases we had made them with Australia and New Zealand, the dimensions Argentina and Uruguay had in common with the other Latin American countries would be more noticeable. For some comparisons in that direction, see Geller, "El crecimiento industrial," and Héctor Diéguez, "Argentina y Australia: Algunos aspectos de su desarrollo económico comparado," *Desarrollo Económico* 8 (no. 32, 1969).

22. The effective market is a function not so much of the total population as of that part of the population subject to capitalist relationships and with a monetary income sufficient for the purchase of mass consumption industrial goods; see O'Donnell, *Modernization,* ch. 1.

23. As always with the exception of Uruguay and partly—and too complicated to be dealt with here—of Chile.

24. It is impossible to quote here all the pertinent references. The data and main sources can be found in Pablo Gerchunoff and Juan Llach, "Capitalismo industrial, desarrollo asociado y distribución del ingreso entre los gobiernos peronistas," *Desarrollo Económico* 15 (no. 57, 1975); and Juan Sourrouille, "El impacto de las empresas transnacionales sobre el empleo y los ingresos: El caso de Argentina" (Geneva: International Labor Office, 1976).

25. See, above all, Juan Ayza, Gerard Fischet, and Norberto González, *América Latina: Integración económica y sustitución de importaciones* (Mexico: CEPAL and Fondo de Cultura Económica, 1976).

26. This was one of the constant themes of the CGE and the CGT after 1955.

27. The subject of the stop-go cycle has elicited important contributions from various theoretical perspectives. See, above all, Carlos Díaz Alejandro, *Devaluación en la tasa de cambio en un país semi-industrializado: La experiencia argentina, 1955–1966* (Buenos Aires: Editorial del Instituto, 1966); Carlos Díaz Alejandro, *Essays on the Economic History*; Marcelo Diamand, *Doctrinas económicas, desarrollo e independencia* (Buenos Aires: Editorial Paidós, 1973); Mario Brodersohn, "Política económica de corto plazo, crecimiento e inflación en la Argentina, 1950–1972," in Consejo Profesional de Ciencias Economicas, *Problemas económicos argentinos, diagnóstico y política* (Buenos Aires: Macchi, 1974); Juan Sourrouille and Richard Mallon, *Economic Policy-Making in a Conflict Society* (Cambridge, Mass.: Harvard University Press, 1974); Aldo Ferrer et al., *Los planes de estabilización en la Argentina* (Buenos Aires: Editorial Paidós, 1969); and Javier Villanueva, "Una interpretación de la inflación argentina," *Revista de Ciencias Económicas,* April–September, 1972. Adolfo Canitrot, "La experiencia populista en la redistribución de ingresos," *Desarrollo Económico* 15 (no. 59, 1975), has a different viewpoint, but is nevertheless an important contribution. For attempts to connect this type of analysis with a more specifically political level, see Oscar Braun, "Desarrollo del capital monopolista en la Argentina," in Oscar Braun, ed., *El capitalismo argentino,* and

Guillermo O'Donnell, *Modernization.* From another angle, the literature already mentioned on the political "stalemate" in Argentina is relevant to this subject. However, not much has been done so far to capture the formation and shifts of political alliances which have stimulated those cycles.

28. On this subject the principal source is Díaz Alejandro's important book, *Essays on the Economic History,* where the slow growth of the physical quantity of these exports and the spectacular lag of pampean productivity with respect to its principal competitors in the world market are shown. Also see Sourrouille and Mallon, *Economic Policy-Making.*

29. I hope it is clear that I am speaking at the class level. That is, the change towards an agribusiness would surely displace more than a few individuals who at present constitute the pampa bourgeoisie.

30. The pampa bourgeoisie's demands and declarations, at least of the last twenty years, constitute a repeated complaint that it does not receive profitable or stable prices.

31. See the microeconomic studies quoted in the works I mention below. The issue is, however, more complicated, as appears from the controversy which took place in *Desarrollo Económico* between Flischman, Braun, and Martínez (see Guillermo Flischman, "Modelo de asignación de recursos en el sector agropecuario," *Desarrollo Económico* 10 [no. 39–40, 1970]; Guillermo Flischman, "Nuevamente en torno de la eficiencia en el uso de la tierra y la caracterización de los grandes terratenientes," *Desarrollo Económico* 14 [no. 54, 1974]; Oscar Braun, "Comentario al trabajo de Guillermo Flischman," *Desarrollo Económico* 10 [no. 39–40, 1970]; Oscar Braun, "La renta absoluta y el uso ineficiente de la tierra en la Argentina," *Desarrollo Económico* 14 [no. 54, 1974]; and Carlos Martínez et al., "Nuevamente en torno al problema de asignación de recursos en el sector agropecuario pampeano," *Desarrollo Económico* 16 [no. 51, 1976]). The central point of these for our analysis is that the differential rent which the pampean region still enjoys and, especially, the great fluctuations of the whole economy and the high (and erratic) inflation rate, made the purchase of pampa land an excellent speculative investment—and a defense against the effects of inflation—for the urban and agrarian capital surpluses. This combines to reinforce the microeconomic rationality of maintaining the region's extensive exploitation. But, from the perspective of this analysis, the subject which these authors discuss seems to be a consequence (although in time it nourishes them in turn) of the economic and political factors I analyze here.

32. Further on I shall complicate this matter by introducing other factors.

33. Not only is the coefficient high but it grows with an elasticity greater than 1.0 with increases in its production level; see Ayza et al., *América Latina: Integración económica.*

34. For data on this point see especially FIEL, *La financiación de las empresas industriales en la Argentina* (Buenos Aires: 1971), and Mario Brodersohn, *Financiamiento de empresas privados y mercados de capital* (Buenos Aires: Programa Latinoamericano para el Desarrollo de Mercados de Capital, 1972).

35. On this point and others closely connected with it, see Guillermo O'Donnell and Delfina Linck, *Dependencia y autonomía* (Buenos Aires: Amorrortu, 1973).

36. See the pertinent data in Brodersohn, "Politica económica de corto plazo."

37. Actually, the price elasticity of pampean production is nil or slightly negative in the short term. This is because for cattle "an increase in relative prices reduces supply and increases the stocks. Besides, an increase in the cattle stock implies a greater use of land due to the rigidity in the supply of land. . . . Therefore, an increase in the relative prices of beef also negatively affects the production of cereals since to the lesser supply of beef is to be added the smaller area for cultivation" (Brodersohn, "Política económica de corto plazo, p. 28).

38. In contrast with what I noted above concerning exports, the income elasticity of imports is extremely high. It was estimated at around 2.6 for the 1947–67 period (Díaz Alejandro, *Devaluación en la tasa de cambio,* p. 356); for the period after 1966, Ayza et al., *América Latina: Integración económica,* p. 13), with a different methodology, estimate an elasticity of 1.8. One piece of information which indicates how internal consumption causes this pincer movement to close on the balance-of-payments in the upward phase of the cycle is that the wage earners' marginal propensity to consume exportable goods (foodstuffs, drinks, and tobacco) is 0.36 and that of nonwage earners is 0.16.

39. This is the briefest of summaries of the principal theme of the works quoted in endnote 27, to which I must refer. A useful presentation of the economic mechanisms operating in the upward and downward phases of the cycles—which unfortunately came to my attention only when this work was substantially finished—is Marcelo Diamand, "El péndulo argentino: Empate político o fracasos económicos?" (ms., 1976).

40. As the upward phase approached the balance-of-payments crisis, state controls were imposed on prices and foreign exchange, thus particularly troubling this fraction. I cannot deal with these points at greater length; suffice it to point out that, as far as price controls, which are typical of the final moments of the upward phase, are concerned, they could only really be attempted with the "leading firms." In other respects, when the balance-of-payments crisis occurred, the imposition of foreign exchange controls and of restrictions on capital transfers abroad became serious hindrances, particularly to firms more closely connected with the centers of world capitalism. Admittedly, none of these controls achieved their goals, nor did they prevent massive flights of capital, but many of the high-ranking staff of large firms (national and transnational) whom I interviewed in 1971 and 1972 said that for that reason they "had" to act "excessively" beyond the pale of Argentine legislation, with consequent uneasiness at times when, during the upward phase of the cycles, "demagogues" and "nationalists" with access to state institutions were not lacking.

41. In terms of their high import coefficient and demand for foreign exchange, and in spite of their better access to international finance, which allows them to make excellent deals in pre- and post-devaluation periods of acute scarcity of foreign exchange.

42. Even within private capital's oligopolistic fraction, the more fully and directly internationalized firms—the subsidiaries of the transnational corporations—are usually the largest (in capital and sales), the fastest growing, and the most capital intensive; see especially Sourrouille, "El impacto de las empresas." Of course this is not peculiar to Argentina; on Mexico see Fernando Fajnzylber and Trinidad Tarragó, *Las empresas transnacionales: Expansión a nivel mundial y proyección en la industria mexicana* (Mexico: Fondo de Cultura Económica, 1976), and Carlos Von Doellinger and Leonardo

Cavalcanti, *Empresas multinacionais na industria brasileira* (Rio de Janeiro: IPEA/INPES, 1975).

43. These in turn carried with them a large part of the nonpampean regions, which also had to "contribute" to these income transfers.

44. At least, the more concentrated and internationalized industrial branches usually responded with greater dynamism to the reactivation.

45. Maintaining a fixed exchange rate—or systematically allowing it to lag behind domestic prices—was the main mechanism which turned relative prices in favor of the urban sector (including wages and salaries).

46. This of course did not prevent these processes from being acutely conflictive. The point is that the capacity of these classes to resist was less than that of the pampa bourgeoisie and that, besides, the cost of such policies—in terms of their short-term impact on the level of internal economic activity and exports—was lower.

47. In the case of the enclaves it obviously was not a matter of modernizing the economy's most capital- and technology-intensive sector, but of renegotiating with international capital the percentages which could be retained locally. In the cases in which "excessive" pressure was exerted (reaching or threatening nationalization, above all) and the enclave's product was as important as the pampa production for total exports (Bolivia and, more recently, Chile) the familiar falls in production, prices, or both—equivalent in this sphere to the pampa bourgeoisie's recurrent "discouragements"—unleashed the consequent balance-of-payments crisis.

48. For the pampa bourgeoisie's insistence on its "discouragement" because of its internal prices and the attempts to "smother it" with taxes, it is enough to consult collections of documents of the Argentine Rural Society (SRA) and the Coordinator of Rural Associations of Buenos Aires and the Pampas (CARBAP).

49. Even by trying to introduce a tax on potential rent which, like so many other things, faded away with the social explosions of 1969.

50. Another exception—less clear, but also a telling one—can be found in the economic policy followed during 1964 and 1965. Then, as can be seen from Figures 1 and 2, high pampean prices coexisted with an improvement of real wages. But this attempt ran into its own limitations, since it entailed the reduction of profits for the urban bourgeoisie—which actively contributed to the 1966 coup—a large increase in the fiscal deficit, and severe restrictions on imports.

51. Since these wage and salary increases encourage economic activity at the same time that other policies, made possible by the transitory easing of the balance-of-payments, raise the employment level, the orthodox warnings that all this feeds inflation matter little—particularly since inflation, with a fixed or systematically lagging exchange rate, accelerates the reversal of relative prices in favor of the urban sector.

52. In Uruguay the lower level of industrialization, fundamentally due to the smaller internal market, weakened both agents much more; the local bourgeoisie has in itself been weaker and in the popular sector the working class has had relatively less weight. In Chile the political expression of the working class in Marxist parties (and the absence of a direct target in the relative price of foodstuffs as in Argentina and Uruguay) made this alliance more ambiguous and discontinuous. In the remaining

countries of the region the relative weakness of the popular sector—due to a greater intranational heterogeneity—deprived the local bourgeoisie of that fundamental ally.

53. These are subjects and terms which recur in the CGE's demands and declarations; see, e.g., its *Memorias Anuales.*

54. At least using as a proxy the relationship between urban wholesale prices and wages.

55. Basically, it was prevented from uniting to defend the domestic market against the internationalized character of export related activities and of the large bourgeoisie.

56. Even ignoring possibilities which would presuppose a change in the capitalist parameters of the situation, tax policies might have cushioned the cycles to an extent which would have modified many of the political aspects we have analyzed. But the ability to extract and reallocate resources by means of fiscal instruments (not only taxes on pampean land) also presupposes the medium-term stability of those instruments and their implementation and a fairly consolidated bureaucracy which can "ignore" immediate pressures from the interests involved. These conditions could hardly be met in the midst of the pendular motions and the consequent colonization and fractionalization of the state's institutional system.

2

Tensions in the Bureaucratic-Authoritarian State and the Question of Democracy

To the memory of Kalman Silvert, whom I admired.

Reality is compelling. In 1974 I wrote an essay in which I focused on the BA states that existed at the time—and was convinced of the imminent reappearance in Argentina of this type of state.[1] In this essay I discussed the conditions that contribute to the emergence of BA states, but my interests had already shifted toward the study of the dynamic generated by the internal tensions of this kind of state and by its impacts on society. Now, at the end of 1978, with Brazil making cautious yet significant advances toward political democracy, with Chile and Uruguay subjected to systems of domination that seemingly face no serious challenge, and with Argentina in the first stages of the implantation of a BA, I would like to reconsider the interrelationship between the internal tensions of the BA and its impacts on society.

In contrast to my earlier essay, I will examine here only the first stage in the evolution of the BA and, within it, the effects of factors which previously I insufficiently analyzed: i.e., strictly political factors and, in particular, the problem of democracy. On a superficial level, that the possibility of a return to democracy is being raised by leaders of the existing Latin American BAs might be attributable to their "false consciousness" or to external pressures. At a deeper level, however, I will argue that profound and abiding issues are involved regarding the nature of this kind of state. I will maintain that the fact that the issue of democracy has arisen at all (regardless of whether it is qualified as "organic" democracy, "responsible" democracy, or even "authoritarian"

First published in English in David Collier, ed., *The New Authoritarianism in Latin America* (Princeton: Princeton University Press, 1979).—Ed.

democracy) is an indication of fundamental tensions within the core of the BA, as well as with the social sectors that this kind of state excludes.

This topic is important because focusing on the superficial features of the BA can lead to erroneous conclusions. The institutions of the BA often appear as a monolithic and imposing force whose rhetoric celebrates the superior rationality which they impose upon the nation in order to save it from its deepest crisis. These institutions also give the appearance of change and adaptation on the basis of the "impartial" and "technical" evaluation of the progress they claim to be making. Yet behind this facade, the BA state is subject to tensions—contradictions, dilemmas, and perils[2]—which reflect the extraordinary difficulties of consolidating a system of domination that can conceal neither the fact that it is founded on coercion nor the fact that its most crucial supporters represent a spectrum of society far more narrow than that of the entire nation which the BA claims to serve. Its domination is particularly repressive because, by the nature of its emergence, the BA entails an anticipated abdication of its own legitimacy. The BA arises from an overwhelming political defeat of the popular sector and its allies, who came to be perceived as a serious threat to basic parameters of society. It is from this perspective that one must consider a topic which, under the BA, might seem as surrealistic as that of democracy.

I. Concerning the State

. . .* The principal mediation [between society and the state] is the nation. I mean by nation the collective identities that define a "we" that consists, on the one hand, of a network of solidarities superimposed upon the diversity and antagonisms of civil society and, on the other hand, of the recognition of a collectivity distinct from the "they" that constitutes other nations. The nation is expressed through dense symbolisms epitomized by the flag and the national anthem, as well as by an official history that mythologizes a shared, cohesive past and extols a collective "we" which should prevail over the cleavages of civil society.

There are two other fundamental political mediations. One is citizenship, in the double sense of (1) abstract equality, which—basically by means of universal suffrage and the corresponding regime of political democracy—is the foundation of the claim that the power exercised by the occupants of governmental roles is based on the consent of the citizens; and (2) the right to have recourse to legally regulated protection against arbitrary acts on the part of the state institutions. The second mediation, particularly important in Latin America, is

---

* At several points in this chapter (each marked with an ellipsis) one or more paragraphs have been deleted because they repeated points made in other chapters in this volume. The notes corresponding to deleted passages were also left out.—*Ed.*

the *pueblo* or *lo popular.** This mediation is based on a "we" that derives neither from the idea of shared citizenship, which involves abstractly equal rights, nor from the idea of nation, which involves concrete rights which apply equally to all those who belong to the nation without respect to their position within society. Rather, *pueblo* or *lo popular* involves a "we" that is a carrier of demands for substantive justice which form the basis for the obligations of the state toward the less favored segments of the population. . . .**

The effectiveness of this idea of the nation allows the state institutions to appear as agents which achieve and protect a general interest—that is, the general interest of a "we" that stands above the factionalism and antagonisms of civil society. Moreover, the effectiveness of the ideas of citizenship and *lo popular* provides another consensual basis for the exercise of power, and ultimately of coercion, by the state institutions. They do this because the state can only be legitimated by referents that are external to itself, and whose general interests the state institutions are supposed to serve. As noted, these referents are normally the nation, citizenship, and, at least in Latin America, also the *pueblo*. From these referents there usually emerge collective identities that stand above the class and other cleavages that potentially arise from civil society. Each of those referents mediates the relation between the state and society, playing a crucial role in achieving consensus and, correspondingly, in legitimating the power exercised by the state institutions.

On the other hand, these mediations are the means through which the social subject, as a member of society, rises above his/her private life. Identifying herself in the symbols of the nation, exercising the rights of citizenship, and eventually making demands for substantive justice as part of the *pueblo*, the social subject transcends daily life and recognizes herself as part of a "we" which is the same referent evoked by the state institutions. Hence, these institutions do not usually appear as organizers and guarantors of social domination, but rather as agents of general interests expressed through the mediations of nation, citizenship, and/or *pueblo*.

II. The Bureaucratic-Authoritarian State

The BA is a type of authoritarian state whose principal characteristics are:

1. It is, first and foremost, guarantor and organizer of the domination exercised through a class structure subordinated to the upper fractions of a highly

---

* These two terms were not translated because the most nearly equivalent terms in English, "people" and "popular," have different meanings. The meaning intended by O'Donnell is indicated in the text.—Ed.

** The remainder of this section is deleted because it refers to themes that are covered in greater detail in chapter 1 of this volume. See also Guillermo O'Donnell, *Bureaucratic Authoritarianism: Argentina, 1966–1973, in Comparative Perspective* (Berkeley: University of California Press, 1988).—Ed.

oligopolized and transnationalized bourgeoisie. In other words, the principal social base of the BA state is this upper bourgeoisie.

2. In institutional terms, it comprises organizations in which specialists in coercion have decisive weight, as well as those whose aim it is to achieve "normalization" of the economy [by means of orthodox neoliberal policies].[3] The central role played by these two groups represents the institutional expression of the identification, by its own actors, of the two great tasks that the incumbents of the BA are committed to accomplish: the restoration of "order" in society by means of the political deactivation of the popular sector, on the one hand, and the normalization of the economy, on the other.

3. It is a system of political exclusion of a previously activated popular sector which is subjected to strict controls in an effort to eliminate its earlier active role in the national political arena. This political exclusion is achieved by destroying or capturing the resources (especially those embodied in class organizations and political movements) which supported this activation. In addition, this exclusion is guided by a determination to impose a repressive type of "order" on society and guarantee its future viability. This order is seen as a necessary condition for the consolidation of the social domination that the BA guarantees and, after achieving the normalization of the economy, for reinitiating a highly transnationalized pattern of economic growth characterized by a skewed distribution of resources.

4. This exclusion involves the suppression of citizenship, in the twofold sense defined above. In particular, this suppression includes the liquidation of the institutions of political democracy. It also involves a denial of *lo popular*: it prohibits (enforcing the prohibition with coercion) any appeals to the population as *pueblo* and, of course, as class. The suppression of the institutional roles and channels of access to the government characteristic of political democracy is in large measure oriented toward eliminating roles and organizations (political parties among them) that have served as a channel for appeals for substantive justice that under the BA are considered incompatible with the restoration of order and with the normalization of the economy. In addition, the BA appears as if placed before a sick nation whose general interest it invokes; yet, because of the depth of the crisis that preceded its installation, the BA cannot claim to be the representative of that nation, which is seen as contaminated by innumerable internal enemies. Thus, the BA is based on the suppression of two fundamental mediations—citizenship and *lo popular*. Furthermore, in an ambiguous way it evokes the other mediation—the nation—but only as a "project" (and not as a present reality) which it proposes to carry out through drastic surgical measures.

5. The BA is also a system of economic exclusion of the popular sector, inasmuch as it promotes a pattern of capital accumulation which is highly skewed toward benefiting the large oligopolistic units of private capital and

some state institutions. The preexisting inequities in the distribution of societal resources are thus sharply increased.

6. It corresponds to, and promotes, an increasing transnationalization of the productive structure, resulting in a further denationalization of society, in terms of the degree to which it is contained within the territorial scope of the authority which the state exercises.

7. Through its institutions, the BA endeavors to "depoliticize" social issues by dealing with them in terms of the supposedly neutral and objective criteria of technical rationality. This depoliticization complements the prohibition against invoking issues of substantive justice as they relate to *lo popular*, which allegedly introduce "irrationalities" and "premature" demands that interfere with the restoration of order and the normalization of the economy.

8. In the first stage of the BA that we are considering here, its political regime—which, while usually not formalized, is clearly identifiable—involves closing the democratic channels of access to the government. More generally, it involves closing the channels of access for the representation of popular and class interests. Such access is limited to those who stand at the apex of large organizations (both public and private), especially the armed forces and large oligopolistic enterprises. . . .

III. Ambiguities in the System of Domination

What goes on behind the imposing facade of power of the BA? In what way is the rhetoric of its institutions, directed at an ailing nation which the state is determined to save even against its will, a sign of uncertainties and weaknesses inherent in this state? The BA is a type of state which encompasses sharply contradictory tendencies. On the one hand, the BA involves the sharp denationalization of society that occurs first as a consequence of the urgent search for the transnational capital which is a requisite for the normalization of the economy, and later due to the need to maintain a "favorable investment climate" in order to sustain the inflow of such capital. At the same time, the BA entails a drastic contraction of the nation, the suppression of citizenship, and the prohibition of appeals to the *pueblo*. This contraction derives from the defeat of the popular sector and its allies; from the reaction triggered by the threat that the political activation of this sector seemed to pose for the survival of basic capitalist parameters of society; and, once the BA is implanted, from the aim of imposing a particular social "order" based on the political and economic exclusion of the popular sector.

Such exclusion appears as a necessary condition for healing the body of the nation, seen from the BA as an organism with infected parts upon which, for its own good, it is necessary to perform the surgery of excluding the popular sector and its "subversive" allies. This exclusion involves redefining the scope of the nation, to which neither the agents that promoted this illness nor the parts that have become infected can belong. They are the enemy within the body of the nation,[4] the "not-we" of the new, healthy nation that is to be constructed by the BA. When the rulers speak of the nation, the referent is restricted, by the very logic of their views, to a far less comprehensive "we" than in the past; only those can belong who fit into their design—socially harmonious and technocratic—of the future nation.

Yet, like all states, the BA claims to be a national state. Lacking the referent of the nation as a comprehensive idea that encompasses the entire population, the rhetoric of the institutions of BA must "statize" the meaning of the nation—at the same time that, in relation to the normalization of the economy, the same rhetoric defends an intense privatization. Such statizing of the idea of the nation implies that its general interest be identified with the success of the BA in its quest to establish a repressive order in society and to normalize the economy. As a result, the state institutions no longer appear to play the role through which they usually legitimate themselves, that of serving an interest superior and external to themselves. Rather, under the BA, when the state institutions redefine the nation in terms of exclusion and of national infirmity, the power they exercise no longer has an external basis of legitimation and cannot but appear as its own foundation. In other words, domination becomes naked and dilutes its consensual mediations; it manifests itself in the form of overt physical and economic coercion. In addition, the suppression of citizenship, together with the prohibition against invoking *lo popular,* radically eliminates other legitimating mediations between the state and society. . . .

The institutions of the BA attempt to fill the void thus created through an intensive use of martial and patriotic symbols. But these symbols must be anchored in some of the aforementioned referents if they are not to be merely grandiloquent rhetoric. The BA leaders also attempt to re-create mediations with society by inviting "participation"; but the state's denial of its own role as representative of the nation and the elimination of *pueblo* and citizenship mean that such participation can only involve a passively approving observation of the tasks that the state institutions undertake.

Under these conditions, the best that the BA can hope for is what its incumbents often call "tacit consensus," i.e., depoliticization, apathy, and a retreat of the population into a highly privatized daily existence. And fear. Fear on the part of the losers and the opponents of the BA, which results from BA's conspicuous capacity for coercion. And fear on the part of the winners, who face the specter of a return to the situation that preceded the implantation of the BA. And there is also the fear, on the part of those who carry out the physical coercion, of any "political solution" that could possibly lead to such a return. This last fear at times appears to drive them down a path of coercion that knows no limits. . . .

There cannot be consensus unless the connection between coercion and economic domination is veiled. Yet the opposite occurs in the BA. Moreover, in the BA the proximity of coercion and economic domination juxtaposes two social actors—the armed forces and the upper bourgeoisie—who usually are separated, on the political level, by the mediations mentioned above and, on the institutional level of the state, by various agencies of civilian bureaucracy and democratic representation. That is to say, the decisive support given to the BA by the upper bourgeoisie, and its "bridgehead" in the state apparatus in the form of the economic policymaking technocrats, intersect directly with the armed forces. The upper bourgeoisie and the technocrats have a strongly transnational orientation, both in their beliefs and in their economic behavior. For them, the political boundaries of the nation are basically a useless constraint on the movement of the factors of production, on the free circulation of capital, and on considerations of efficiency at the transnational level. These views clash with what is perceived by these same actors as the narrowness of the nation and of "nationalism." Furthermore, these actors are the most fully and dynamically capitalistic members of these societies: they are unabashedly motivated by profit, the driving force behind a highly concentrated accumulation of capital that they claim will, in due time, contribute to the general welfare.

But a great problem in the BA is that its other central actor—the armed forces—tends to be the most nationalistic and least capitalistic of the state institutions. With their sense of mission, the martial values with which they socialize their members, and their doctrines of national security which presuppose a nation characterized by a high degree of homogeneity, the armed forces are the state institution most predisposed to define appropriate political behavior as that which is inspired by an introverted and exclusivist vision of the nation. In addition, the profit motive appears to most members of the armed forces to be at most of secondary importance, and sordid in comparison with the larger concerns and ideals that derive from their own orientations. Profit may be necessary, but in any case it should not become "excessive" or work against the mission of homogenizing the totality of the nation.[5] . . .

IV. The Nostalgia for Mediations or the Question of Democracy[6]

The existence of a BA is comprehensible only as an alternative in the face of the abyss of a severe perceived threat—both in the past and potentially in the future—of elimination of the capitalist parameters of society. I have presented the reasons for this assertion, but it is appropriate to summarize here the principal ones: (1) the BA drastically curtails or suppresses mediations on the basis of which consensus is normally established; (2) it reveals starkly what is the underlying, but not normally the exclusive, reality of the state—coercion;

(3) it likewise reveals the fact that the upper bourgeoisie is the principal—and, at least in the initial period of economic normalization, virtually the only— social base of this state; (4) as a result of the historical context in which these countries have evolved, this fraction of the bourgeoisie is conspicuously their least national element; and (5) the organizations specialized in coercion acquire enormous importance within the institutional system of the state, while the values and behavior of these organizations are not consonant with those of the principal social base of that state—i.e., the upper bourgeoisie.

The suboptimal character of this type of political domination manifests itself in the fragilities that derive from the shrinking of the legitimating referent of the nation, the suppression of the mediations of citizenship and *lo popular*, the political and economic exclusion of the popular sector, and the fear by its incumbents of the reactions that may be brewing beneath the silent surface of society, as a result of the heavy costs that derive from the imposition of order and normalization. . . .

Yet how can mediations be created that would resolve for the BA "the difficulties that derive from the solitude of power"?[7] One solution would be, of course, to reinvent the Mexican political system with its dominant party, the PRI, which provides these mediations and at the same time efficiently helps prevent popular challenges. However, the PRI can be only a nostalgic aspiration because its origin is precisely the opposite from what occurred in cases with which we are concerned here: a popular revolution, rather than the terrified reaction that implanted the BAs. Another possibility would be that of a corporative structuring of society. But for corporatism to truly take the place of the missing mediations, it would have to incorporate in a subordinate fashion the entire society rather than simply restricting itself to being a form of state control of workers. Yet this is precisely what the upper bourgeoisie cannot accept. With good reason, it has no objection to the reimposition of strict controls over the popular sector, but why should the upper bourgeoisie, an indispensable supporter of the BA, accept to be incorporated into a state that subordinates it? For this reason corporatist ideology, in spite of its important influence on many actors in the BA, is a utopia as archaic as it is unachievable. Corporatism can serve—in the form of tight control over unions—to consolidate a class victory, but not as a means of replacing the mediations between state and society that the BA suppresses.[8]

If some version of the PRI is not possible, if corporatism cannot replace the mediations which are lacking, and if the state's exhortations for "participation" bounce off of the silence of society, then the only solution that remains is the aspiration for the very thing that the BA radically denies: democracy. The use of this term from the BA would be inexplicable if we did not recognize that it reflects the fundamental problem of a state without mediations and, hence, of a system of naked domination. If political democracy were to be restored, at the very least the mediation of citizenship would reappear. As a result, many members of society would once again be treated as, and would see themselves as, participants in a form of abstract but not insignificant equality—in addition to the implication of the restoration of some basic legal guarantees. In this way, the basis of state power could be attributed to this source exterior to the state—a condition which is not sufficient, but yet is necessary, for its legitimation. The restoration of political democracy would also permit the resolution of another problem that arises from the lack of mediations and from the militarization of the state: that of presidential succession. From the perspective of the upper bourgeoisie, solving this problem would have the advantage of reducing the institutional weight of the armed forces, of allowing it to cushion its ties with the armed forces through various civilian groups, and—ultimately—of reducing the visibility of the coercion through which the BA supports its social domination.

But what kind of democracy? From the perspective of the BA, it would have to be one that achieves the miracle of being all of this and that at the same time maintains the exclusion of the popular sector. In particular, it would have to be one that sustains the suppression of invocations in terms of *pueblo* and class. Such suppression presupposes that strict controls of the organizations and political movements of the popular sector are maintained, as well as controls over the permissible discourses on the part of those who occupy the institutional positions which democracy would reopen. The search for this philosopher's stone is expressed in the various qualifying adjectives that, in the rhetoric of the BA incumbents, customarily accompany the term "democracy."

How long can a kind of domination endure which is based in "tacit consensus" and which is so overt—and particularly so overtly coercive? How long can a state apparatus sustain itself in the face of the silence and opacity of civil society? How many Franco's Spains and Salazar's Portugals can there be nowadays? How can the leaders of this kind of state help but search for solutions that would permit the system of political domination that the BA embodies, and the social domination which it supports and organizes, to believe that it can be extended into the distant future, and become hegemonic? These questions point to the weaknesses of a state which proclaims itself to be, and for a time is widely perceived as being, an imposing power. The terror of the incumbents and supporters of this kind of state in the face of the silence of civil society, their aborted attempts at introducing corporatism, and their nostalgia for democracy are oblique yet crucial expressions of the difficulties faced by a type of power that lacks both mediations and legitimacy.

But, how to democratize? It seems clear to the rulers that any move in this direction can open the Pandora's box of popular political reactivation, along with invocations in terms of *pueblo* and eventually of class, which could lead to a renewal of the crisis that preceded the BA. And for the BA alliance this outcome would be worse than continuing to rule without mediations and legitimacy. Moreover, if the BA emerged in response to threatening political activation, and if the silence that it imposes on society does not hide the heavy costs of economic normalization and the imposition of "order," is it not reasonable to fear that this threat would reappear even more acutely as soon as the dike of exclusion that the BA has constructed is even partially opened? Because of this fear, the restoration of some of the mediations of democracy is both the hope and the dread of this system of domination.

The philosopher's stone would be a kind of democracy which is carefully limited, especially in the sense that invocations in terms of *pueblo* or class are prohibited, but which at the same time is not such a farce that it cannot provide the mediations and, ultimately, a legitimacy that could transform itself into hegemony. The question of how this kind of democracy could be achieved severely tests the ingenuity of the "political engineers" who offer their expertise to accomplish a task which amounts to squaring the circle. Yet the goal which the most enlightened actors in the BA seek to achieve is clearly this type of restricted democracy. In cases of a high level of prior threat and crisis, as in Chile, a democratic alternative was not proposed by the state apparatus and was introduced instead by members of the initial BA alliance who subsequently withdrew their support: the Catholic church and the Christian Democrats. In the case of a low degree of prior threat, Argentina in 1966, the issue of democracy was posed almost at the beginning of the BA, as an alternative to the corporatist leanings of the governing military group. In Argentina in 1976, as a result both of the "lesson" derived from this earlier experience and of the underlying tensions discussed in this text, no pro-corporatists have appeared and the goal of restoring democracy also has been mentioned from the start, although the obstacles that must be overcome in order to achieve this goal appear more difficult than they did in 1966. In Uruguay, the topic of democracy continues to be mentioned, accompanied by curious contortions intended to preserve an image of civilian government in the form of a figurehead president completely subordinated to the armed forces. In the case of lower previous threat, Brazil, there was even an attempt during the Castelo Branco period to retain some of the institutions of political democracy. The authoritarian dynamic of the situation took the process in a different direction, but some of the initial elements nonetheless remained: the parliament, two official parties, and periodic elections for some governmental positions. In this country the experience with elections, albeit tightly controlled, has made quite evident the potentially disruptive dynamic that is set into motion when the alternative of democracy is raised, regardless of how surrealistic this alternative may appear to be when it is done by, and under the aegis of, a BA.

The nakedness of BA domination and of the alliance that supports it, as well as the highly visible character of its negative social consequences, generate the great issues raised by those who oppose the BA: human rights, economic nationalism, and demands for substantive justice. The great dread of a system of domination which is simultaneously so imposing and so insecure is the fear that the opponents—who, despite their silence, quite clearly exist— will galvanize themselves around these issues into one great explosion that will destroy not only the BA but also the social domination that it has helped to reimpose. The [1969] "Cordobazo" and the events that followed it are the symbol of this possibility, and not just in Argentina. The unsuccessful attempts to reestablish a cohesive and harmoniously integrated nation, the prolongation of the ominous silence of society, and the notoriety of the domination which the BA supports are the basis of the insecurity of this system of domination, which often tends to make it more dangerous and coercive. This coercion further biases the institutional system of the BA toward a larger role for the armed forces and further deepens the silence of society, which is exactly the opposite of what should happen if the BA is to achieve some legitimacy. Nevertheless, democracy continues to be mentioned, at times eclipsed but then reemerging in the official rhetoric or as the proposal of one or another of the groups that struggle for power in the BA.

The issue of democracy is important not only because it indicates the Achilles heel of the BA, but also because it contains a dynamic that can be the unifying element in the long-term effort to establish a society that is more nearly in accord with certain fundamental human values. The proposal from the BA for a limited form of democracy, without *pueblo* and ultimately without nation, is not the gracious concession of a triumphant power, but the expression of its intrinsic weakness. The ambivalence with which democracy is mentioned from the institutional apex of the BA and by its principal allies, and the evident fear of transgressing limits beyond which it would be too risky to advance in a process of democratization, does not generate its own contrasting negation as do other policies and impacts of the BA. The antithesis of the distorted and limited democracy proposed by the BA's incumbents and supporters does not have to be the political and social authoritarianism which is, precisely, the true and evident reality of this state. As a result, the issue of democracy, even the mere mention of the term, remains suspended in political discourse, and thus liable to be expropriated by giving the term meanings that supersede the limitations and qualifications that the voices heard from the BA try to impose.

The possibility of democracy may simply represent an invitation to opportunism for those who wish to use it just to enter into a game to be played with rules predetermined by the BA's incumbents. This possibility may also invite the imbecility of rejecting democracy out of hand because it is initiated from above and because there is such a careful effort to impose limits upon it. But what democracy can also be, if indeed the powers-that-be are not the only ones who have learned something from the tragedy of the Southern Cone, is the discovery of a purpose and style of politics that would not be limited to a careful calculation of the limits up to which it can be expanded at each point in time. It would be, more fundamentally, a struggle for the appropriation and redefinition of the meaning of democracy, oriented toward impregnating itself with the meanings carried by those who are excluded by the BA and constituting, together with them, the basis for an alternative kind of state.

There are circumstances in which the discussion of certain topics can seem useless nostalgia. But the fact that nowadays certain words, such as democracy, are employed at all cannot simply be attributed to idiosyncracies, to tactics of accommodation with the international situation, or to false consciousness. Under the BA, the evident contradiction between the mere mention of democracy and the reality of daily life is much more than this. This contradiction is a key to understanding the weaknesses and profound tensions of the present system of domination. It is also an indication of the immense importance of what remains behind the superficial appearance of these societies—the importance of those who are excluded and forced into silence, who, on one hand, are the focus of any hopes for achieving legitimacy for the BA and yet, on the other hand, as seen from this same BA, are a Pandora's box that must not be tampered with. This implicit presence of those who are excluded and silent is a source of the dynamic and tensions of the BA, to no less a degree than that which occurs in the grand scenarios of this state.

Later on, after the first period of BA—that of its installation, on which this essay has focused—its dikes of exclusion begin to crack, fear dilutes, and some of the voices which had been silenced are heard once again. Then, more or less obliquely, but with a meaning that no one can fail to understand, these voices resound, not only throughout society but also within the state apparatus. These changes do not just involve the end of the silence imposed on those who were defeated by the installation of the BA, nor the thousand ways of demonstrating that the "tacit consensus" in fact represented a suppressed opposition. Nor are these changes merely a search for mediations on the part of some incumbents in the BA who know, on the one hand, that without these mediations they cannot continue to rule for long and, on the other, that by attempting to restore the mediations they revive the ghosts which they attempted, at such high risk and cost, to destroy. At such point, the fissures of the BA which are opened by its absence of mediations pose a great opportunity. The response to this opportunity—in terms of the scope of the potential democratization that it involves—in large measure depends on those who in the phase of the implantation of the BA are so radically excluded. But for a whole series of reasons, this still unmapped future lies beyond the scope of the present analysis.

Notes

1. Guillermo O'Donnell, "Reflections on the Patterns of Change of the Bureaucratic-Authoritarian State," *Latin American Research Review* (winter 1978): 3–38, presented first at the "Conference on History and the Social Sciences," University of Campinas, Brazil, and published as CEDES Document, GE-CLACSO, no. 1, 1975.

2. A similar argument is presented by Philippe C. Schmitter, "Liberation by *Golpe:* Retrospective Thoughts on the Demise of Authoritarian Rule in Portugal," *Armed Forces and Society* 2 (no. 1, November 1975): 5–33.

3. I use this phrase to refer to the tasks undertaken by the civilian technocrats in charge of the economic apparatus of the BA, whose aim is to stabilize certain crucial variables (such as the rate of inflation and the balance-of-payments) in a manner that will gain the confidence of major capitalist interests—above all, in the first stage of the BA, of transnational finance capital.

4. This organic image is, of course, reinforced by the doctrines of "national security."

5. After closely examining the orientations of the armed forces in the countries in which the BA has emerged, I am convinced that this is a valid generalization. However, this assertion does not preclude the possibility that in some cases the upper echelon of the armed forces might be controlled by groups more favorably disposed toward the orientations of the upper bourgeoisie. This greater affinity would doubtless mitigate the problems which I analyze below—but it does not eliminate them, since it seems to mean that the control over the armed forces exercised by this military leadership will be more precarious. The most important case of such congruence between the attitudes of high level military leaders and the upper bourgeoisie and the officials in the economic team of the BA is that of Castelo Branco and his group in Brazil, from 1964 to 1967. Another case is that of the Lanusse presidency in Argentina, from 1971 to 1973. However, in this case it was not the consolidation of the BA that was being attempted, but rather the negotiation of its liquidation.

6. No discussion of this theme is complete that does not mention the fundamental contributions of Fernando Henrique Cardoso. See especially his *Autoritarismo e Democratização* (Rio de Janeiro: Paz e Terra, 1975).

7. Phrase used by the Argentine president, Lt. General Videla, as quoted in *Cronista Comercial*, April 27, 1977, p. 1.

8. I have dealt with this topic in "Corporatism and the Question of the State," in James M. Malloy, ed., *Authoritarianism and Corporatism in Latin America* (Pittsburgh: University of Pittsburgh Press, 1977).

PART II
Despotisms

3

Democracy in Argentina: Macro and Micro

This essay is about daily life in Buenos Aires during the most repressive years of the BA that today is crumbling. In the pages that follow I do not conceal its subjective and testimonial character, just as I—a political scientist to the end—do not refrain from analyzing some micro/macro relationships that seem important to me.

The tone of this text is not due solely to the characteristics of its subject matter. It also arises from the particular difficulty of trying to understand social relations under a kind of rule that is bent on brutally and systematically suppressing much of the information that is available under conditions of reasonable freedom. In my experience such suppression raises crucial questions about the criteria used to investigate situations where normal research methods cannot be put into practice. Situations like the ones we Argentines have experienced in recent years demonstrate the inadequacy of many social science concepts, especially those associated with the problematic of authoritarianism. At least, in situations this extreme, I and others began to pay close attention to the microcontexts of the social world—the textures of everyday life—so that, beginning at this level, we might trace their relationships to the macroarenas of politics. This occurred in part because of the impossibility of obtaining adequate aggregate data due to the secrecy imposed by harsh authoritarian rule, and also because of a genuine emotional and intellectual need to understand those microrelations. Another consequence of trying to

Prior to being translated for inclusion in the current book, this text was first published in Oscar Oszlak, ed., *El "Proceso," crisis y transición democrática* (Buenos Aires: Centro Editor de América Latina, Biblioteca de Politica Argentina, 1984).—*Ed.*

work under circumstances of severe and pervasive repression is that the values by which—and because of which—the legitimacy of a critical intellectual practice can still be asserted must be made explicit, even though for a time it is only possible to do so in the small circles that somehow survive the repression.

On the other hand, in the present days of celebrating the collapse of this accursed BA, perhaps it is not too much to raise questions about the scars, not all of them easily perceptible, left behind by those years, including the consequences that they might have for the consolidation of democracy in Argentina.

I

In these pages I discuss some aspects of daily life in Argentina between 1976 and 1980. As I pointed out, it was impossible, due to the harsh repression that engulfed us, to reliably know the overall situation of the country. The opinion surveys that I imagine were conducted were, and continue to be, like so many other things, a state secret; for this reason I cannot bring in reasonably reliable data to corroborate the impressions I convey in the present text.[1] Nevertheless, I believe it worthwhile to discuss some themes that may have subtle but important consequences for the future.

In other works I have analyzed the characteristics of the authoritarian period inaugurated in Argentina in March 1976.* One is its enormous repressiveness, not only in the quantity of horrors that it inflicted but also in its terrorist and clandestine nature. Another is the political significance of its economic and social policies as a historical vengeance against the "plebeian, populist, and immigrant" Argentina of the preceding decades.[2] These aspects are crucial for understanding what the incumbents of this BA did and tried to do. But there is a third aspect that seems to me no less important even though it has received less attention, probably because it took place on less spectacular terrain. I refer to the systematic and relentless attempts by the state to penetrate society in all contexts its long arm could reach, in order to implant "order and authority." This purpose was modeled on the radically vertical, authoritarian, and paternalistic vision held by the incumbents of this BA—its military and civilians, and at least initially, their many supporters in society. This attempt to penetrate society with a deeply authoritarian *pathos*, along with the destructiveness of the BA's economic policies, are two features that

---

* See chapter 2 in this book. Other articles by the author that address this theme include "Reflections on the Patterns of Change in the Bureaucratic-Authoritarian State," *Latin American Research Review* 13 (no. 1), and "The Armed Forces and the Bureaucratic-Authoritarian State in the Southern Cone of Latin America," *Research Monographs* (Berkeley: Center for Latin American Studies, University of California, 1982).—*Ed.*

link Argentina with contemporary Chile and Uruguay, and which distinguish these cases from more restrained BAs such as post-1964 Brazil and Argentina 1966–73.

The widespread violence that occurred in Argentina prior to the March 1976 coup and the savage paranoia of the military and its allies led them to the diagnosis that the entire "social body," even its most microscopic "tissues," had been "infected" by "subversion." (I suspect that few times in history the far right has used and abused its characteristic organic metaphors like it did during those years.) According to them, "chaos," "subversion," and the "dissolution of authority" were to be found not only, or so much, in the macroarenas of politics and in the actions of guerrilla organizations; this sickness also existed in every corner and niche of society, from where it had nourished the more visible "symptoms" found in the macroarenas. Based on this diagnosis, a microscopic "cure" was formulated, directed at penetrating all the layers of society and "reorganizing" them in such a way that the central goal of the rulers would be guaranteed forever—that the authority of those who had, in every microcontext, both the right and the obligation to rule would never again be "subverted."

Consequently, we were not only stripped of political citizenship but also, in the contexts of daily life—in the social relations and patterns of authority that mark day-to-day existence—an attempt was made to subjugate us and turn us into obedient infants. Those who had the "right to rule" would rule tyrannically in the workplace, the school, the family, and the streets; those who had the "duty to obey" would do so meekly and silently, unanimous in their acceptance that even the most despotic demands made in these microcontexts were, like those of the state, for the good of their subjects. If this were not so, how would it be possible to separate the wheat from the chaff, the obedient from the subversive? After all, according to these views it had been demonstrated beyond doubt that the "insolence" of "inferiors" led to chaos. This conception of authority could not be any more vertical, authoritarian, and depreciative of the autonomy of those whom it sought to subjugate, nor could it conceal, despite the paternalistic tone that adorned its arguments, the massive violence (not only physical) on which it was sustained. Thus we lost the right to walk down the street if we did not dress in the civilian uniform (short hair, jacket and tie, dull colors) that the bosses—civilian as well as military—considered appropriate; it became highly inadvisable to be "different," or to give unconventional opinions on even the most apparently trivial topics; in educational institutions, where everyone was expected to learn passively, it was anathema to ask questions, to doubt anything, or even to meet with more than a few others; and in many workplaces (including, but not limited to, factories) there was constant persecution of anyone who was not absolutely obedient. This pattern was repeated even within families, in part because the authoritarian mindset apparently found important echoes there, in part because many parents felt that by "retaking command" they could assure the depoliticization of their children and thus save them from the deadly fate that had been suffered by so many other young people. Our interviews with psychologists and psychoanalysts suggested that the repressive and infantilizing traits of many families were accentuated during this period, reproducing the patriarchal model that was constantly propitiated by official and commercial propaganda.[3] I cannot even bring myself to mention the treatment given to anyone even remotely connected to "hippies," drugs (starting with marijuana, that terrible weapon of subversion against Western and Christian civilization), or "sexual perversion."[4]

II

It is not my intent to reel off a dreadful inventory. The point I wish to make is that the information we gathered indicates that, at least in its initial years, the rulers' efforts met with considerable success. Many gave in, kept quiet, disguised themselves, and dissembled in the face of enormous pressure to act like obedient children, ready to leave it to those "who knew" (in the economy, in the administration of terror, on the streets, and in so many microcontexts) what, supposedly, would be best for everyone—and which had to begin by putting everyone "in their place," from the woman in the home, to the former citizen toiling in the street, up to the military officials and cadaverous oligarchs ruling in the BA. The second point is that although the pressure to accept such infantilization was enormous, it was not enough (nor could it ever have been enough) had it come solely from state officials—not even with their phenomenal authoritarian desire to control our behavior in such detailed fashion. For such control to occur there had to be a society that patrolled itself. More precisely, there were many persons (I do not know how many, but surely quite a few) who, without any "official" need to do so, simply because they wanted to, because it seemed good to them, because they accepted the vision of order that the regime presented as the only alternative to the perpetually invoked images of pre-1976 chaos, took it upon themselves to zealously exercise their own authoritarian *pathos* in whatever microcontext they commanded. These were *kapos*[5] who, assuming the values of their aggressor, we often saw going well beyond what the rulers demanded of them.

It is not easy to raise this issue, but it seems to me that the problem of democracy in Argentina, as in every case in which similar atrocities have been committed, must pass through the painful recognition that there was not only a state and a government that were brutally despotic, but that there was also a society that during those years was much more authoritarian and repressive than ever before—and that even though we will never know their number, many persons had a hand in the cruel repression that took place in numerous microcontexts. Just as with the dead and disappeared produced by this BA by the tens of thousands, these microhorrors can only be ignored by paying the price, individual and collective, of every denial: the inability to see ourselves as we really are. By engaging in denial, we flee from the painful yet creative possibility of reformulating our identities and values in order to prevent the reemergence of our most destructive aspects.

Perhaps I am exaggerating. Perhaps I kept silent too often, and loathed too much the sadism of the *kapos* that we encountered daily during those years. Perhaps it is an exaggeration, but it would be a far greater—and more dangerous—mistake to project everything onto that accursed BA and hence to excuse ourselves from fully seeing, and trying to understand, what took place during those years in Argentina. In those times I often reflected on a metaphor: that the implantation of merciless authoritarian domination unleashes the wolves. I refer not only to what the rulers command but also, more subtly and powerfully, to the permission they grant so that many feel free to exercise their minidespotisms on workers, students, and every other kind of "subordinate," from passers-by to children (to say nothing of what the military later showed they could do, following this same terrible logic, with the soldiers they sent to death in the crazy adventure of the Malvinas/Falklands war). Those of us who did not want to exercise this type of power (or who were unable to) learned, through the persuasiveness of inversion, what the absence of a reasonably democratic environment meant: to be at the mercy of the wolves because we had no rights, and if some rights still belonged to us in theory, we had no chance to enforce them. Given this, and the authoritarian *pathos* that the BA exuded, our society, riddled with *kapos* and with the patrolling of behavior (including the hair length of passers-by) that many "volunteers" practiced, we bowed to state and social despotism. Some adopted this repression as their own credo and others endured it in angry silence. We will never know how many were on each side, but certainly neither was lacking in numbers.

III

Now that the regime has begun its demise and many voices that once were silenced have begun to be heard, and now that the right to be different begins to be exercised again, it is important to recognize the considerable success that the BA and its supporters had in affecting society and, I fear, the degree to which many of these successes have not been reversed. It is not only that so many *kapos*, those microdespots, continue in their positions. Nor is it only that during those years many people refused to know what was going on with the thousands that were murdered, kidnapped, and tortured, attributing these events to malicious rumors, or—when there was no way to deny certain horrors—blaming the victims (that terrible condemnation of "They must have done *something* . . ." that was said so often during those years). These are echoes of things that we would like to believe can occur only in other parts of the world until we are forced to confront them ourselves. Nor is it that many of the *kapos* and those who turned a blind eye today vent their rage* against the BA for the economic disaster it has provoked, for the Malvinas/Falklands fiasco, and for the phenomenal corruption of the military—as if that were all that occurred (and do so with the impassioned tone of those who must unconsciously deny having had anything to do with horrors that are no longer defensible). In addition to all of this is yet another problem that I believe is even more fundamental to our future—the persistence of extremely authoritarian patterns of behavior in many microcontexts.

What I have said so far raises two questions that I will present, not really answer, in these pages. The first refers to the reasons why the BA was successful in making Argentine society so much more authoritarian. On this score, just as in Europe in the era of denazification, it is our responsibility not to reach for easy answers. As already argued, the most obvious—and most escapist—answer would be to project all responsibility onto the rulers of recent years (and by this I do not mean to minimize the enormous responsibility that belongs to them). On the other hand, for several years the great ideological victory of the BA was to trap many people in the dilemma of either accepting the brutal "order" which it offered or returning to the "chaos" preceding the 1976 coup.[6] To the extent that this was perceived to be the case, in a situation in which all public spaces for formulating and recognizing alternative political identities had been suppressed, the possibility of opposing the BA's attempts to penetrate and "reorganize" society remained obstructed. There is little doubt that after years of intense mobilization and hyperpoliticization during the first half of the 1970s, many were predisposed to accept what the post-1976 repression and propaganda set out to achieve: a decisive turn inward, toward the privatization of lifestyles, a generalized aspiration to reduce the uncertainties of life (for which it was made clear that one had to obey the wishes of those in power), and the no less generalized sensation that during the years preceding the 1976 coup the patterns of authority—not only in politics but also in innumerable microcontexts—had reached a point of personally intolerable and socially suicidal anarchy.

The question, then, of why this BA was successful in its authoritarian vocation in many contexts of society can be partly answered by reference to the extremely violent, and in many ways truly crazy and chaotic years that pre-

---

* For discussion of the relationships between this kind of reaction and "cycles of repoliticization," "rebound effects," and the "resurrection of civil society," see chapters 4 and 6 in this book.—*Ed.*

ceded the coup of March 1976. It seems that after a period perceived as the height of danger and uncertainty, a politically and psychologically regressive tendency was at work: to hope for the emergence of a supreme power that could guarantee almost any kind of order. This tendency, which Hobbes and some analysts of fascism understood well, suggests some of the less visible, but no less severe, costs that a period of extreme violence and radicalization like the one prior to the 1976 coup can generate.

In light of what I have said, the discussion could easily become centered on whether the pre-1976 or post-1976 period should be assigned the greater explanatory power (and blame) with regard to the questions I have raised. I do not believe that such a debate would be very useful, not only for the obvious reason that we do not know how to assign relative weights to such complex phenomena, but also because the question itself is insufficiently posed. To assert that the advance of social authoritarianism in Argentina during 1976–80 was a direct consequence of the BA, and that the opportunity and predisposition for this were largely sown in the years immediately prior to the coup, is true but not fully satisfactory. At least, insisting on the themes I stress in the present text, another question remains: the degree to which the conceptions and patterns of authority in everyday contexts were influenced by, and influenced, a long history marked by the repeated failure of Argentine social and political actors to achieve more democratic, and ultimately more humane, ways of articulating social and political life.

IV

It is beyond the reach of this essay (and of its author) to provide an answer to the question posed above. But even though we may not know how to answer it, we cannot avoid raising it. This question is, perhaps, the key to recognizing some authoritarian tendencies long present in Argentina; it may allow us to understand the recent past as the brutal accentuation of these tendencies, not as a novelty solely brought about by pre-1976 or post-1976 experiences at the macrolevel. On one hand, if it is true that in recent years many micro-despotisms have become more widespread and, perhaps, more deeply rooted in a variety of social contexts, and if the principle causes of this can be found in the macropolitics of the period immediately preceding or following the 1976 coup, then the problem of democracy in Argentina could be resolved by democratizing only the political regime and the aegis of the state apparatus. Under this view, the causal arrows go from the macro to the micro, and a stable democratic solution may be accomplished in a relatively short period. Unfortunately, the problem, as I have suggested, is more complicated and far-reaching.

I do not mean to deny the importance of the kind of politics played out on the great stages of national life by politicians and other actors. But I do believe that the interpretation outlined above falls into a dangerous politicism. By this I mean that too much emphasis is placed on the democratization of the regime and of the aegis of the state, while the mutual reinforcements that the diffusion of democratic values and practices on both levels (micro and macro) could generate are denied or seriously underrepresented. From the classics to today, we could fill an entire library with works relevant to the study of relationships between different levels of social action. Even if our reading of these texts would lead us to conclude that there is not much that can be said with certainty, we may still hazard a few propositions of interest to our topic. One is that micro/macro relationships are neither so direct nor so linear that a significant degree of social democratization is a necessary or a sufficient condition for the implantation of a democratic regime. A second proposition is that, nevertheless, the practice of democracy, even at the macropolitical level, entails a long-term process among actors involved in complex interactions, and that this practice is greatly helped by a conception of citizenship through which the individual emerges as a subject endowed with rights that he or she must learn to use and to make effective. Such learning processes (even if they were oriented only toward the recruitment of those who would be players in the grand scenarios of politics, which is not the case) can take place to the necessary extent only if diverse contexts of daily life, from childhood to adulthood, lend positive reinforcement to such practices. A corollary to this proposition is that important advances in the democratization of society are a necessary, if not sufficient, condition for the consolidation of a democratic political regime and, even more, for its expansion in the direction of greater participation and social justice.

This is the point that may be obscured by a politicist and historically myopic vision. To put my views plainly, I believe: first, that the problem of the consolidation and expansion of democracy in Argentina is linked as much to society as it is to the state and macropolitics, and second, that the authoritarian strands found within our society, though greatly accentuated in the 1970s (especially after 1976), are to be found in a longer and deeper past.

Unfortunately (or thankfully) in this social sphere there is no Gordian knot that could be severed with one swing of the axe. If the problem I have noted is real, it can only be confronted by means of a perspective that knows that it is essential to achieve a democratic regime but that also recognizes that this alone is not sufficient to resolve the long-standing enigma of the failure of democracy in Argentina.

If, despite its methodological limitations, I have so far relied on our proto-investigation to support my arguments, at this point in my reasoning I can no longer resort even to that. I have recourse only to some hunches, which I now outline. I believe that one of the problems has been that many Argentines (myself included) have committed an error that classical thinkers (including minds as dissimilar as Hobbes and Tocqueville) did not incur: failing to recognize that a society (like Argentina's, at least until 1976) can be comparatively quite egalitarian and yet at the same time highly authoritarian. From the time that universal suffrage left the Argentine political right without votes yet in control of the pampas' land, of crucial financial circuits, and of a cultural prestige as noteworthy for its anachronistic quality as for its strength, our country followed a bumpy road toward social equalization. First with the Radical party and later with peronism, by the mid-1970s Argentina had achieved, by Latin American standards, a quite remarkable degree of socioeconomic equality. But in politics, none of the main forces was (to put it mildly) immune to attacks of acute skepticism regarding democracy, especially after the right began to display systematic disloyalty toward the democratic game. From this emerged a particularly weak political society, repeatedly overwhelmed by the corporatist logic of various social forces and easily dispensed with whenever these forces (indeed including the more armed of these forces, the military) agreed, or whenever there was a prolonged political impasse. As a result, Argentina's political regime ended up looking more like a case of anarchic corporatism (a strange invention, indeed) than anything else. Especially after 1976, the resulting conflicts, lacking institutional mediations, ended up demonstrating that those who lose the most are those who are the weakest in a class-based society. Before 1976, the main kind of mediation between social and political actors increasingly consisted of violent confrontations—which, by their own logic, tended to become re-monopolized (in the worst possible way, and for the worst reasons) by those with the most armed force. Thus before the 1976 coup we reached the terrible limit of a confrontational semi-egalitarianism that lacked any convivial vision, a vision that could only have derived from the very thing that this brinkmanship was making less and less possible: that is, from institutional mechanisms that could generalize and widen the crude corporate and institutional interests that monopolized, and primitivized, this style of politics.[7]

My purpose in the present text was to see if it was possible to recognize echoes of the style depicted above in the microcontexts I have described. It is my impression that, even before 1976, despite the rather noteworthy egalitarianism of interpersonal and interclass relations in our country and the sharp awareness of the rights that correspond to each class or occupational category (elements that in another political context would be very congenial for establishing and expanding a democratic polity), the social relations, the patterns of authority in diverse microcontexts, and even the criteria for perceiving and evaluating the "other-who-is-not-as-I-am," have long been authoritarian and intolerant in Argentina. The puritanical and hypocritical moralism of the right, and often of the left as well; the ever-renewed paranoid and Manichean views of our history and its failures; the racism of many, expressed not only in anti-Semitism but also in the arrogant myth of a "white" and "European" country lodged in a Latin America of indians and mulattos; the frequent repression of sexual identities and practices; the interaction between repressive and infantilizing conceptions of educational authority on the one hand, and rebellions of youth's anomic rage on the other; the frequent reproduction of a rigidly patriarchal model of family organization; the hard gesture that erects barriers to cooperation and is backed by the presumption that only idiots think beyond themselves, their family, or the social sector to which they belong—the widespread and long-term presence of these and other signs marks what is perhaps the main paradox of our history and, at the same time, the most important enigma to be solved in this new attempt to construct democracy in Argentina: the course followed by a country that quite early achieved a relatively high degree of prosperity and egalitarianism but repeatedly failed to translate these achievements into values and practices from which reasonably compatible views of the social order could be derived. Instead, each failure seems to have taught a perverse antagonistic lesson, in a spiral that ensured that the next failure would be even more violent and catastrophic.

V

After having believed it many times in the past, it seems that this time we Argentines really have gotten to the bottom of the hole that we have been digging over the past generations. There, at the bottom, we did not find, as it was sometimes said, our "Bolivianization," but the scarred face of Argentina itself: ruined, violent, and under the heel of its history. In the aftermath of the terrible period inaugurated in March 1976, it is perhaps possible that, for the first time, we will derive lessons congruent with (to use the crudest term that comes to mind) more civilized social and political arrangements.

This hopeful side follows not only from the collapse of the BA and the now nearly unanimous condemnation of the horrors that its incumbents committed, but even more so from the fact that today many voices are calling, with apparent sincerity, for the conquest of the democracy that has eluded us for so long. But I have argued here that for this to occur and for democracy to be sustainable, it will be necessary to look inward, at ourselves. It is in the microlevel struggle against the manifold authoritarian tendencies present in our country—in the persistent struggles of democratic citizens who are also democratic and tolerant in their microcontexts—that the enormous challenges that we face today reside, no less than in other, more macro and visible levels.

Notes

1. Those of us who were truly opposed to what was going on (by "truly" I mean totally and unconditionally, not just unhappy about this or that aspect of the BA) adopted curious ways of first, surviving, and second, not going (literally) crazy in the face of the extreme isolation to which we were condemned. For my former wife Cecilia Galli and I, such a way consisted of conducting a proto-investigation of various aspects of daily life in Buenos Aires. I say "proto" investigation because we carried out interviews only with those persons from various sectors and social activities who we thought, under the circumstances, we could get away with interviewing without fear of being denounced. We had no pretension whatsoever of "representativeness" in our sample; we simply interviewed those who we were not too afraid to interview. We did other things as well: we approached, "with due discretion," various educational institutions and professional organizations; we read (and, the height of masochism, forced ourselves to watch on television) the speeches of BA leaders, observing their self-images as projected in official propaganda. And since we were condemned to a phenomenology of daily life, we observed streets and various professional activities through the lens of our concern as to whether we could discover there impacts of the horrors and terrors of the BA. From this mélange of information emerged something like an ethnography of the consequences, often unconscious for the actors themselves, of living under an exceptionally repressive regime.

2. On this matter I find particularly illuminating Jorge Schvarzer: "Martínez de Hoz: La Lógica Política de la Política Económica" (Buenos Aires: Ensayos y Tesis CISEA, 1992). Roberto Frenkel and I made an early attempt to discuss some of these themes in "The Stabilization Programs of the IMF and Their Internal Effects," in R. Fagen, ed., *Capitalism and the State in U.S.–Latin American Relations* (Stanford, Calif.: Stanford University Press, 1979). I took up other related themes in "Modernization and Military Coups: Theory, Comparison, and the Argentine Case," in Abraham Lowenthal, ed., *Armies and Parties in Latin America* (New York: Holmes & Meier, 1976).

3. We noted the frequency with which both official and commercial propaganda reproduced a scene that perhaps captures best the preferred self-image of this regime: a "correctly dressed" (by the standards imposed at the time) man, returning home from a day at work, tired but happy, lovingly received by his wife, who is no less happy for having stayed home cleaning, cooking, and caring for the children. Another typical character in the scene was a grandmother or grandfather, kind and revered, conveying the image of a deeply rooted past in which this wonderful family found its sense of continuity. On the other hand, there were absolutely no teenagers or young adults (potentially subversive images, of course), only very young children—smiling, squeaky clean, and totally obedient. Assuming that the repetition of this stereotypical image in commercial advertising was due to instructions from the government, we interviewed some advertising executives. Apart from the "moralizing" prohibitions imposed upon television (which did not restrict publicity only to the kind of image I have described), to our surprise we were told by our interviewees that their clients themselves often requested this kind of socially and psychologically regressive scene. To our further surprise, according to the former, their market research showed that this was the kind of image that sold the most products. Ironically, the publicity that frequently departed

from this scheme (and even showed young people) was that of some affiliates of multinational firms which reproduced the advertising packets of their headquarters.

4. Néstor Perlongher, "La represión a los homosexuales en la Argentina" (unpublished manuscript, São Paulo, 1982) contains a grim and moving description of the cruelty that the repression of homosexuals reached during these years.

5. In the Nazi concentration camps, "kapos" were prisoners who were charged with carrying out numerous aspects of "discipline" within the camps. Memoirs of survivors consistently report that these individuals were often even more cruel than the S.S. officers.

6. Many of our interviewees showed that they had swallowed this false but, for the rulers' purposes, efficacious dilemma. When in 1979 we invited them to compare their feelings about their lives and our country's affairs with any previous period, most of them chose the years immediately prior to 1976. This period was selected because it was perceived as one of unbearable chaos, violence, and uncertainty, to which any alternative of order seemed preferable. This did not prevent many of these same respondents from being unhappy with various aspects of the policies of the BA. But, to the extent that their outlook was trapped in the "chaos-order" dilemma, these dissatisfactions did not lead our interviewees to modify their factual consent to the BA nor the extremely depoliticized lives they had adopted. In some cases this privatization had reached such a point that they told us that, until our interview forced them to, they had not thought about "political" questions for quite some time. Certainly this narrowing of the general outlook of our interviewees (which corresponded to the deprivation of citizenship that was taking place at all levels) was precarious; everything indicates that this narrowing began to erode with the obvious intra-military conflicts that marked the presidential transition from General Videla to General Viola in 1981 and then disappeared with the Malvinas/Falklands fiasco.

7. On this theme, see Marcelo Cavarozzi, *Autoritarismo y democracia en la Argentina* (Buenos Aires: Centro Editor, 1983).

4

On the Fruitful Convergences of Hirschman's *Exit, Voice, and Loyalty* and *Shifting Involvements*: Reflections from the Recent Argentine Experience

I

As this volume abundantly, albeit partially, shows, the works that Albert Hirschman has addressed to the economic and political development of Latin America have had enormous impact on the students (and often on the social and political leaders) of the region. Hirschman's influence on Latin America, however, goes well beyond those writings: his more general or theoretical publications, including those that were written more with the developed world in mind, have been extremely useful to many Latin Americanists from various disciplines. In this essay I use some of the ideas developed by Hirschman in *Exit, Voice, and Loyalty (EVL)*,[1] and in *Shifting Involvements (SI)*[2] raised by the hectic and violent politics of my country, Argentina. By "transplanting" those ideas to a deeply repressive and authoritarian context, I hope to show that they can be further extended in ways that enhance their comparative and theoretical import.

II

The coups that implanted bureaucratic authoritarianism in South America in the 1960s and 1970s occurred after, and to a large extent as a consequence of,

First published in Alejandro Foxley, Michael McPherson, and Guillermo O'Donnell, eds., *Development, Democracy, and the Art of Trespassing* (Notre Dame, Ind.: University of Notre Dame Press, 1986).

serious economic crises, great waves of popular mobilization, widespread
politicization, and—quite often—high and increasing levels of violence.[3] In
most cases, however, as happened with the emergence of fascism in Europe,
those phenomena had already peaked before the respective military coups.
This was certainly the case in Argentina before the 1976 coup: the massive
mobilizations, the extensive and intense politicization of many individuals
from practically all social sectors, and even the challenges posed by urban
guerrillas had been declining for approximately two years before the coup.
Although relevant data is sparse, it is clear that many individuals, tired of intense political involvement and threatened by the chaotic violence that characterized the post-1969 period in Argentina,[4] had quite eagerly returned to
private pursuits before the 1976 coup.

In *SI* Hirschman persuasively discusses the factors that seem to account for
the cycles of (to use terms which are equivalent to Hirschman's but which are
more appropriate for my purposes here) politicization and privatization observable in many countries. As Hirschman points out in *SI*, there are important
differences in these cycles depending on whether or not the general political
context is democratic. Pursuing this distinction further, we may note that
when individuals opt for privatization in a democratic context, they are not
haunted by the possibility of being victimized for whatever political reason.
Furthermore, in those circumstances, the regime and, in general, the rules that
regulate events in the public sphere remain unchanged, except for the lowered
political participation entailed by the turn of many individuals to their private
pursuits. On the other hand, when a new wave of politicization occurs, the
costs eventually incurred by each individual are those resulting from his/her
changed allocation of time and efforts. A quite different matter are the additional (and eventually much more important) costs that may result from the
actions of a government determined to prevent and, if necessary, repress such
repoliticization. As we shall see, both *SI* and *EVL* are useful for studying some
processes that occur under bureaucratic-authoritarian rule, but further specifi-
cation of the contextual assumptions of those works is needed: first, BA
regimes were committed to preventing the repoliticization of their subjects
and were ready to apply extremely harsh repression for that purpose; and second, even while living very privatized lives, many individuals had reason to
fear reprisals motivated by their former political involvement.

In such situations, in Argentina as well as in Chile and Uruguay, many
persons exited: they went into exile, some literally to save their lives, some
because they could not stand the existing climate of pervasive fear and uncertainty. But many had not, or thought they had not, such an option. Their main
alternative was the antonym of voice—silence—which is not discussed in detail under the contextual assumptions of *EVL* and *SI*. Silence and, as we shall

see, "oblique voice" are, however, prime alternatives when the exit option is foreclosed and one is subjected to a repressive power.[5]

A situation such as the one I have sketched entails a sharp reduction of voice in at least two senses: first, in respect to the kind and number of individuals who can address the rulers without serious personal risk and, second, in what pertains to the permissible content and style of whatever voice is allowed to remain. Notice that I have referred to the type of voice that Hirschman analyzes in *EVL* and in the papers subsequently published in *Essays on Trespassing*.[6] This voice is addressed to the "top," by customers or citizens, toward managers or governments. This is what I shall call "vertical voice." This kind of voice is indeed crucial, but I shall argue that there is another type of voice that is no less important, and in some senses even more important, since it is a necessary condition for the exercise of vertical voice. This other kind of voice I shall call "horizontal."

In a democratic context, we assume that we have the right to address others, without fear of sanctions, on the basis of the belief that those others are "like me" in some dimension that at least I consider relevant. If we actually recognize ourselves as a "we" (for example, as workers who have the right to unionize), we have taken a necessary, and at times sufficient, step towards the formation of a collective identity. Such an identity entails not only that we share some basic (if often fuzzy) ideas about what it is that makes us a "we," but also that we share some ideal and/or material interests, the pursuit of which supposedly will guide our collective action.[7] When I am addressing others, or others are addressing me, claiming that we share some relevant characteristics, we are using horizontal voice.

Horizontal voice may or may not lead to the use of vertical voice. There exist collective identities which are not interested in addressing those "in power." On its part, vertical voice may be individual, such as when a customer writes to management or a citizen to a member of parliament or when an entrepreneur enjoys direct access to a public agency. This may be the usual mode of vertical voice in business organizations, but in politics—particularly in democratic politics—the more important mode of vertical voice is collective. Collective vertical voice at times is used directly, such as when individuals take to the street together to express their grievances. But the more frequent mode of collective vertical voice is indirect, particularly in the densely organized world of contemporary societies: i.e., when some individuals speak to the authorities claiming that they are doing so in representation of some reasonably ascertainable constellation of individuals.

Whether in its direct or indirect modes, collective vertical voice, at least if it has reasonable hope of being heard, must be based on the plausible existence of a constellation of individuals whose ideal or material interests it invokes.

This usually means that some process of collective identity formation has occurred. Horizontal voice is one of the mechanisms that lead to such identity formation. Certainly, collective identities may be created or reproduced by the discourse of those "on top" toward their subjects. But the possibility of using horizontal voice without serious restrictions or dangers is a constitutive feature of a democratic (or, more generically, a nonrepressive) context. Horizontal voice is a necessary condition for the existence of the kind of collective vertical voice that is reasonably autonomous from those "on top." This, in turn, is a necessary condition for the existence of a democratic context.

Notice that I am not referring to all sorts of social communication. Even though the analytical boundaries are fuzzy, here I want to confine myself to collective identities that are political in a rather narrow sense: those that somehow wish to address themselves to the existing governmental authorities, or those that for whatever reasons want to change those authorities. An important case (important at least in regard to the intensity with which it is likely to be felt) of political collective identity is that of those who oppose a repressive regime and who, even though they may disagree in other important respects, converge in the common purpose of terminating such a regime. I shall argue that this kind of situation demonstrates the importance of horizontal voice and, consequently, the convenience of extending Hirschman's framework to include the former.

III

. . .* Then the 1976 coup took place. For reasons I cannot discuss here, the state was, plainly, terroristic. Not only did it apply severe and cruel repression to many individuals, it did so in a decentralized, largely unpredictable, and usually clandestine way. That this was so is sufficiently well known today, so I do not need to go into details here. I must only stress that the risks were as high as they were difficult to gauge. Almost anyone (because he/she had been politically active in the past, or simply because he/she knew somebody whom some repressive agency suspected of "subversion") could be abducted, tortured, and murdered without even knowing the "reasons." Furthermore, since in keeping with its terroristic nature the BA refused to issue any clear rules about what was and was not punishable, it was practically impossible to feel safe—in our melancholic encounters with Chilean and Uruguayan friends

---

* The first two paragraphs of this section are deleted because they describe topics already discussed in chapter 3 of this book, the "proto-investigation" conducted by O'Donnell and Galli during the BA (chapter 3, note 1), and the violence that preceded the 1976 coup (chapter 3, section III).—*Ed.*

we found ourselves envying them because of their no less repressive but more bureaucratized, and hence more predictable, states.

IV

There was, however, one major prohibition that was clear, not because somebody decided to make it explicit but because it is inherent in the very nature of repressive, deeply authoritarian rule—not only at the level of the nation state but also, with a logic that reverberates through all social contexts, down to the more microlevels. That logic means that occasionally one may address the rulers, on some issues and in the forms that they determine and may modify at their whim; but what one should never do is to address other subjects of the rulers in terms of the shared condition as such subjects. This is the logic of divide and rule, not only as a useful strategy for maximizing power but as the very core of authoritarian domination, made nakedly explicit at its more repressive limits.

Accordingly, during those years in my country, with some risks and slight chances of success, one could think of using some vertical voice (i.e., "respectfully petition the authorities" on some thoroughly depoliticized issues), but what meant almost certain death was any attempt to use horizontal voice. Individuals had to be isolated, obedient subjects of the state, happy to devote themselves to their private pursuits—work and family—avoiding the dangerous world of public affairs, of which the rulers claimed they were taking good care. Any attempt to keep alive former collective identities (such as those of members of a political party, or workers who had conquered certain rights, or students who could ask questions) was a sure signal of "subversive contamination." Even apparently innocuous activities (such as being part of a music or theater group, or participating in a study group on whatever theme, or simply joining other persons chatting in the street) were suspect and, therefore, dangerous.[8] Getting together, in any of the manifold forms of sociability one takes for granted in more benign contexts, was suspect precisely because it meant getting together. Since it was potentially even more subversive to address relevant others beyond face-to-face relationships, the media were strictly controlled by perverse mechanisms that it is not the occasion to narrate here. This was not only with respect to overtly political messages which, in any case, nobody except the rulers and their propagandists would have dared to convey through the media. Controls were also applied—as a linguist at the service of the regime told a theater director we interviewed—to messages that "even if apparently apolitical, could trigger semantic series of subversive potential."

It goes without saying that attempts to extend mutual recognition as opponents to the BA—the crucial type of horizontal voice at stake under the
circumstances—were especially dangerous. We shall see, however, that this
kind of voice was not entirely suppressed, and I shall argue that, in contrast
to what a repressive state can do, at least for a time, with vertical voice, not
even the most efficiently terroristic state could ever completely suppress
horizontal voice. But before making this argument we must undertake a
digression.

V

. . .* The repression that the state applied for achieving the depoliticization of
its subjects was successful for some time. Such success was based not only on
the fear raised among those who disagreed but also—at least in our sample—
on the fact that there were many who, even before the emergence of that BA,
were in full swing away from the politicized pole of the Hirschmanian cycle
of involvements. In the often repeated words of those interviewees, the
previous period had been "too much"—crazy years in which they had been
"intoxicated" with politics, when they had believed, and at times done, things
that now lingered on dangerously in their lives. Thus, even though, as mentioned, after talking to us for a while some sadly recognized that they had lost
something important in the shift toward their profoundly privatized lives,
those respondents felt that they had become "more realistic and mature."
After all, what life was about was work and family and, eventually, with
some luck, the purchase of the imported junk that the BA at the time was
making available as the *panem* for its subjects. The *circus* was a one-shot event:
the vicarious (but practically unanimous) experience of politically sanitized
(but ecstatic) participation manipulated by the state after the victory of the
Argentine team in the world soccer cup of 1978.

Furthermore, many of those respondents seemed to agree so fully with the
already mentioned injunctions of the government that they declared that, for
reasons that in most cases they could not articulate, they had also drastically
reduced other forms of apolitical sociability. But those reasons became clear
when they talked about their children, or when we interviewed adolescents'
psychologists and psychoanalysts. Any form of sociability that could not be
controlled by the family or by the school (which, of course, became more authoritarian than ever) was inherently dangerous: "bad influences" could operate or, even if such were not the case, the son or the daughter could be linked
to someone that the government (and the various groups that abducted and

---

* Again, the first paragraph of this section has been deleted because it refers to aspects of the
"proto-investigation" discussed in chapter 3, note 1.—*Ed.*

killed as part of the terroristic strategy of the BA) could at any time, and without possible appeal, define as "subversive."

These data have many implications, both political and psychological, which I cannot deal with here. But I hope that the underlying argument of this section is plausible: that it may be illogical but it is not existentially impossible that those individuals felt two very different things at the same time. On the one hand, they agreed with the government that they should live thoroughly privatized lives and that they should do whatever they could to prevent their family members from transgressing that norm. On the other hand, at a less immediately conscious level, they felt something of which, as some of them put it, they became aware only by talking to us about some public issues they had been striving to ignore: that, by so extensively privatizing their lives, they had lost something very important. They seemed to feel as if they had amputated an important dimension of their lives and that this loss was not only the suppression of their rights *qua* citizens, but also something that impoverished them in very intimate dimensions. Thus, many of our interviewees, at least at the level of their superficial beliefs, agreed with the regime about what was meant by a "good Argentine": half-time *homo economicus*, half-time jealous and authoritarian parent, and all the time an obedient subject of threatening powers.

In *SI* and further works, Hirschman, in a cogent critique of the usual assumptions of economic theory about stable and transitive individual preferences, makes the argument that, as illustrated among other things by the shifts between public and private involvements, "men and women have the ability to step back from their 'revealed' wants, volitions, and preferences and consequently to form metapreferences that may differ from their preferences."[9] The fact that many of our interviewees behaved as I have described but that, at the same time, they felt a deep sense of loss, supports Hirschman's argument. Our interviews suggest that, at least in cultures that share a common root in classical Greece, the idea that many of us have of a "well-rounded," properly self-esteeming individual includes both an active public life and an intense involvement in private concerns. But we cannot have both at the same time—not to the degree that our more or less conscious normative images demand. So we tend to shift from one kind of involvement to the other. Thus, while we have chosen one kind of involvement over the other (and have dressed such choice with the remarkable talent we have for giving ourselves good reasons for our preferences), at a less conscious level we may be nostalgic for that "other world" which, at least for the time being, we have abandoned. Angst, omnipotence, denial of death, hubris, and innumerable related terms point to a much more inherently dissatisfied and tense animal than the chooser between two or more preferences that mainstream economics—and, to a large extent, political science—present to us.

That the interplay between public and private impulses may be an unsolvable tension is suggested by the negative connotations that in our cultures evoke persons who give the impression of being entirely devoted to public or to privatized concerns. An entirely public man (not to say anything about the "public woman," as Hirschman reminds us in *SI,* that euphemism for prostitution which, in the sense I am discussing here, is not too different from the connotations of an "excessively public man") is suspected of having nothing behind the mask he wears, just shallow, "dehumanized" emptiness. This may be why the ultimate public persons, the politicians, find it useful to show that, in spite of their heavy public obligations, they have a beautiful, intense family life. On the other hand, a person entirely dedicated to his private concerns (his, because women are supposed to be so dedicated, which means, precisely, that in an important sense they are "less" than men) raises connotations of selfishness and pettiness, of a life which is "too small" and without a dignified purpose. This may be why, when they have been successful in the very private pursuit of earning money, some rich persons feel obliged to show their "public consciousness." One way or the other, the language we use, as well as the innumerable portraits that the literary imagination has drawn of the manifold variations of these archetypes, express the feeling that a person "excessively" immersed in a public or a private life is less than "fully" or "truly" human.

If, as I am suggesting, a shift toward a very politicized or privatized life is deeply conflictive and leads to guilt feelings that we usually repress from our consciousness, it follows that the strength of the "rebound effects" from private to public involvements that *SI* discusses, is dependent upon the general contextual situation. In a democratic setting, the decision to live a very private life is, in principle, a free one; if afterwards I decide to involve myself politically and then I look negatively at my "excessively privatized" previous period, short of acute neurosis I cannot but criticize myself. The situation is different in repressive contexts. As we saw, our interviewees were living extremely privatized lives for reasons more complicated than the coercion that the government was applying. But when, as we shall see, a new cycle of politicization occurred, those persons could project upon an obvious target all the blame for what they now recognized as deep losses during the period through which they had just lived. That target was the BA. The availability of such an external (and, of course, in many senses, very appropriate) target exempted those persons from self-criticism and, thus, unleashed the full intensity of their guilt feelings and grievances against the BA. This is why Hirschman's "rebound effects" are likely to be stronger when a politicized cycle occurs after a period of privatization that has been backed by a repressive power. This strengthened rebound effect, even if not particularly useful in terms of the self-knowledge of the individuals concerned, is a powerful weapon against authoritarian rule. Through it we may understand another theme often tackled by the literary imagination: the scenes of liberation from authoritarian rule, where those who have fought against it are the more serene, while those who have been passive or in some senses collaborated are the more cruel and vengeful. But for this enhanced rebound effect to occur, some horizontal voice must have reappeared. This theme will occupy us in the following pages.

VI

The remarks of the preceding section can now be put in a different way: at its limit, the logic of authoritarian domination tends to exercise full control of the collective identities of its subjects (as we saw, in our case, the constellation of attributes connoted by the idea of "a good Argentine"). This is a monological structure. Those "on top" address their subjects and allow very little, and strictly controlled, vertical voice; furthermore, they forbid the dialogical structure entailed by horizontal voice. This results not only in the suppression of the specifically public dimension of the subjects, but also in severe loss of their sociability. The themes of loneliness, of cold as opposed to the warmth of spontaneous sociability, and of darkness as the expression of the cognitive difficulties resulting from the suppression of most channels of free communication are recurrent in literature, psychology, and history (as they were in our own feelings and in those conveyed to us by our interviewees) in the depiction of the experience of repressive rule. He who must listen but cannot speak is the infant in the authoritarian family. Such an infant cannot possibly know what is good for him, much less for others; he must be told who he is: with whom, how, and why he should identify.

In a nation state (as well as, I surmise, in many organizations) the obliteration of horizontal voice has some crucial consequences. First, it is a sufficient condition for the severe decay of vertical voice. Even if an authoritarian state would leave unobstructed the preexisting channels for the use of vertical voice, the suppression of horizontal voice entails that such information as does get through to the top consists exclusively of individual—and in a sense perversely privatized—messages. This means that collective vertical voice (which, as we saw, presupposes collective identities which in turn presuppose the use of horizontal voice) is suppressed. Furthermore, the obliteration of horizontal voice means that those social sectors whose mode of voicing cannot but be collective are condemned to silence; consequently, as we descend the ladder of social stratification a deeper silence is imposed. Thus, whatever vertical voice remains is not only drastically diminished, it is also inherently biased. A second consequence is that, since all sources of collective identity not monopolized by the authoritarian rulers are prohibited, they place extraordinarily jealous demands on another theme of *EVL*: loyalty, in this case the loyalty due to the collective identity that those rulers wish to impose. This is a jealous demand because it pretends to exclude all others and, thus, defines *a contrario* the most dangerous category in any authoritarian context, from repressive states to street gangs: those who do not "truly deserve" to be considered members. A third consequence is that the more repressive a state is, the more exclusive and paranoid it becomes toward autonomous sources of voice. The resulting closure to potentially relevant information entails the lack of the "corrective mechanisms" discussed in *EVL*[10] and, at the limit, is equivalent to the clinical definition of madness—this is why these systems are disaster prone, as was superbly illustrated by the Malvinas/Falklands fiasco of the Argentine BA.

Another consequence of the suppression of horizontal voice—already suggested—has to do with the subjects of repressive rule: the atomized life they are forced to live, the extreme privatization of their concerns, and the caution and mistrust with which the few remaining occasions of sociability must be approached. These restrictions entail a sharp impoverishment, as our interviews and observations in Argentina showed, even of very personal and not at all political dimensions of human life. As research on political culture shows, in all countries there are many who never use vertical voice, probably do not feel the tensions between the public and private discussed above, and still may be quite happy human beings. But life with horizontal voice severely repressed is plainly awful. If I have not become a perfect *idiotes* and, thus, if I have opinions about the politics and economics of my country, I need others, who even if they disagree, confirm that my opinions and beliefs are not senseless. Without the emotional and cognitive anchoring that such communications furnish to my personal and social identities, the very assumptions about what is real and valuable may enter into flux. Short of the psychological disintegration of the individual—of which our interviews with various sorts of psychological therapists gave sad and quite extensive evidence—the resulting tendency converges with the purposes of the BA: to take refuge in an extremely privatized life, "forgetting" the dangerous and cognitively uncertain "outside world." On the other hand, if in such situations one still tries to use horizontal voice, some interesting things happen. This will occupy us in the following section.

VII

It is conceivable that an extremely repressive state could, at least for a time, entirely suppress vertical voice. But the trick with horizontal voice is that, even if such a state might get quite close to it, it can never completely sup-press or control it. Not only through personal experience in Argentina but also in a comparative study of authoritarian rule[11] that I undertook with a group of colleagues, the importance of what I shall call "oblique voice" be-came evident. This is a particular kind of horizontal voice. It intends to be understood by "others like me" in our opposition to a repressive state and, at the same time, it hopes not to be perceived by the agents of the latter. After the March 1976 coup there was not much horizontal voice in Argentina but there was something, enough for not falling into utter despair. Certain unconventional (slightly so, there was not room for more that that) ways of dressing, clapping hands with excessive enthusiasm in front of the public au-thorities, going to the recitals of singers or musicians who were known to dis-agree with the regime, some quick glances in the streets and other public spaces—these were some of the ways with which, in this most fertile area of human imagination, one could recognize and be recognized by others as op-ponents to this BA. Notice that such signals did not intend other behavioral consequences, such as the ones that members of a resistance movement ready to enter in action might exchange. Notice also that there were no instrumental rewards expected, and that oblique voice always entailed some degree of risk. But these signals had great emotional and cognitive import, as the way to rec-ognize that each one was not entirely alone in his or her opposition to the state. This was the untransposable limit of the violence of the BA, that residue of oblique, nonverbal horizontal voice which one could still exercise when all other forms of voice had been suppressed. As Hirschman notes in *SI* and other works,[12] there are some activities that gratify because of the very fact that they are undertaken; this is why some forms and moments of political participation cannot be reduced to a utilitarian calculus nor, consequently, are subject to the free-rider problem.[13] This is suggested by oblique voice, that irreducible core of political involvement: by exercising it one obtained the crucial cognitive gratification of confirming a shared collective identity, as well as the no less crucial emotional benefit of asserting one's self-respect as a *non-idiotes*. Notice, finally, that even though oblique voice is practiced in an apparently depoliticized context, it has an intrinsic reference to a very public involvement. It is this capacity of linking the most personal with the most public, not only of oblique but also of all sorts of horizontal voice, that makes it so important politically.

This argument can be further illustrated *a contrario* with another piece of the story I began to narrate above. I was living in Brazil when the Argentine government launched the invasion of the Malvinas/Falklands. As soon as it happened, I felt a strong urge to go to Buenos Aires, hoping that I could find others who shared my unconditional rejection of such an adventure and of the war it would predictably trigger. But I was immensely distressed to find

that an overwhelming majority of my acquaintances, including many of those
who opposed the BA, enthusiastically supported the invasion and, later on,
the war. "Before anything else we are Argentines" was the argument I heard
ad nauseam. Until appalling defeat occurred, the government was enormously
successful in establishing a hypernationalistic collective identity that practically erased all others. Even oblique voice almost disappeared; almost everyone was trying to "help the country" win the war. This led me into quite a few
painful discussions in which many accused me of "thinking like a foreigner,"
if not worse. The rather lonely reflections with which I tried to stand fast to
my opinions and values were not enough, not even when I recognized in myself a well-known psychological problem: the immense difficulty of holding
on to values and even to elementary factual opinions when most social interactions refute them. This had been quite easy to do before the war, while
some oblique voice existed. But it became immensely difficult when even
oblique voice was practically obliterated during those awful days. Then,
faced with the arguments of most relevant others that I was at best misinter-
preting everything, I realized I was losing the social support—cognitive and
affective—needed in order to stick to basic opinions and values;[14] even what
was and was not real became doubtful. Afterwards, chatting with persons
who had shared my views during those days, they told me that they had suffered similar problems; some of them had ended up by supporting the war.
(My own part of the story is that, in despair, in the midst of those events I exited to Brazil, where, even in a deeply polemical milieu with fellow Argentines,
I found enough supportive interactions to enable me to stick to my opinions
and values.)

VIII

As is well known, the Malvinas/Falkland adventure ended in the complete
defeat of the Argentine troops. It soon became evident to the population that
the government had lied outrageously about the developments of the war,
and that the behavior of many officers of the armed forces had been remarkably inept and cowardly. The BA thus entered into collapse, eroded by its
internal conflicts and recriminations, and pushed by the rage with which suddenly many demanded rapid democratization. The atrocities that the rulers
had committed, as well as the abysmal corruption of most of them, began to
be publicly exposed. These facts, which many had refused to acknowledge or
had until recently justified, fed still further the moral indignation with which
most Argentines suddenly found themselves agreeing in their demand for
democratization.

Even though the circumstances made this process particularly rapid and intense in Argentina, in the study on transitions from authoritarian rule, we found that this "resurrection of civil society," as Schmitter and I call it, is a typical occurrence.[15] At some moment, and for reasons too varied to be discussed here, many individuals who have been formerly passive, depoliticized, acquiescent, or simply too afraid to do anything converge in a broadly shared (and often daring) demand for the termination of authoritarian rule. Whether successful or not in the achievement of its goals, such a convergence is a powerful driving force in the transition.

As I suggested above, the mechanisms that lead to this—for the actors, at least—surprising emergence are more complex than the existence, under the aegis of the authoritarian state, of many individuals who purposely conceal their opposition until the situation becomes ripe for acting. Undoubtedly there are such individuals but, if the lesson from the Argentine case has any value, there are also many who are at best politically passive or indifferent during that period, but who as the contextual conditions begin to change quite suddenly repoliticize in determined opposition to the authoritarian state. When the BA in Argentina was already collapsing, in a rather perverse move—with the pretext that I had lost the transcript of their former interviews and needed their help for reconstructing them—I reinterviewed some of the more depoliticized and acquiescent individuals in our sample. On this second occasion, most of them were full of rage against the BA, the armed forces, its behavior in the war, and the atrocities it had committed in the country. Furthermore, some of those respondents had again become politically active. All of them "remembered" what they had told us before in a way that sharply contrasted with what they had actually told us. They were wrong, but evidently sincere, as they had been sincere before, in telling me, in the reinterviews, that they had always strongly opposed the regime and had never accepted its injunctions. In the first interviews some of those respondents had given distressing responses to our probing concerning the abductions, tortures, and murders that were going on: these were only "rumors" or "exaggerations" and, at any event, "there must be some reason" why some persons were so victimized. Refusal to know and in some worse cases, identification with the aggressor and blaming the victim were ugly mechanisms about which we had read in studies on Nazi Germany. To our deep sadness because, quite naively, we had not expected these mechanisms to operate in our interviewees, we had to recognize them during our research; most of those persons told us on the second occasion that "only now" had they become aware of those atrocities and that, "of course," they energetically condemned them.[16]

The persons I reinterviewed gave me the impression that they had just "discovered" what they subconsciously felt they should have believed during the years of harsh repression. As a consequence, they had rewritten their memories to fit that discovery. The sense of continuity of their personal identity was preserved and, thus, they could look at the past without conscious guilt or shame: they had had "nothing to do" with the atrocities perpetrated by the BA (which was true in the real but partial sense that they had not personally participated in repression), and had known little or nothing of those atrocities. It is my impression that these important although unacknowledged changes were closely related to the previous obliteration of most forms of horizontal voice and, at the moment of the reinterviews, to the rapid recuperation of all sorts of voice that was taking place.

During our first round of interviews, trying to find a not entirely dark side to our data, we told ourselves that the refusal of many interviewees to recognize what was going on was a defense mechanism that preserved them for better times. Given the extremely repressive conditions, short of conscious identification with the regime and, consequently and necessarily, with its atrocities, the actual alternative for such persons was to plunge into an absorbed private life, and to refuse to know what was going on "outside." This, at least, preserved them (more specifically, their self-esteem) for the moment when it eventually would become not too dangerous to "know" and, thus, to become indignant about what had happened. Imagining that they had "always" been opposed to the BA and only coming to terms with reality after the BA had begun to collapse are expressions of well-known defenses such as psychological rationalization, selective memory, and cognitive dissonance. The aspect of these complex phenomena that interests me here is how their occurrence may be triggered by changes in the political context.

As we found in the already mentioned study of transitions, there are—generalizing beyond the Argentine case—circumstances that lead to the collapse or, less dramatically, to the obvious decay of authoritarian rule. There are, then, some noble individuals who have the courage to say that the emperor is naked (some of them even had the courage to say it before, but then very few listened). There are, also, other no less noble individuals who dare to spread such, shortly before, unimaginable opinions. The exemplary character of those statements leads others, and then others, to address others saying that what really matters is to act together for the purpose of getting rid of authoritarian rule. In other words, civil society has resurrected, horizontal voice has reemerged, its "subversive" implications operate again, oblique voice becomes unnecessary, and—as a consequence—vertical voice aimed at changing those who are "on top" is heard. In the first stages of this process, repression by the crumbling authoritarian state may be and usually is harsh, but it tends to be erratic and, above all, few believe that it can restore the hold the state previously had on individual lives.[17] In such circumstances, horizontal voice again appeals to the public self of individuals, in ways that allow them to recover a feeling of integrity: now they can demand the rights that pertain to them as citizens, and they again have moral standards with which to take a stand against authoritarian rule. This is why the rebound effects toward public involvement are so widespread and intense in these cases: many repoliticize themselves, electoral campaigns draw big crowds, attempted authoritarian reversions are usually defeated with the support of an active and mobilized public opinion, and electoral participation in the founding elections of a more or less democratic regime is unusually high. Whatever free riding may exist does not weigh enough to weaken such processes, and there seems to be nothing like the perception of the "paradox of voting": on the contrary, participating in the demise of authoritarian rule and voting (the very act of symbolic and, to a significant extent, also practical negation of authoritarian rule, which constitutes not only the democratic authorities but also the voter *qua* citizen) are undertaken, as Hirschman argues, because those activities are felt as extremely rewarding in themselves.

What is clear in the admittedly exceptional circumstances of the demise of authoritarian rule, may well also be true—although less intense and, thus, more difficult to perceive—of many forms of political participation and re-politicization occurring in more normal circumstances. The sense of personal worth and self-respect, the feeling that one is not an *idiotes,* the hope of achieving valued goals by means of collective action, the motivation of overcoming the "coldness" and "darkness" of an isolated life through the emotional warmth of sociability and collective identity, and the cognitive reassurance that comes from the public sharing of values and opinions with many others—all these are crucial phenomena of political life, even if often they fade away and then, again and again, reappear under old or new faces. These phenomena cannot be accounted for on utilitarian grounds, so we should not expect that they will be subject to (or, at least, that they should be dominated by) the dilemmas and paradoxes of the kinds of social action for which utilitarian assumptions are reasonably realistic. Horizontal voice has crucial importance for the emergence and reproduction of such phenomena, as well as for the very existence of a democratic context.

Notes

1. Albert O. Hirschman, *Exit, Voice, and Loyalty: Responses to Decline, Organizations, and States* (Cambridge, Mass.: Harvard University Press, 1970).

2. Albert O. Hirschman, *Shifting Involvements: Private Interest and Public Action* (Princeton: Princeton University Press, 1979).

3. See especially, David Collier, ed., *The New Authoritarianism in Latin America* (Princeton: Princeton University Press, 1979).

4. These processes are analyzed in Guillermo O'Donnell, *Bureaucratic Authoritarianism: Argentina, 1966–1973, in Comparative Perspective* (Berkeley: University of California Press, 1988).

5. For a similar argument, see Jean Laponce, "Hirschman's Voice and Exit Model as a Spatial Archetype," *Social Science Information* 13 (no. 3, June 1974): 67–81.

6. Albert O. Hirschman, *Essays in Trespassing: Economics to Politics and Beyond* (Cambridge: Cambridge University Press, 1981).

7. On this point, Alessandro Pizzorno, "Political Exchange and Collective Identity in Industrial Conflict," in Colin Crouch and Alessandro Pizzorno, eds., *The Resurgence of Class Conflict in Western Europe since 1968*, Vol. 2 (London: Macmillan Press, 1978), pp. 277–97.

8. It even became dangerous to participate in psychological therapy groups: the repressors soon discovered that, if appropriately pressured or tortured, members of such groups were excellent informants about any other members whom they suspected. Many psychologists and psychoanalysts stopped working with groups. As it often happens, this high uncertainty and risk has been better expressed in literary works; see, e.g., Humberto Constantini, *De dioses, hombrecitos y policías* (Buenos Aires: Editorial Bruguera, 1984).

9. Albert O. Hirschman, "Against Parsimony: Three Easy Ways of Complicating Some Categories of Economic Discourse," in *American Economic Review* 74 (no. 2, May 1984).

10. The tendency of authoritarian states to close themselves to crucial information and the destructive consequences that follow from this are cogently discussed in David Apter, *Choice and the Politics of Allocation* (New Haven: Yale University Press, 1973).

11. Guillermo O'Donnell, Philippe Schmitter, and Laurence Whitehead, eds., *Transitions from Authoritarian Rule: Prospects for Democracy* (Baltimore: Johns Hopkins University Press, 1986).

12. Especially Hirschman, "Against Parsimony."

13. As we shall see below, this is why Brian Barry's critique of *Exit, Voice, and Loyalty* to the effect that this work fails to take into account free riding and its consequences for political action misses the target at least with respect to some, often very important, forms of collective action; Brian Barry, "Review Article: 'Exit, Voice, and Loyalty,'" *British Journal of Political Science* (February 1974): 79–107. Of course, the reference to "free riding" is to the *locus classicus* of Mancur Olson, *The Logic of Collective Action* (Cambridge, Mass.: Harvard University Press, 1965).

14. Some readers may find it interesting to know that, in those circumstances, it was helpful to me to remember the classic experiment of S. E. Asch, which had fascinated me when I studied in graduate school. See S. E. Asch, "Effects of Group Pressure on the Modification and Distortion of Judgments." First printed in H. S. Guetzkow, ed., *Groups, Leadership and Men: Research in Human Relations* (Pittsburgh: Carnegie Press, 1951); reprinted in H. Proshansky and B. Seidenberg, eds., *Basic Studies in Social Psychology* (New York: Holt, Rinehart and Winston, 1965), pp. 393–401.

15. O'Donnell, Schmitter, and Whitehead, *Transitions*. [See also chapter 6 of this book.—*Ed.*]

16. An obvious question that we posed ourselves from the beginning of our research was whether the respondents concealed from us their true opinions due to fear and mistrust. We are sure this was not the case because practically all the interviews,

after a tense beginning, became very emotional. Often our respondents cried and gave other unmistakable signals of the deep emotions they were feeling as they talked to us about themes related to the public sphere and/or their own past that—as some of them insisted—they had "forgotten." Both factually and emotionally the more difficult moment for us was not to begin but to end the interviews. In no less than half of the cases the respondents asked us to continue (after an average of two and a half hours of interview) or to make another appointment with them, arguing that the very fact of talking to us was very important for them.

17. These processes are discussed in O'Donnell, Schmitter, and Whitehead, *Transitions.*

5

"And Why Should I Give a Shit?"
Notes on Sociability and Politics
in Argentina and Brazil

I

For several years I tried to give the impression that "I have read it, too" every time someone mentioned *"Você sabe com quem está falando?"* ("Do you know with whom you are speaking?"). For some time, Roberto DaMatta's book[1] had been staring invitingly at me from my library shelf, but only recently did I read and admire it. Passing through that magnificent array of parades, carnivals, processions, *malandros* (rogues), and *caxías* (uptight asses), guided by an author so knowledgeable about Brazil, a country and a culture that thoroughly seduce me, I understood why I had delayed so long in approaching DaMatta's analysis of *"Você sabe com quem está falando?"*: I suspected, correctly, that I would read it in a schizophrenic mood, attentive to the Brazilian realities that the text reveals but rushing to contrast them with my own country, Argentina—so close, so Latin, and yet so different. Many times I heard similar expressions in Argentina, often with the tone of *"¿Quién se cree que soy yo?"* ("Who do you think I am?") rather than the less aggressive *"¿Usted sabe con quién está hablando?"* ("Do you know with whom you are speaking?"). In the former expression, the phoneme "creeeer" is accentuated in a staccato that places the entire weight of the question on the other who is clearly "out of place." In Argentina, like Brazil, the question is posed to reinforce social hierarchy. As DaMatta observes of *cariocas* (natives of Rio de Janeiro), *porteños*

The original version of this text was prepared for the "Oportunidades e Limites da Sociedade Industrial Periférica: O caso do Brasil" Seminar (IUPERJ-Berkeley-Stanford), held in Nova Friburgo, July 18–20, 1983.

(natives of Buenos Aires) perform this ritual as a means of "bringing to the actors' attention the differences necessary to carry out social routines in situations of intolerable equality."[2] In both locations it is an act of aggression, "to be used when other means of establishing social hierarchy in a given situation fail irremediably." But instead of the silence, apology, or submissive gesture which according to DaMatta ends this ritual among *cariocas*, a *porteño* is likely to receive a different response: *"¿Y a mí qué me importa?"* ("What do I care?") and, quite often, *"¿Y a mí, que mierda me importa?"* ("Why should I give a shit?"). Unlike DaMatta's *cariocas*, the *porteño* finds himself engaged in a genuine exchange, confronting another who replies, often by stating explicitly and unceremoniously that he does not "give a shit" about the first speaker and the social hierarchy he is invoking.[*]

What is interesting about this exchange is that even though in Buenos Aires the social hierarchy is impugned, it is ultimately reaffirmed—just as in Rio. It is clear to both parts that the initiator of the exchange occupies a higher place in the social hierarchy; that is why the message is an implied threat. By responding "Why should I give a shit?" the "inferior" neither denies nor negates the other's hierarchical status. Indeed, he affirms it in the most irritating manner possible; the hierarchy invoked may be exercised and his brashness may cost him dearly, but he is determined that no one will "push him around." If that is the end of the matter (as is generally the case), the hierarchy has been aggressively reaffirmed by both sides but its validity in the current situation has been ridiculed and sullied: What could be more insulting for those who solemnly invoke their hierarchical status than for the other to "not give a shit"?

Consider, too, that in Buenos Aires the original question-epithet is not issued in the informal voice (*"vos sabés con quien estás hablando"*) but in the formal one, *"Usted sabe . . ."*[**] In contrast, the typical response—with or without vulgarities—does not require the speaker to choose between *"vos"* and *"Usted."* Unlike DaMatta's *cariocas*, the "superior" *porteño* refers to the other as *"Usted"* even as he is trying to put him in his "inferior" place. When he does not do so, in this and other contexts that attempt to reinforce social hierarchy, the most frequent response is *"¿Y a Usted quién le dio permiso para tutearme?"* ("And who gave you *[Usted]* permission to address me informally?") with the words *"Usted"* and *permiso* forcefully accentuated. If, instead, the reply is *"¿Y a vos, quién te dio permiso para tutearme?"* ("And who gave you *[vos]* permission to talk down to me?") the situation is on the brink of physical violence and,

---

[*] Although gender is not clear in the Spanish text and I considered using the he/she format, I decided to use the masculine pronoun because exchanges of this sort are much more common among men.—*Ed.*

[**] In Argentine Spanish, the use of the word "Usted" connotes respect or a position of inferiority, while "vos" is used among peers.—*Ed.*

should it erupt, it is not at all clear that the socially superior individual would come out on top. In Rio, the violence of the initial question is usually met with submission; in Buenos Aires, it is reciprocated. Is this better or worse? Neither; it is different. But there is one important commonality: each society, in its own way, presupposes and reaffirms its awareness of inequality.

Allow me to continue with my contrasting memories. In Rio, when waiters, store employees, taxicab drivers, and others do their job well according to their own view, they are solicitous and congenial "servants," and, if necessary (which it rarely is), they themselves interpose the appropriate social distance. Their equivalents in Buenos Aires employ a series of gestures, approximations, and omissions to make it clear that they are not serving, but working. Workers need not be obsequious; it is enough that they complete the required tasks. If there is going to be some intimacy, it is usually initiated by the worker.

This seems excellent to me, even though it does not always guarantee pleasant meals, trips, or shopping. But this moment of leveling has to be placed in the context of a social hierarchy which is challenged and at the same time reinforced in other situations. Brazil is distinctly and profoundly hierarchical, at times hiding this aspect behind its *homens cordiais* (affable men). But Brazil also has its moments of magical (though not entirely unreal) transmutation of this hierarchy, especially in its carnivals, as DaMatta helped me see. In contrast, Argentina—a hierarchical society as well, though much less so than Brazil—reveals a more egalitarian (or, to be more precise, leveling) attitude to social distance at almost every opportunity. As the "Why should I give a shit?" interchange encapsulates so well, the urge by both sides to underscore and simultaneously deny the differences, if only for a minute, is vigorously enacted. A society can be relatively egalitarian and, at the same time, authoritarian and violent.

Another recurring sensation goes to the same point. Old gypsy that I am, one of my problems is getting reaccustomed to driving cars in various countries. It is never easy for me to return from Europe and the United States, where traffic laws are enforced and do regulate traffic, to that fantastic disorder that is Rio's traffic. In Rio, traffic laws, including signals and lights, are mere suggestions that drivers might follow at times, but only under conditions that are sufficiently clear to others that they will not be smashed from behind (or assaulted from the side), when, for example, stopping at a red light at night. In Buenos Aires, the disorder is less, but that, too, has its price. In Rio, the police are often absent. On those rare occasions when they are present, they usually concern themselves with minor infractions, or intervene in order to get a *gorjeta* (bribe), obliquely reaffirming the intermittent force of the law. They will usually help out persons like myself (with my obvious foreign accent) who rarely know how to get where we want to go. In contrast, in Buenos Aires, where fines are very steep, the police have gone into hiding, using the same clandestine *modus operandi* with which other powers are committing much more horrid acts.* A police officer in hiding has a much greater chance of "hunting down" violators[3] who only realize they were caught when the multifigure fine arrives in the mail. In Rio, when a police officer does intervene, he assumes that anyone driving a car is from the upper end of the social hierarchy and *tudo se ajeita* (everything is worked out informally) while the traffic mess continues undisturbed. In neither city the police order traffic, but the personal contact that usually allows infractions to be taken care of informally in Rio is a lot more problematic in present-day Buenos Aires, where all sorts of powers-that-be hide in order to punish more often and more severely. The result: In Buenos Aires, one develops a sixth sense for places that are dangerous (not for accidents, but for hidden police). There one does everything according to the book only to return, in the very next block, when the danger has passed, to the law of the jungle.

I invite you to recall a common experience: entering an avenue from a side street during rush hour. In the United States entering the avenue usually presents little problem, given the general obedience to traffic lights and the rule to proceed according to the order that one arrives at the intersection. In Rio it is definitely a problem, but it does not take long to resolve it, because someone will voluntarily give up those few seconds that will allow one to squeeze into the flow. It is, of course, more complicated than the U.S. system, but as soon as I readapt to it I tell myself that it has a congenial aspect: usually in this circumstance, one is the recipient of something that another talented observer of Brazilian society, Roberto Schwarz,[4] has analyzed as an important part of its functioning—a favor. This favor is often accompanied by a friendly nod, answered with a thumbs-up gesture which I have not yet encountered a DaMatta to decipher.

In Buenos Aires, we are apparently equals: the rule is that if there is no police officer in sight (and if it is unlikely that one is hiding out nearby) each driver should go first. Therefore, the crux of the matter is to impede the passage of others. The way to do this, illegal but universally practiced, is *meter la trompa,* that is, to edge one's car in front of another's, to "sneak it in," or "slide it in."[5]** As a result, the cars at the intersection advance to the point where they almost hit one another. One line of cars is crossing bumper-to-bumper (so that those who are coming from the other direction cannot get through), and the cars in the other line are millimeters away from the doors and fenders of the crossing cars, ready to take advantage of the tiniest hesita-

---

* The author is writing during and about the 1976–82 period in which the Argentine BA engaged in the disappearance (the unacknowledged abduction, detention, and often, execution) of those it deemed to be its enemies.—*Ed.*

** This is a very loose approximation of the expression "meter la trompa." This Argentine expression is explicit about what is being put in or slid in, partially conveyed in English by the use of the word "it."—*Ed.*

tion in order to "sneak it in" and victoriously inaugurate the flow that now begins from the cross street, until someone else *achique* or *arrugue* ("gives in" or "chickens out") and therefore opens the way once again for cars coming from the other direction. The consequence of all this, of course, is monumental inefficiency, insults, fights, and often that gesture of a thumb and index finger closed in an evocative circle which celebrates one's "sticking it" to the other who is left *frenado y con rabia* (stranded and humiliated) (this sounds like the title of a tango) a few millimeters away from the car now sliding forth in victory.

The problem, as I rediscovered not long ago, is that there is no way *not* to play this game. Accustomed as I was to the more peaceful traffic of Rio, with my self-esteem less dependent on my ability to cross first (and also, I must admit, because the reflex to sneak it in tends, like so many other things, to atrophy without practice) I began to drive in a manner that, with imprecise pedantry (after all, nobody disliked the state of nature more than Hobbes) I described to one of my sons as "non-Hobbesian." But this was worse, for reasons that should be obvious: at every intersection, those who came behind me, and therefore depended on me to sneak it in, punished me with the stigma of loud honking and rude commentaries on my hormonal state. (For anyone interested, the story ends with me returning to the home of the friend who had lent me his car, fighting ferociously at every street corner).

This aggressive leveling is not without its own rules and hierarchies; however, they are neither the order of arrival, as in the United States, nor the "go-ahead" favor, as in Rio. He who hesitates for that crucial second that allows the other to get through is generally the driver of the smaller car,[6] or the driver of any car when the rival is a bus *(colectivo)* or a truck. There are other subtle gradations (for example, anyone who drives a rusty car has an important psychological advantage over the driver of a new one) that interact in complicated fashion with the "size variable."[7] There are also situations that are admittedly unsolvable, such as the encounter between two buses, or worse yet (because it challenges the professional pride of each) between a bus and a truck. But, apart from these inherently catastrophic situations, the major problem revealed by my data is the 87 percent probability of coming bumper-to-bumper with an automobile of approximately the same size and condition as one's own, so that in most instances the only way to resolve the matter is to play chicken.[8]

Could it be that these hierarchical scenes at the micro level (the encounters, services, and jobs that occasionally link persons of different social positions), and the more egalitarian (since nearly everyone who drives is from the middle or upper classes, or is chauffeuring someone from one of those classes) street intersections, tell us something about similarities and differences between our societies that we may also recognize, with transmuted but perhaps not fictitious congruence, at other, "more important" levels?

II*

That some relationship between levels does exist becomes apparent after a clarification that is, at this point, indispensable: When I referred to Argentina, I should have used the past tense or, more to the point, I should have noted that much of what I described remained suspended for several years. The state implanted in Argentina in 1976 engaged in widespread kidnappings, torture, and assassinations. . . . This made it very, very dangerous to respond, "And why should I care?" with, or without, the expletive. The rulers never tired of repeating that subversion had permeated Argentina and so infected society that everything had to be put back "in its proper place." . . . Bus and taxi drivers and other public "servants" (with the exception of the little-admired "Servants of the Fatherland"—the military—who did not dare wear theirs in the street) had to don uniforms: a light blue (patriotic color) shirt, and, of course, that perfect symbol of everything rigid and constricting, a necktie.

More importantly, the use of *vos* was prohibited since it was essential to "reinstate the principle of authority" as far as the long arm of the state could reach. This was quite far indeed, and where the state could not reach, many others—also full of hatred toward this insolent and aggressive people—enthusiastically imposed their own microdespotisms. Between oppression, repression, and the increase in unemployment, workers had to conceal their identities and behave as servants, permeated by the fear that someone, assuming the familiar form of address denied the rest of us, would ask, "*¿Vos sabés con quién estás hablando?*"—and that this person would have over us, without any recourse whatsoever, the power of life or death, employment or hunger. All of this affected life on the streets: as mentioned above, even the traffic police began to operate clandestinely, emulating those occupied with more serious "diseases of the body politic and society."

For their part, the security forces (a curious designation under the circumstances) became obsessed by the subversive potential of youth, especially those without jackets or ties but with plenty of long hair. This made my own sons frequent candidates for being *enderezados* ("straightened out," while their hair was cut military-style) during the periods they would have to spend in some police station being inculcated with the proper respect for order and authority. We were afraid to edge our car in front of those who, with gangster-esque weapons and anonymity, might literally do anything they wanted to us. The street and the school, the work place and the public office became places of submission and fear, or, to use a concept from political science, of the com-

---

* Some sentences and paragraphs in Part II have been deleted because they repeat the depiction previously made in chapter 3, "Democracy in Argentina: Macro and Micro."—*Ed.*

plete loss of citizenship. The experience of arbitrary violence by which the inhabitants of the shantytowns were repressed became everyone's experience to an extent and a degree never experienced in Brazil, even during its most repressive periods. In those terrible years, all of us submitted to the violence that previously had victimized only the very poor, and we became equal through the common experience of keeping our mouths shut—just in case—when faced with anyone assuming an air of command.

But this is not the place to vent my anger. My point is that Argentina—like Brazil, but in different ways—was already authoritarian and violent. Unlike Brazil, it was also fairly egalitarian. So the use of *vos* and the "I am a worker, not a servant" attitude, the "Why should I give a shit?" retort, and, in general, everything that was "out of place" in this rebellious and insolent society became the target of a fiercely repressive *pathos*. The violence directed against these styles and customs, not only by the BA but also by the numerous *kapos* who appeared during those years, was directed against behavior that truly upset the civilian and military bosses, both in itself and for what these bosses understood that it meant: an insolent and aggressive populace who had succeeded in spreading their plebeian attitudes to a substantial part of the population. Post-1930 Argentina, with its succession of factories, magnates with strange-sounding last names, powerful unions, full employment, demagogues, and, encompassing all of these things, peronism—this country that was "ungovernable," was finally, beginning in 1976, going to be put in its place once and for all.

It is lamentable that Argentina was far from being a democratic country even before this. Without having to go back any further than the period of rampant violence that preceded the coup of 1976, the absence of democratic values, discourses, and practices in politics, as well as in the principle organizations of society, was notable.[9] I insist here on two points: that egalitarianism and individualism are not the same as democracy, and that to tell someone who invokes the social hierarchy that you do not give a shit does not overcome or dissolve that hierarchy but actually reaffirms it, even as it sows hatred and resentment.

Albeit much less so than Brazil, Argentina was a socially inegalitarian country, even though it was basically true that "*aquí nadie pasa hambre*" ("Here, no one goes hungry"). Today, after the meticulously executed attack on the Argentine popular sector that began in 1976, our country is much more unequal than before, and yet we may have a better chance of becoming more democratic and civilized in our social and political life. This is so not because we are more unequal, but because the incredibly brutal means that were used to achieve these inequalities may have made it possible for certain democratic and consensual values and practices to become more widely accepted—even if traffic patterns remain the same and the *kapos* that I knew remain at their posts in schools and workplaces, blaming everything on "the disaster of the Malvinas.'"*

But let us return to Brazil.

III

I am struck less by the distance and clear demarcation of social hierarchies, so evident in Brazil, than by the country's ability to reproduce this hierarchy in almost every context I have observed. To choose one example: whenever my studies on intersections, vulgar expressions, and transit patterns permit, I find it fascinating to observe the complex social system in the apartment building where I live, and of the pleasant block in Leblon where it is located. Beneath the president of the condominium and the distinguished residents extends a complex and strongly hierarchical social structure: principle doorman, assistant doorman, night watchman, and janitors. There is also the permanent coming and going of domestic workers and deliverymen, and of residents who take it for granted that one of the above will rush to help them with their shopping packages. In this pecking order I am always surprised by the distant tone with which residents give orders and receive services[10] and, even more so, by the strongly hierarchical relationships among the "servants." In a similar setting in Argentina there are, first, fewer employees (a consequence of long years of full employment). Also, the Argentine doorman has not the slightest idea that he *should* open the door for us or help us with our packages, and when he does, it is clear that such help is a voluntary act and he should be warmly thanked for it. Moreover, when there is more than one doorman, even if one is the "head" and the other the "assistant," they either establish some leveling agreement between them (which I suspect includes a pact not to become "excessive" in their services to the tenants, somewhat like a shop floor pact not to speed up production) or, before long, one or both of them will have slammed the front door on their way out to their union.

On the flip side of this is carnival. Also *umbanda*** (fascinating by anthropological accounts, but about which I know very little) and other rituals that Brazilians know much better than I. Yet there are aspects that can probably be better discerned by foreigners. One of these is the extraordinary warmth with which Brazilians treat children. For someone who comes from a country that

---

* The "disaster of the Malvinas" (or of the Falklands) is a reference to the war between Argentina and Great Britain over the Malvinas islands off the coast of Argentina. Argentina's defeat in that war accelerated the demise of the military regime.—*Ed.*

** The *umbanda* is a form of spirituality that is extremely popular in Brazil. It includes syncretized African gods, Catholic saints, and dancing in its rituals.—*Ed.*

at times seems enamored of death, including displays of acute necrophilia and necrophobia, these tender gestures seem magnificent demonstrations of love for life, for that which is still fragile, and for the future. Another example, which is going to outrage some of my Brazilian friends, is something that to me seems incredible coming from such an exploited people *(povão)*: the joy with which I have seen them work, and their ability to make music—lively, joyous, and with *swing*—while working, or before or after days of hard work and long commutes. I gather that this is not the world of the factory—which I do not know in Brazil—nor the world of the *Baixada Fluminense** and its equivalents, which I have scarcely seen. But there are many Brazilians, whether they live in the *Baixadas* or not, and whether or not they travel pinned inside those horrible buses for hours on end, who have, under the circumstances, a prodigious capacity for smiling and good humor.

I am aware and will argue (not very originally) that everything I have mentioned constitutes an extremely efficient means of consolidating the high social inequalities that exist in Brazil. But there is no need to jump to sweeping conclusions, especially if one keeps in mind other societies and the tradeoffs they, in their turn, make. So, for now, I will start down a perilous road warning that I am about to make a leap from the "micro" to the "macro" level.

IV

I begin with Argentina, an individualistic society full of confrontations that resolve nothing but provoke the fury of the powerful. It is also a society that lacks a vigorous liberal tradition, and which, in spite of a certain democraticness in interclass relations, has not experienced anything resembling democracy for many years, and never long enough for it to take root. On the contrary, Argentina's style of social relations tends to stir up authoritarian regimes that are more violent, radical, and all-encompassing than the ones Brazil has endured. A confrontation of the "Why should I give a shit?" sort, not only impugns a hierarchy it fails to overcome; its generalized use—I now add—precludes the emergence of stable social relations that are reasonably acceptable to all parties concerned. Until a resolution is found, the only alternative is to continue to act and reenact the confrontation, or for the "superior" party to violently impose another, "more respectful" relationship.

This tendency to close off spaces for the generalization of social relations is manifest at macro levels as well. The principle actors of Argentine politics have been corporations: the armed forces, capitalist's associations, unions, and even "privatized" segments of the state apparatus, all of them directly

* The *Baixada Fluminense* is a sprawling settlement of working class neighborhoods on the outskirts of Rio. Not all are slums but many suffer violence and high crime rates.—Ed.

defending what they understand to be their interests. This anarchic corporatism, a true mass praetorianism, has left few opportunities for the formation
of a viable political society and, with it, for the emergence of political parties
as mediators and interest aggregators.[11] Behind scarcely mediated confrontations, the state apparatus has danced to the rhythm of social forces, functioning more as a battlefield than as an institution for defining common interests
which transcend the particularistic interests in conflict. If the minidramas of
individual confrontations give an appearance of equality while ratifying existing social distances, at this more aggregated level a curiously similar phenomenon occurs. The confrontations of anarchic corporatism, the outgrowth
of a complicated history I cannot recount here,* give an appearance of equality (so much so as to justify the great argument of the right that in the last
thirty years Argentina's greatest problem has been peronism and, behind
that, and above all, the unions) sustained by the fact that at some points the
unions and other popular forces succeeded in reversing policies that affected
them adversely.[12] But behind this appearance other, quite different, realities
emerge. One is that these confrontations have nothing to do with democracy;
on the contrary, the game is played with resources and with conceptions of
the "other" that repeatedly annul the spaces available for agreement, cooperation, and the establishment of more or less stable and generally shared rules.
In addition, as in the micro examples, this apparently equal game presupposes and in fact reinforces social inequalities and profound differences in the
distribution of power. So, in contrast to what some authors have argued, the
Argentine situation has not been a stalemate since 1955, 1966, or even 1976.
On the contrary, after several twists and turns—during some of which, it is
true, the popular sector appeared to be winning—it is undeniable that the
Argentine popular sector has suffered a hugely disproportionate amount of
the damage that the country has inflicted on itself.

Without arenas, then, for generalizing interests, discourses, and goals,
Argentina has been restricted to a protopolitics in which—just as on street
corners—the winner in the short run (always the short run, for in a game like
this only the short run counts) is the one who can most threaten and damage
the others. In this kind of situation, neither parties, parliament, or other democratic institutions have taken root. Indeed, there is nothing weaker than
the parties and parliament (which have functioned only intermittently in any
case) in the face of this anarchic corporatism. Each of these forces has tried to
"stick it in," until some players are exhausted (not coincidentally, the weakest
ones in a class society) and others turn, once again, to the supreme violence
that this time—weapons in hand—they hope will finally put everyone "in
their place."

* Some of this history is recounted in chapter 1.—*Ed.*

The repeated military coups in Argentina, as well as their repeated failures, can be understood from this perspective: One power, the more armed one, seeks, at gunpoint, to become the supreme power and then, with the help of its long-standing allies (the upper bourgeoisie and the countless authoritarians that proliferate in a context like this) attempts to "reorganize society": those on top, on top and commanding; those below, below and obedient (and thankful to the former for the benefits that will be bestowed on them once social relations are straightened out), and those in the middle, acting out their eternal schizophrenia, commanding and obeying, well aware of whom to command and whom to obey. Yet in Argentina, the repeated and violent victories of those who have sought to impose this kind of order have always been transitory. No sooner than the bosses feel victorious, they—doing what they learned first and then taught the rest of society—begin to devour one another.[13] When this happens, those on the bottom exploit the resulting divisions among the rulers, and those in the middle no longer know whom to order and whom to obey. In this kind of situation, neither the victors nor the losers have much chance to discover democratic values or mechanisms, and in the next round, when the antagonistic motives and visions of each side seem ratified, the game becomes even more confrontational, and the attempts to impose "order" more authoritarian and brutal. All of this may now change, but for that to happen the logic of this vicious spiral must be understood.

To be sure, the guerrilla movement contributed greatly to the brutality of the 1976 coup. On the other hand, the guerrilla movement itself, the popular support that it received at one point,[14] and the irresponsibility with which a substantial part of the intelligentsia legitimized its favorite violent group, be it from the right or the left—all of these were products of the perverse lessons learned in preceding spirals. But in addition to the brutality of what took place before, we should note the fine-tuning of repression that began after the 1976 coup: Far from limiting itself to macrolevel political actors and guerrillas, repression extended to all corners of society, affecting even the most innocent aspects of daily life. In the view of BA incumbents, it was necessary to eliminate the true cause of "subversion," which resided *not* in the state apparatus, political society, or the upper echelons of anarchic corporatism, but in the microcontexts of society—in a game in which, if no one folds, the cards are revealed, and the one with the ace of spades wins. This is why the 1976–83 BA was so "extremist," so violent, and, as some realized only at the very end, so insane.

Again, this authoritarian experiment in Argentina failed. This failure, the penultimate turn in the destructive spiral that lacked only the Malvinas/Falklands fiasco to be complete, makes clear the enormous costs—and the ever more biased distribution of these costs—of not embracing the alternative democratic pole (that is to say, a democratic regime, a set of rules to guide a reasonably civilized competition) for a society that simultaneously invites and forcefully rejects these authoritarian tendencies. If, in Brazil, there has recently appeared a fear of "Argentinization," in Argentina we spent decades fearing that we had touched bottom and before long would experience our "Bolivianization." Now, with the sobering discovery that what awaited us at the bottom of the well was our own desolate skeleton, perhaps the need for a new, democratic regime will be acknowledged.

V

I ask the reader's tolerance for what will be another change in tone in the present text. I can speak more calmly of Brazil than of Argentina, not because I lack strong feelings about it but because, with all its problems, injustices, and the current crisis, Brazil has not endured the catastrophes that have marked Argentina's history.

DaMatta's book impressed me because it reveals relationships and dimensions of order and disorder that reappear, transformed but recognizable, in other, more macro contexts. Brazil is, from way back, a hierarchically ordered society with sharply drawn social demarcations. For this reason, as DaMatta suggests, one of its principle rituals—carnival—is a moment of egalitarian reversal. Argentina has no carnival. Instead, it has two main types of national ritual. One is the military parade and other ceremonial presentations of state power which signify the antithesis of Argentina's tumultuous pseudoegalitarianism. The other great ritual is the large political demonstration which directly expresses, in songs and drums, the popular and plebeian bent I have been discussing.

In Brazil, the popular classes have long been "in their place." Admittedly, the history of Brazil, from the time of slavery until the present, has been punctuated by rebellions that illustrate the extent to which this order is an imposed one. But these rebellions have not succeeded in crystallizing organizations and collective identities occupying an autonomous space removed from the shadow of the dominant classes. We also know that this order is sustained by various forms of violence, beginning with daily life in the *favelas*, grinding poverty, unemployment, and the lack of basic labor rights which workers in Argentina, Chile, and Uruguay have taken for granted for decades (despite their brutal suspension under the latter's recent BAs).[15] I am saying that Brazil is a more authoritarian *society*, its subordinated classes are less class-like, and the violence that guarantees its order is much more institutionalized than it is in Argentina, Chile, and Uruguay.

Moreover, in Brazil this order is reimposed daily on the popular sector by extraordinary police violence which teaches both those who suffer it in the flesh and those who witness it about their lack of basic rights. The violence that reinforces the inequalities of Brazilian society is protopolitical. That is, it is notably independent of the political affiliations and opinions that the victim may or may not have. This pattern, dominant in urban Brazil,[16] contrasts with the modest degree of protopolitical repression in Argentina. But it also contrasts with the extremely high degree of direct and explicitly political repression that is unleashed from time to time against the Argentine popular sector (especially in the post-1976 period but also during the previous authoritarian turns of the Argentine spiral). Moreover, as I pointed out, these periods of political repression unleash the wolves of protopolitical repression, stripping the popular sector not only of political but also of civil citizenship.* These more discontinuous patterns of repression reflect—and reproduce—the oscillations and the strongly antagonistic perceptions operating in Argentine politics. The more permanent and protopolitical patterns in Brazil also reflect and reproduce macrophenomena, especially the comparatively high degree of depoliticization of a popular sector that is subject to a violence that is not obviously political. These are different forms of violence, and each has consequences that reinforce or subvert the "order" that the violence is intended to preserve or impose.

Personally, I find the systematic, institutionalized, and covert violence of Brazil to be the worse. But precisely because Brazilian society is so hierarchically structured, the Brazilian BA has been less brutal and authoritarian than its counterparts in the Southern Cone. And this, especially if we consider what the latter have done to their respective popular sectors in the past decade, is better. This is neither a paradox nor a possible choice but a difference and, as such, it deserves to be explored.

Let us consider the respective coups. In Chile, where political society occupied a much larger space than it ever did in Brazil or Argentina, the parties were the articulators of a society they truly represented, serving as its mediators and aggregators in the political arena and the state apparatus. In this intensely politicized society, it was through the institutionalization of these parties and the regime that the left came to control part of the state apparatus. The principle targets of repression after the 1973 coup were thus clear: leftists in the government, the leftwing parties, and the dense network of popular organizations (including unions) affiliated with these parties. Because the threat that the left constituted ran vertically from the bottom to the top of political society, repression in Chile, with the perverse logic that such things have, has been both brutal and extensive.

Now let us contrast this with Brazil in 1964. There the threat that the coup tried to eradicate occupied comparatively little space in society and only a little

---

* See chapter 3 of the current book.—*Ed.*

more in the state apparatus. Compared to Chile, Uruguay, or Argentina, there was little mobilization by either workers or peasants in Brazil, and when a popular movement was beginning to gain some momentum, the coup was already underway. In addition, the radicalizing discourse in Brazil was more moderate and ambivalent than that of the Popular Unity in Chile and emanated from only a few persons in the state apparatus. These individuals, with scarce social or political support, neared the abyss not so much because of their ideology and goals, but because of their ambiguities with respect to such touchy issues as military discipline or their own willingness to play the constitutional game. This was so much the case that Castelo Branco and his advisors believed that if they purged these individuals along with some politicians, military officers, and leaders of popular organizations, things would quickly return to the "normal" course of a very elitist democracy governing a very stratified society. They even believed that *those* parties and *that* Congress (after some purges, to be sure) could continue to function, a belief that was inconceivable in the Southern Cone. It was not even deemed necessary to censure the mass media, since "subversion" did not seem to have penetrated a society that had mobilized more to demand the coup than to support those who would be overthrown. Nor were the coups-within-the-coup that followed the one of 1964 a result of popular upheaval against this BA, despite a couple of strikes that were in good measure noteworthy because they were exceptions to the general atmosphere of compliance to the BA. Even the student protests and the guerrilla activity of 1968–70 were pale shadows of their Uruguayan and Argentine counterparts, and their actions failed to touch a chord in the larger population.

Having thus reinforced a social domination that it did not invent but did accentuate, the Brazilian BA offered to a rapidly expanding international economy the great collateral of the economic "miracle": a "social peace" that seemed guaranteed for a long time and ensured a cheap labor force. Also, even though successive crises suggested that it would not be a bad idea for this BA to seek ratification through elections (which, unlike its more "extremist" Southern Cone counterparts, it had the good sense not to abolish completely), Brazil offered political stability and immunity from the "demagogic temptations" that repeatedly seized its neighbors. As a result, Brazil grew spectacularly: it expanded its productive base enormously, its working class and modern middle sectors multiplied, it further reinforced its social inequalities—and it raced headlong into the current crisis.

In contrast, Chile and Argentina (Chile by paths that were still democratic, Argentina via its increasingly authoritarian spirals) had popular sectors that were far more politically active and organized than Brazil's. The last thing that these countries could guarantee during those crucial years of global economic expansion was "social peace" or vaccinations against "demagogy."

And so, after a thousand bends in their histories, Chile and Argentina suffered a more brutal authoritarianism than Brazil's (as did Uruguay, a country with a unique history and social structure that make it difficult to lump in with Chile and Argentina). Chile and Argentina also confronted a deeper social and economic crisis than Brazil, their productive base and working class diminished, and many members of their modern middle sectors went into exile.

Let us now examine the Argentine coups. What was true of the 1976 coup was already true in 1966: the "subversives" against whom the coups were directed were not in the state apparatus (as in Chile and Brazil), the political parties (as in Chile and, partially, in Brazil), or even in the upper echelons of the unions (as in Chile). On the contrary, the government, the parliament (for the little that it mattered), party leaders, and the top labor leaders, long before 1976, were doing everything *except* fomenting the political activation of the population, much less its radicalization. Where, then, was the "subversion"? Of course it was in the guerrilla organizations—but they had been in retreat since 1975, and their political clout had greatly diminished after Perón excommunicated them in a terrible ceremony in the Plaza de Mayo.[17] The problem, thus, was not deemed to reside in the state apparatus or in the great arenas of politics, but in society: in countless wildcat strikes, in belligerent negotiations over salaries and work conditions (not infrequently carried out at gunpoint), in innumerable day-to-day behaviors that those at the top perceived as unacceptable insolence,[18] and in universities gone mad.[19] Subversion was also found in the lunar landscape of the streets at night: transforming, but also reaffirming some of the themes I have discussed, in the years preceding the 1976 coup the night streets belonged to anonymous assassins who killed or kidnapped victims, often just as anonymous. The military, already preparing the coup, publicly washed their hands of these matters but privately supported López Rega (Isabel Perón's Minister of Social Welfare and principle advisor) and his henchmen as they organized the system of assassinations and kidnappings the military would later extend and perfect—no holds barred—after March 1976. The guerrilla practiced its own version of "justice" through terror and death, creating—almost—the appearance of dual power while remaining far away from their anticipated revolution. There were also the real gangsters, some with links to certain union leaders and business groups, others "private," "apolitical" thugs, but all with firearms, and with kidnapping and blackmailing schemes. Then, as if in a premonition of what would happen after the March 1976 coup, the police went into hiding. They, too, were filled with fear. At night the police entrenched themselves in their stations and waited, like everyone else, for daylight to give them some security; the nocturnal streets they left for any and all assassins to stick it—with their machine guns—to whomever they wanted. This experience (which only some Central Americans can empathize with) would reach its zenith after the coup of March 1976, with the complete appropriation of the street, day and night, by the band of triumphant assassins licensed by the state. This was a grotesque exaggeration of an old story: the appropriation of the public sphere by unmediated conflicts (or, rather, by conflicts mediated only by increasing violence) by actors ever more private and particularized, and, behind this, the destruction of civilized coexistence.

For this reason, the assassins who in Argentina took over in 1976 killed few of those in the upper echelons of society and politics (at the most they accused them of corrupt practices which, even if true, the subsequent BA exceeded a thousandfold). Instead, they spread their repression and terrorism to the interstices, the micro levels of society. For it was there that the enemy was supposedly hiding; it was there that one could find the countless variations of "Why should I give a shit?" that this coup wanted to liquidate once and for all.

Chile, a social formation vertically articulated by *politics*, after the 1973 coup was massacred along this axis. In Brazil there is a socially imposed authoritarianism, exercised with comparatively little state repression. In Argentina, a country of nondemocratic egalitarianism before the 1976 coup, there was little left to decapitate; the problem, as the military and their allies maintained, was the whole "social body."

If we could add up the micro and macrohorrors of each type of authoritarianism—those that are *socially implanted* and those that are *politically imposed* on more rebellious societies—the sum of this futile exercise would be similar. But the two are not the same, even though the implications of their differences are difficult to trace and even more difficult to evaluate from the perspective of human and democratic values. Now I propose to explore these themes from an angle that is less melancholy: that of the *possible* paths toward democracy in these countries, so similar and yet, as I have emphasized, so different.

VI

Perhaps because authoritarianism is so socially rooted in Brazil, the state apparatus has been and, perhaps more importantly, has appeared powerful and decisive and has monopolized center stage during the great episodes of national life. It may be that my impression is overly influenced by the contrast between Brazil and Argentina (as well as its contrast with Chile, Uruguay, Bolivia, and Peru; Mexico, on the other hand, seems more like Brazil in this respect) though I cannot help but wonder how a state could seem anything but powerful if, on the one hand, it is rooted in, and, on the other, it reinforces and guarantees, a social order that, at least until very recently, has been markedly hierarchical. Without intending to make of this a question of the chicken and the egg, it is interesting to note that political society has been as weak in Brazil as in Argentina, albeit for opposite reasons. In Argentina, the unmediated forces of society recurrently destroyed the potential spaces for politics and for a reasonable degree of state autonomy; therefore, the state apparatus has been particularly weak and disarticulated. In Brazil the highly hierarchical arrangement of society has favored an even more radical inversion of the social and political relations envisioned by the classical (liberal) models of political representation. Simply put, there has been little to represent in politics from a society whose popular sector has been prevented from generating political organizations and identities that are relatively autonomous from the dominant classes. At best, the Brazilian popular sector reached a "regulated citizenship"[20] which, instead of serving as a channel for the expansion of its rights, has obstructed opportunities for such expansion, irrespective (until now at least) of the type of political regime. Without the presence *qua* citizens of a good part of the popular sector, there is little chance for the emergence of a political society in which the members of this sector can be *politically represented* in their double condition as citizens and as members of "the people."[21]

The space in which a political society could have emerged in Argentina— and with it, a democratic regime—was swept away by an avalanche of highly organized social forces that included the popular sector. In Brazil, the space in which a political society could emerge is much too narrow; there is no system of political representation that includes those for whom mediation is most important—those at the bottom of a sharply delineated social hierarchy. Without such a system, Brazilian political society is as narrow as it is elitist. Relations with the popular sector are not politically mediated except when some of the latter's aspirations and interests are digested at the highest levels of the social hierarchy or state apparatus lest they become a political concern. Therefore, even those policies that take the Brazilian popular sector into account tend to paternalistically reproduce the social hierarchy that impedes the popular sector's effective representation. The concept of political representation implies the existence of a reasonably autonomous subject that is not subsumed under other subjects. A political system without effective representation does not fit the mold of a democratic regime—or it may have fit the institutional architecture of oligarchic republics, but cannot do so in a country as socially and regionally unequal, but also as complex, industrialized, and dynamic, as Brazil.

For these reasons, neither Argentina's razed political society nor Brazil's excessively narrow one, have mattered much—they have been eliminated or manipulated by the dominant powers as often as the latter have deemed it "necessary." Thus, in neither country has democracy had an institutional space in which to operate, much less consolidate.

Consistent with what I am arguing, let it be noted that during its most openly authoritarian periods, the Argentine state apparatus, in so many ways weaker than Brazil's, was more thoroughly authoritarian. As I mentioned, even before 1976 but especially afterward, the state intervened with unusual violence in almost every aspect of daily life. During authoritarian rule in Brazil, by contrast, the state apparatus, in other areas more dynamic and decisive than Argentina's, penetrated society to a much lesser degree and proposed much less radical goals. Given the parameters already in force (that did not have to be "adjusted" much) of a strongly hierarchical system of social domination and of "regulated citizenship," the state of such a statist social formation was nevertheless much less interventionist in the microcontexts of society, than was the more disarticulated and less weighty state of authoritarian Argentina.

VII

Brazil is a country whose "social peace" was only marginally shaken by pre-1964 processes and where after the subsequent purge of a narrow political society, the BA's governments were able, for a number of years, to focus on "other things," especially managing the rapid growth and transnationalization of the economy. In Argentina, society was perceived to be the problem. It was there that, according to the perpetrators and supporters of the 1976 coup, everything was out of place. Nothing important could be achieved, nor would the cruel victories of the perpetrators be worth anything, if the destruction of the basis of such "disorder" was not accomplished. The country's evil elements *(la Argentina maldita)* had to be eliminated; i.e., the political identities of the popular sector, its unions, and, as we have seen, their insolence in daily dealings with "superiors." To accomplish this the repressors cared little whether or not the economy grew. The economy could be taken care of later on, once the repressors had completed what they referred to as the *"indispensable saneamiento"* ("indispensable cleansing") of these ills. In a word, the social quiescence that authoritarian Brazilians took virtually for granted was at the heart of the problem as defined in Argentina. Returning to Chile, the repression its BA applied was similar to Argentina's. There, too, though for different reasons as we have seen, the perpetrators and supporters of the coup believed in the need to "put the popular sector in its place" and to destroy forever the foundations that might allow it to *"desubicarse"* ("lose its way") again.

But the fast growth and economic internationalization of Brazil's economy made clear, even before the presently suffocating effects of the foreign debt, the exponentially increasing costs of "success." Even in this relatively moderate

BA, the ravaging logic of repression made clear to both the perpetrators, supporters, and beneficiaries of the coup the dangers of this violent power. Furthermore, the triumphant arrogance of the state eventually alarmed that great and exaggerated winner of the day, the Brazilian bourgeoisie. These tensions created the first spaces from which clear and courageous voices began to be raised, before the present economic crisis accentuated these and other problems.

In Argentina the BA's success must be measured by what it was able to destroy. And its abysmal failure is nowadays revealed in the resurgence of a popular sector, weakened though it has been by the onset of unemployment and poverty, that today demands redress of the hardships imposed on it since 1976.

In both countries, I think, the road that must be followed is as clear as it is difficult. In Argentina, the obvious issue is whether this time, under conditions that are objectively less favorable than ever (due to the urgency of each sector's demands in a context of drastically reduced material goods and very high inflation), but perhaps subjectively more favorable (due to the learning that some seem to have undergone as a result of the destructive dynamic of anarchic corporatism), we will stop sticking it in at each intersection—if not in the streets (an excessively utopian dream), then at least in relations among the social forces that the BA did not completely destroy. Is this wishful thinking? Possibly, but unless we can establish a system of representative mediations, there is little doubt *"que seguiremos a los tumbos y cuesta abajo"* ("We will continue on our bumpy road downhill"—another tango title). The great novelty, the source of hope, is that nowadays many claim to have learned this lesson.

In Brazil, as usual, the situation is more nuanced, less all-or-nothing. The transition that began in 1974 accelerated with the strikes of 1978 and 1979 and then slowed down. Today, with an economic crisis that is particularly traumatic for a country so addicted to growth, Brazil also confronts the unresolved enigma of how to build a political society and, behind it, a democratic regime. The great virtue of the transition process begun in 1974 is that beyond the interactions of politicians and top-ranking members of the state apparatus, other actors and tendencies are coming into play that might weaken the hierarchical character of Brazilian society, at least in the urban centers where an important part of the population is concentrated.

If the praetorian style of doing politics in Argentina generated the spirals described above, the highly elitist style of doing politics in Brazil has also reached a point of diminishing returns. Democratic politics in a society as complex as Brazil's can be reasonably representative only if they include the popular sector for whom citizenship can be postponed nowadays only by resorting to a level of repression that is more extensive and penetrating than any yet practiced in Brazil. However, in today's Brazil, the progressive and democratic discourse coming from some parties and members of congress is directed much more toward the state apparatus than toward society. This is because the gap with society is much greater than the discourse suggests, revealing the weakness of political society and of the vast segments of society who are scarcely represented. As a consequence, during the present Brazilian transition, there arose what could be the world's record of electoral legislation stratagems, imposed repeatedly and with impunity by the BA's incumbents. As a friend of democratic politicians in Brazil and Argentina, sometimes I feel that in Argentina they are devoured by anarchic corporatism, while in Brazil they are forced to revolve around the orbit of the state because there are so few ties to keep them within society's gravitational field.

The sufferings endured by Argentina and Brazil have the advantage of raising problems that might otherwise continue to be postponed or ignored. In Brazil, perhaps the greatest problem is that the limits of "normality" as it has historically been conceived by those on top have become too narrow to be minimally democratic. When viewed from this perspective, what today is called in Brazil a social and political crisis is, at least in part, a condition for the possibility of creating a democratic regime. That there are and will continue to be strikes; that day by day the government controls fewer of the economic and political variables on which its iron grip was, until quite recently, either praised or vilified; that popular and middle sectors are beginning to impose demands and dilemmas that go beyond their traditional relationship to the state; that urban violence has spread from the *favelas* to feed the fears of the middle and upper sectors; and that the economic crisis not only punishes the poor but also affects many who, like the regime itself, believed the "miracle" was going to last forever: today, all of these themes underlie speculations over whether the armed forces will continue the transition or will reinvade the state apparatus in order to exorcise these (for Brazil) unusual or, in any case, forgotten disorders.

VIII

My purpose here is not to analyze the democratic transitions in Brazil and Argentina. Instead, the concern of this essay continues to be certain differences that each country must resolve in its own manner. Chile (and Uruguay, too) had, and will probably have again, a political society that truly mediates between the state and society. The principle problem for Argentina in its quest to consolidate its democracy is to strengthen political society against the unmediated assaults of society; in other words, to defend the space needed for aggregating interests without the suffocations provoked by anarchic corporatism. The main problem for Brazil—in order to attain democracy, as well as to consolidate it—is to strengthen political society vis-à-vis the state apparatus.

A society that submits to *"Você sabe com quem está falando?"* is articulated in such an authoritarian manner that it lacks the strength to push beyond the freedoms that those who do speak may see fit to grant. Such a society tends to generate kinds of authoritarian rule that are more self-assured, probably more successful, and generally less repressive than Argentina's. In a society like Brazil, I can assure you, it is much more agreeable to be a member of the "elite"; one gets accustomed to a deferential treatment that in other cultures one should best forget. Given these and other aspects—including the enjoyment of the temporary reversal of all this in the ritual of carnival—it may be particularly difficult for the dominant classes in Brazil to relinquish with reasonable grace part of their extraordinary privileges.

Brazil's transition, zealously controlled since 1974, has already been prolonged for a period of time that is unusual in the twentieth century. This transition is exceptional in other ways as well: the liability for horrors committed in the recent past is relatively slight (and no one seems willing to demand retribution); the popular sector raised its head in the strikes of 1978–79 but then returned to a level of protest that would be considered idyllic by the initiators of other transitions; the great specter of other transitions—angry protests by middle sectors experiencing a deterioration in their economic conditions—is only now beginning to appear; the political right controls a significant part of the vote and none of the parties or candidates who enjoy broad electoral support represent the slightest threat to the country's basic (capitalist) parameters; and, finally, the opposition, which currently governs several states, recognizes the basic realities of the existing national distribution of power, reaffirms the Brazilian style of doing politics, and bends over backward to find grounds for cooperating with the national government. In a society and a transition like this one, it would require an extraordinary rigidity by those on top—as well as a historically absurd attachment to privileges unheard of in other modern, complex societies—for the military and their social supports to acquire sufficient support to abort the democracy that is currently in sight.

IX

This essay now comes to an end, not because I am going to reach a conclusion, but because I will return to where I began. Although it may not always have been evident, the subject of this essay has been democracy in our countries—seen from the perspective of certain antidemocratic obstacles and the possibilities of overcoming or at least sidestepping them. We simply cannot (actually we can, but the consequences are not positive) tell a power that is stronger than us that we do not give a shit, nor can we "stick it to 'em," especially if this power is accustomed to asserting itself from time to time with as much violence as good conscience. On the other hand, we can remain silent, or do what we are told. But in that case some people will become too accustomed to speaking for both themselves and the voiceless, and will get very angry when others—even those without subversive intent or vulgar language—try to say something on their own. Behind both kind of situations is a serious lack of citizenship.

Argentina has been programmed to generate multitudinous and episodic democracies, aborted by ever more brutal coups. Brazil, on the other hand, has been programmed to generate elitist democracies that are rather easily discarded as soon as they show signs of expanding. Behind these fragile flowers lie, in Argentina, a political society razed by political violence and anarchic corporatism, and, in Brazil, a political society that represents some sectors so much, and others so little, that it cannot constitute a stage on which the tragedies and comedies of democracy can be played out. In both cases, it is not only or even primarily the state that needs to be democratized, but society. Without aspiring to utopias or imagining revolutions, I have in mind a *reasonable* democratization. Applying this less-than-rigorous concept to Argentina, I mean that its strong horizontal collective identities—as members of classes, sectors, and social factions—have to become more vertical. That is, these identities must be attenuated by a complementary identity as citizens who share an interest in establishing stable and predictable mediations between their otherwise crude interests. With regard to Brazil, I mean exactly the opposite while making the same point. Instead of being so vertically and fragmentedly submissive to those on top, the popular sector must develop horizontal identities in order to become collective subjects who can be represented in political society.

Looking at the history of both countries, these changes seem improbable. Nevertheless, it is my impression (and that is why I wrote this essay) that through the recent authoritarian experiences and crises, and by the strange twists of history, these changes—different in their content yet convergent in their destination—have now become possible. For this to happen it should not be necessary for the Argentine *pueblo* to stop proclaiming its rights, nor for the Brazilian *povão* to lose its amiable nature. In both countries, and in both senses, the argument of these pages is that the construction of democracy implies much more than accommodating the paranoia of the powerful. It implies deciphering, each in its own way, the still unresolved enigma of both countries: how to establish, in the context of a democratic regime, effective political representation for the popular sector. Here I have suggested some criteria—or, if one prefers, necessary conditions—for this to occur: With respect to Argentina, to partially dehorizontalize and then to politicize in a more appropriate manner (i.e., with more ties to political parties and, in general, to a more autonomous political society) its intensely mobilized society; with respect to Brazil, to horizontalize popular collective identities, defending them from the immense power of a social architecture that is highly clientelistic and corporatist and, therefore, statist. When all is said and done, I do not see how democracy can expand and consolidate without the support of social relations and interactions in which neither side submits nor responds with curses to the one who spoke first and more forcefully.

Notes

1. Roberto DaMatta, *Carnivals, Rogues, and Heroes: An Interpretation of the Brazilian Dilemma* (Notre Dame, Ind.: University of Notre Dame Press, 1991). The book was previously published in Brazil: *Carnavais, malandros e herois* (Río de Janeiro: Zahar, 1978).

2. DaMatta, *Carnivals*.

3. This is the response, perfectly logical under the circumstances, we were given in 1979 when we asked several police officers why they hid themselves. [The author refers to the "proto-investigation" narrated in chapter 3.—*Ed.*]

4. Roberto Schwarz, *Ao vencedor as batatas* (São Paulo: Livraría Duas Cidades, 1977), pp. 13–25 and passim.

5. If the reader sees sexual connotations in the use of this language, I admit that I do too. But neither my disordered readings nor the years I have spent on the couch allow me to make productive use of this insight.

6. I say "generally" because not everyone respects all rules at all times. This is what gives the sport its thrilling character.

7. Another complicating factor occurs when the driver is a woman. In our cultures, women are considered genetically incapable of driving a car correctly, so that, as a taxi driver once told me, "*Aquí las minas empiezan perdiendo*" (Loosely translated, "Here the babes start with two strikes against them"). When two women collide, it is *quod erat demonstrandum*; when a woman and a man collide, it is also *quod erat demonstrandum* since the woman is surely at fault.

8. The supermacho U.S.-style game of chicken has many variations, but the principle version, at least as far as I know, consists of two automobiles approaching one another head-on in the same lane; the driver who veers away first (the "chicken") is the loser. Sometimes both win and die in glory.

9. This theme and others relating to the period before the 1976 coup are discussed in Guillermo O'Donnell, *Bureaucratic Authoritarianism: Argentina, 1966–1973, in Comparative Perspective* (Berkeley: University of California Press, 1988).

10. Another characteristic that surprises me (and which I suppose has something to do with the submissive response, whether verbal or not, presupposed by "*¿Você sabe com quem está falando?*") is that almost no one looks at the subordinate persons when giving an order or receiving a service from him or her. It is as if the person were not there and only the act existed. In Argentina the "*¿Usted quién se cree que soy yo?*" of one

who in addition arrogantly refuses to look at the interlocutor, runs the risk of a response I am not going to repeat here so as not to continue sullying this paper.

11. Samuel Huntington, *Political Order in Changing Societies* (New Haven: Yale University Press, 1968).

12. I have analyzed part of this history, and its various twists and turns, in "State and Alliances in Argentina, 1956–1976" [chapter 1 of the current book.—*Ed.*]

13. There is little doubt in my mind that historically it was the right wing, lacking votes and ever-fearful of the "plebeian" behavior of the popular sector fomented by its own behavior, who inaugurated in Argentina the authoritarian and confrontational practices I discuss here.

14. Although the methodology employed may have caused relatively wide margins of error, it is remarkable that a government-sponsored survey conducted during the initial period of guerrilla activity in Argentina (1971) showed 49 percent of the respondents in support of the guerrilla's actions (poll taken in the cities of Buenos Aires, Rosario, and Córdoba). Later, as the guerrillas lost their Robin Hood image, and their confrontations with various sectors of peronism—and ultimately with Perón himself—became evident, support declined dramatically even prior to the 1976 coup. In any case, such a degree of support (probably similar only to the support given the Tupamaros in Uruguay, also at the beginning of their actions), shows how central the guerrilla phenomenon was in Argentina compared to Brazil, a centrality that enabled it to undertake many more, and more ambitious (and crazy) actions. We must also consider that, in contrast to Brazil in 1968–69, the heyday of the Argentine guerrillas (approximately 1970–75) coincided with a great wave of strikes and popular mobilization. The data mentioned here are discussed in *Bureaucratic-Authoritarianism: Argentina,*" chapter 10.

15. See Renato R. Boschi, ed., *Violência e cidade* (Río de Janeiro: Zahar Editores, 1982), and Rubén G. Oliven, ed., *Violência e cultura no Brasil* (Petrópolis: Editora Vozes, 1982).

16. It would be beyond my expertise to say anything about the rural sector.

17. A good study of the principle guerrilla organization and its various incarnations is found in Richard Gillespie, *The Soldiers of Perón: Argentina's Montoneros* (Cambridge: Cambridge University Press, 1982).

18. An anecdote: In 1975, while walking in downtown Buenos Aires, I ran into a former classmate of mine, then the director of one of the main private banks in Argentina. With utter fury he dragged me several blocks to see what was happening to "his" bank, explaining on the way that he did not mind that the employees were on strike or that he was forbidden to enter the premises, since these things happened all the time; what was really serious was what the employees were doing at that very moment. I must confess that I was amazed to see that they had pushed the furniture against the walls, split up into two rambunctious teams, and were playing an enthusiastic game of soccer. But my friend's anger was nothing compared to the rage, compounded by fear, that many businessmen were forced to swallow. Like the military, who had taken to living in fortified quarters, these businessmen hired bodyguards for themselves and their families and changed their routes to work every day, a reasonable precaution

since kidnappings and assassinations of their peers had become an almost everyday occurrence.

19. Even considering the tendency of Latin American universities to hyper-radicalize, what happened in Argentina during those years, especially in the public universities, surpassed all previous limits. The mix of Perón (selectively read, to be sure) with Fanon, Guevara, and Mao was particularly intoxicating, and contributed significantly to the horrible hangover we all suffered later. The phenomenon reached down to the high schools; years later, directors and teachers revealed to us the hatred of "young people" they had developed as a result. As the man in charge of "discipline" in a prestigious public high school in Buenos Aires told me: "These kids are bad, very bad; they must suffer so they will learn to obey." [See also discussion in chapter 3.—*Ed.*]

20. Wanderley Guilherme dos Santos, "Praxis liberal no Brasil," in *Ordem burguesa e liberalismo político* (São Paulo: Duas Cidades, 1978).

21. That is, as members of a relatively underprivileged group that therefore has, in addition to the classic rights of citizenship, certain aspirations for substantive justice; for a discussion of this theme, see *Bureaucratic-Authoritarianism: Argentina*, chapter 1.

PART III
Transitions

6

Notes for the Study of Processes
of Political Democratization in the
Wake of the Bureaucratic-Authoritarian State

The present text does not pretend to offer substantive answers to the mani-fold questions raised by the exit from authoritarian situations. Instead, my goal is to propose several focal points around which the study and compari-son of transition processes might be organized. Despite the fact that they typically occur within a short period of time, such processes present a great number and variety of elements for analysis. Accordingly, the title given to the following pages is not entirely appropriate; the processes by which a BA terminates do not necessarily lead to stable political democracy, as is demon-strated by the case of Argentina during the 1970s. On the contrary, such processes may provoke relapses that intensify the characteristics of earlier authoritarian rule. Histories of success in the consolidation of political democ-racy, and their determinant factors, should be compared with histories of fail-ure, in order to isolate the decisive elements therein.

Of course, to speak of "successes" and "failures" implies a value judgment. I consider intrinsically valuable the move away from authoritarian forms that

This chapter first appeared as "Notas para el Estudio de Procesos de Democratización Política a Partir del Estado Burocrático-Autoritario" (Documento de Trabajo, CEDES 2 [no. 9, 1979]). It was edited by John Rieger for inclusion in this book.

Strictly speaking, the present notes are a working paper, the first fruits of a Guggenheim fel-lowship granted to me for the study of the theme indicated by the title. I have prepared the pre-sent text for a project on the same theme that is being developed in the Latin American Program of the Woodrow Wilson Center for International Scholars. Basically, it is intended as material for discussion among program participants; my hope is that it will prove useful for authors of the case studies to be carried within the project. Given the nature of this work, I have omitted de-tailed bibliographical references.

leads to a regime of reasonably consolidated political democracy. From the normative standpoint I am adopting, the achievement of political democracy—both on the level of competition for governmental authority and of the effectiveness of basic individual and associative rights—is an immense advance over the conditions imposed by a BA.[1] Furthermore, under the circumstances resulting from the previous existence of a BA, the achievement of political democracy may present the most viable route, if not the only one, along which to address issues related to the expansion of democracy at social and economic levels.

Other prefatory remarks are in order. First, I will not be concerned with the dynamics of the BA nor, therefore, with the tensions that contribute to the termination of this type of political domination.[2] Second, I will discuss the transition from a BA toward another sort of rule focusing on properly political factors and processes and paying scant attention to an issue that merits separate treatment: the fluctuations and problems of economic policy that typically accompany the political processes that concern me here. The third remark is that the present notes refer only to the transition from one kind of authoritarian state—a BA—not to transitions from any kind of authoritarian rule. It is possible that some of the reflections presented here are valid for transitions from other forms of authoritarianism, but the BA has characteristics that correspond to social and economic specificities, which influence the kind of political transition that may arise from this type of rule. In particular, it should be borne in mind that the emergence of the BA is an expression of the fear of the dominant classes and various segments of the middle class regarding what they perceive as a high degree of threat posed by a politically activated popular sector—a popular sector not only politically mobilized but also underpinned by an organizational network that, at least during the period directly preceding the inauguration of the BA, is notably extended and autonomous from the dominant classes. A popular sector with these features is characteristic of an economic and social structure endowed with large urban concentrations and extensive though immature industrialization. Such a structure generates a large and strategically located working class along with many dependent layers within the middle class, especially public employees.[3] Furthermore, the existence of a popular sector (including a working class) that has "been there"—that is, fully incorporated into the political arena, and in such a way that in the period preceding the establishment of a BA it was perceived as a threat to the continuity of basic parameters of society (particularly, its international affiliations and its condition as a capitalist society)—signals important differences between the BA and other kinds of authoritarianism—oligarchic and populist—in which the political activation of the popular sector has not occurred and the economy has not attained the level of complexity and industrialization typical of cases of BA. In any event, these are speculations that it will be necessary to explore comparatively through case studies that examine transitions from authoritarian forms other than the BA.

We should now address the problematic foci that, to me, appear fundamental for a case-by-case and comparative study of transition processes: the first consists of some conceptual clarifications regarding the "whence" and the "whither" implied by the very idea of political transition; the second focal point is the identification of the main coalitions involved in this process; the third, which complicates the strictly political analysis to which the earlier topics tend, is what I will call the resurrection of civil society. In a final section I attempt to bind up some loose ends.

I

The first problem with which one is confronted in thinking about the transition from a BA to another political form is the analytical determination of a point of departure—the point at which such a transition is understood to begin. Here, a strictly circumscribed definition of the authoritarian state (or regime, depending on the theoretical orientation of each author) that precedes the transition to be studied is an advantage. The problem of beginnings is an important one; only in one contemporary case that I am aware of (Portugal) did a swift transition from authoritarian rule to political democracy occur. In other cases, the situation remains authoritarian during a not insignificant period; yet, in order to conceptualize the transition itself, we must be able to distinguish between the *subsequent* authoritarianism (itself in fluid transformation) and the BA that preceded it. With this in mind, I propose that we are dealing with a BA whenever all of the following conditions still hold:[4] (1) the maintenance of what in previous works I called the political exclusion of the popular sector, manifest (in what directly interests us here) in the coercive prohibition of the formation of organizations that publicly claim to represent the interests of the popular sector and/or the working class, as well as in rigid state control of unions, (2) the nonexistence or merely formal existence of institutions of political democracy, and (3) the restriction of the political arena, basically, to processes internal to the state apparatus, the actors in which are members—civilian and military—of this apparatus, as well as leaders of large private organizations. The disappearance of any one of these three conditions implies that the BA has ceased to exist. Yet that this occurs is a necessary condition for the emergence of political democracy, not a sufficient one. One characteristic of the kind of transition I discuss here is that, beginning from the time one or all of the just-stated conditions ceases or cease to remain in effect, the situation remains authoritarian; the latter, however, is no longer the specific type of authoritarianism that we refer to as a

BA. Furthermore—and this is part of what we must come to grips with— throughout the transition such an authoritarian situation bears within it the probability, which we should not underestimate, of reversion to further in-stantiations of a BA. Political democracy is only one of several possible out-comes of a process that entails much more than the elimination of certain characteristics of the BA.[5]

Of course, it is usually impossible to pinpoint an exact "moment" at which the transition from a BA starts, but I hope that the categories I have just pro-posed may facilitate the identification of the beginning of such transitions with adequate precision. What, then, would be the "point of arrival"—the threshold at which our analysis would end? Here it is important to recall that one of the issues at play during the transition is the building of a new political regime.[6] The BA has a political regime, though usually not a formally institu-tionalized one, that may outlive this kind of state itself; but, at one moment or another, that regime dissolves,[7] and there begins, also at this level, a transition that may lead to political democracy. In any event, the degree of formaliza-tion[8] and other characteristics assumed by an authoritarian regime are among the fundamental issues put into play in and by the transition. Although his-tory remains open, one may plausibly conclude the analysis of a transition whenever a new political regime—democratic or not—with apparently rea-sonable chances of enduring over the medium term emerges.

We now turn to more specific issues.

II

The transition from a BA toward another type of rule may begin for various reasons: opposition activities that betray the fragility of a BA's social supports and coercive arm (Argentina during 1969–73, and Greece), a perception that the BA is so firmly consolidated that its leaders are lured into seeking legiti-mation by way of elections (Brazil), or prospects of the more or less imminent disappearance of a leader central to the regime (Spain) together, as in Brazil, with a perception of rather high regime consolidation.

The degree of control exercised by the ruling alliance over the transition— especially its capacity to impose the rules of the game under which the transi-tion is to proceed—depends upon the manner in which the process begins.[9] If the transition begins for fundamentally extrinsic reasons (that is, as a direct result of opposition activities), as it did in Argentina and Greece, then the con-trol of the ruling alliance over the process will be weaker. If the transition begins mainly at the initiative of the ruling alliance itself, then its degree of control over the subsequent process will be greater. Furthermore, given that the ruling coalition will typically prefer gradual advances, guaranteed against the risk of "a leap into the void," then, other things being equal, the more control the ruling coalition has over the transition the more protracted it will be.

As we will see, there are also important variations from case to case in the characteristics of the parties or groups that succeed in being recognized as the principal voice of the opposition. They may represent quite moderate stands, as did the Greek opposition, or, as occurred in Argentina during the period 1969–73, they may embody an even more threatening radicalization than that which preceded the emergence of BA. The ruling coalition's initial degree of liberalizing commitment also varies across cases: their intentions may be limited to re-coating the BA in a more legitimate hue (as in Brazil 1973–74), or, their intentions may extend to the establishment of what we might properly call a political democracy (as they did in Spain during the Suárez period).

There are equally important case-by-case variations in the institutional forms that survive the BA or are created during it. The restoration of the monarchy in Spain and, in Brazil, the survival of the parliament and the BA's own creation of two parties (which, although they sometimes appeared devoid of real significance, subsequently took on a life of their own) contrasts sharply with the institutional devastation produced in such cases as Chile, Uruguay, and Argentina. These differences may be crucial in determining the rhythms, issues, and risks that each actor faces. But, without ignoring such differences (here I am only able to take into account some situations by way of example, until such time as a properly comparative study furnishes the requisite data) I wish to highlight several common characteristics that may be gleaned from a broad observation of transition processes. I hope that these remarks serve as a conceptual axis that helps organize the wealth of empirical material of the cases to be studied.

One common characteristic of the transition is the formation of a "liberalizing coalition" that cuts across the typical BA alignments in a new fashion. This coalition is formed, on one hand, by members of the ruling alliance in the BA who, for any of the reasons already mentioned, opt to lead a process of political liberalization—these I will call the BA softliners. Their partner in this coalition is a segment of the opposition that I will refer to as the moderate, or truly democratic, opposition.

While the type of state and regime that the softliners wish to move toward may still be authoritarian, their decision to liberalize[10] and, thus, dissolve the BA, places them in direct conflict with the hardliners within the BA—those opposed to any kind of political transformation. Such opposition to change may be based on their commitment to the BA's unlimited duration, or it may be rooted in the belief that the right moment at which to "decompress" the political situation has—"still"—not arrived.[11] For their part, the softliners must take into account not only the many actors within the state apparatus who remain undecided about these matters (principally, within the armed forces) but also, and no less importantly, among the dominant classes. To all of the above, the softliners must present a plausible argument to the effect that the transition they propose is "better" than the alternative of continuity advocated by the hardliners. In cases of spectacular opposition emergence (such as those of Greece, and Argentina during the period 1969–73), the soft-liners argue that liberalization will neutralize the most threatening oppo-sition elements and, as a result, more effectively safeguard the fundamental interests of the members of the BA alliance than would be the case under the hardline alternative. By contrast, when liberalization is initiated in decisions essentially internal to the BA, then the softliners' argument is that the rough edges of existing domination must be rounded off through the legitimizing reestablishment of certain electoral mechanisms and/or—as in the case of Spain—by filling in inevitable institutional vacuums.[12] In either case, the softliners must persuade themselves and be capable of convincing other members of the ruling alliance that their fundamental interests will not be less effectively safeguarded (and, in the long run, will be more effectively so) than they would under the continuist hardline alternative.[13] Most important in this respect are the "fundamental interests" of the armed forces and of the dominant classes that form the principal social base of the BA.[14]

What are those fundamental interests? An a priori and abstract reply to this question is impossible; such interests cannot be determined outside of the transition process itself. Indeed, the ongoing redefinition of the content of such interests is one of the central themes of the transition. At its beginning, both the upper bourgeoisie and the armed forces typically define their fundamental interests very broadly. Later, following the rhythm of changes in power rela-tions that the transition itself provokes (in reality, the transition *is* those changes) such interests tend to be redefined in a more limited way by the members of the BA alliance. Quite early in the transition, these actors find themselves adopting positions that they would have rejected outright at the start of the process. But even though the flexibility of these actors turns out to be greater than they themselves originally supposed, it is not infinite. For the armed forces, a point of non-negotiability seems to be reached if attempts are made to alter their hierarchical lines of discipline, especially those that sepa-rate officers from noncommissioned officers and soldiers. For the upper bour-geoisie (in addition, obviously, to the continuity of society *qua* capitalist) a fundamental point is to obtain a reasonable guarantee that it will retain its po-sition at the dynamic vanguard of the economy; however, this bourgeoisie may be prepared to accept an outcome in which its supremacy is attenuated or partially relinquished due to advances in various forms of state capitalism and/or state tutelage of selected local capital sectors.[15] Another non-negotiable point—more fundamental because it applies to the entire bourgeoisie, not only to its upper fractions—is that its cellular domination in society remain beyond question. In other words, the bourgeoisie's prerogatives to control the organization of the workplace and decide about the allocation of the capital it accumulates should not be challenged. The remaining interests of the armed forces and the bourgeoisie remain vaguely defined and are ultimately subject to the vagaries of the transition; but those that I have just mentioned seem to be the core, the bottom line that the armed forces and the bourgeoisie cannot even contemplate negotiating. Were this nucleus of interests put in play, the higher echelons of the armed forces and/or of the bourgeoisie, as the case may be, would feel that the transition was leading to a catastrophic outcome; consequently they would adopt behaviors sharply antagonistic to it.

Let us revisit the political game played by the liberalizing coalition. Among their allies in the BA, the softliners will always find some hardliners. Furthermore, neither the softliners nor the hardliners are homogeneous.[16] Among the softliners there will be differences regarding how far the liberalization should go; accordingly, different kinds of softliners will seek different interlocutors within different sectors of the opposition. Among the hardliners there will be those unconditionally opposed to liberalization and those who believe that it is "still" not the right time for liberalization. These latter will allow for limited negotiations with the softliners, as will other members of the BA alliance: prominent figures, groups, and organizations that remain undecided, fence-sitters disposed to "wait and see" what happens with liberalization. One of the central problems faced by the softliners is the potential fusion of the hardliners and the undecided, along with the thinning of their own ranks that would follow from this; such a convergence might be brought about by a convincing argument to the effect that the liberalization process, far from having generated the results promised by the softliners, has led to a situation in which catastrophic harm is about to be done to the fundamental interests of the members of the BA alliance (however broadly those interests happen to be defined at the time of an eventual antiliberalizing fusion).

The danger of this fusion (and the subsequent coup—military or otherwise—that it would provoke) is very real; indeed, it is one of the most important problems that the softliners must face. On the other hand, the threat of such a fusion is a trump card that the softliners hold over the opposition. It is on this very basis that they pressure the opposition to "not demand too much"; in this way, the softliners endeavor to ensure that, at each stage of a very dynamic and uncertain process, the opposition is satisfied with whatever is possible "under the circumstances" over the short and medium term. In their negotiations[17] with the opposition, the softliners may always argue that, were it in their power, they would pursue greater and swifter liberalization; however, goes the argument, this is impossible, because it would trigger a hardline reaction, setting the process back to a situation much worse than that implied by the "realistic goals" of the softliners. One variation on this type of case—which appears when the leadership of the softliners is in the hands of those who control the armed forces—is illustrated, although under very different political circumstances in each instance, by the actions of President Lanusse (1971–73) in Argentina (a liberalization imposed on the BA from outside), and by those of President Geisel (1975–79) in Brazil (a liberalization initiated by decisions taken within the BA). In this kind of variation, it is the leader of the softliners who brandishes the threat that, if the opposition fails to recognize and respect the limits of the situation, he "will be forced" to clamp down on the transition.

However, quite soon it becomes evident that the softliners are so committed to liberalization and, therefore, opposed to a hardline coup that, were such a coup ever to occur, it would be aimed as much at the softliners themselves as at the opposition. It follows that even though the liberalization advances considerably beyond the softliners' initial intentions, to the extent that the latter wish to preserve their governmental positions—among other reasons, in order to attempt "still" to lead the process back toward a path more in keeping with their own preferences—their efforts to forestall a hardline coup make them vigilant guardians of the transition.

On the side of the opposition the situation is no less complicated. There will always be an opportunistic opposition (or pseudo-opposition) ready to accept practically any proposal made by the softliners. Objectively, this part of the opposition is an obstacle to democratization; to the degree that it succeeds in becoming the dominant voice within the opposition, the transition process will grind to a halt at a stage that closely reflects the initial proposals of the softliners—which is to say, short of political democracy. Another segment of the opposition will be maximalist, unwilling to negotiate anything with any sector of the BA. If other members of the opposition do so, the maximalists will execrate them as traitors who have "sold out" to the BA. Furthermore, maximalists will typically depict the proposed liberalization as a trap laid by the softliners and opposition traitors. The maximalist position within the opposition and the position of the BA's hardliners feed on each other. It is the maximalists who, with their words and actions, offer the best reasons for the hardliners to reaffirm their views, and provide them with ammunition for persuading the undecided to take a stand against liberalization. If maximalists succeed in imposing themselves as the dominant voice of the opposition, the consequences are more complex than those that would result from the victory of the opportunists within the opposition camp. The first such consequence is that the risk of a coup increases dramatically because the maximalists explicitly refuse to extend guarantees to any of the interests of the BA alliance. But, as is demonstrated by the Argentine case of 1969–73, the deterioration of the BA may be so severe (as manifested in a high degree of factionalization of the armed forces and an inability on the part of the upper bourgeoisie to envisage minimally coherent political tactics) that a maximalist triumph in the opposition camp does not lead to a coup, despite the risk of the same continually surrounding the process.[18] In such a case, the short-term result is speedy democratization extending beyond the purely political sphere; with the consequent demise of the BA, the barriers to radicalization at the microlevels of society collapse. In other words, in cases such as these, none of the fundamental interests of the BA alliance are safeguarded. Moreover, the resulting democratization tends to be more the byproduct of maximalist supremacy in the political and social arenas than the result of conscious efforts aimed at the construction of a politically democratic regime.[19] When such a regime nevertheless emerges, as did today's regime in Portugal,[20] it is due to vicissitudes of the process that I cannot discuss here. In other cases of transitions culminated under maximalist supremacy, such as Argentina in 1973, the resulting democratic regime could not be minimally stabilized. Yet, in both cases, a maximalist triumph in the opposition camp that is not interrupted by a coup entails not only the collapse of the BA but also, at a more profound level, an acute crisis of the state (understood as guarantor of the relations of domination, including the capitalist relations of production).[21] For its part, such a crisis signals that what has emerged is, at the least, a prerevolutionary juncture; a situation of dual power may ensue, in which power is shared between whatever remains of the repressive power of the state apparatus and the various organizational forms in which the maximalist opposition is embodied (among others, militias, guerrilla groups, and even sections of the state apparatus that have passed over to the maximalist camp). Nevertheless, in none of the contemporary cases—and despite the fact that in Portugal the process extended to an advanced degree of expropriation of the upper bourgeoisie and of restructuring of the armed forces—has the triumph of the maximalists provoked a leap outside the capitalist condition of society. In addition to immense objective difficulties, this is due to the splintering and lack of strategic programs typical of an opposition that is better suited to destroying the BA than to governing over its ruins. As a consequence, the fundamental interests of the former BA coalition once again make their weight felt, accompanied by a backlash against what (after the initial euphoria) is viewed by many sectors of the population as excessive "disorder." Under these circumstances, it is inevitable that a highly speculative economy will emerge. The combined effect of these factors is to encourage the adoption of policies— either by the maximalists or by those into whose hands the government has fallen after the exhaustion of the former—that effectively ratify the capitalist nature of society. Such policies—basically, economic "austerity" and social "discipline"—mark the Thermidor of maximalist victories and portend their ejection from the positions of governmental and social power which they have attained. In a case such as the Argentine transition of 1969–73, and in every other case in which the fundamental social positions of the bourgeoisie and the armed forces have remained intact[22] (no matter how shaken and weakened by the transition these forces may have been), the violation of their fundamental interests provokes reactions that drag the situation back to conditions that are even more repressive than they were under the previous BA. In synthesis, the maximalist opposition may eventually cause the collapse of the BA and generate a prerevolutionary situation, but it does not seem capable of pursuing the transition to the point at which the capitalist parameters of society cease. This, in turn, implies that, in the best of cases, a transition in which the opposition is dominated by the maximalists tends to reach a democratic conclusion not very different from that at which the moderate opposition aims all along—only that, under the maximalists, the route is likely to be longer and more costly. In the worst and, I fear, most probable of cases, a maximalist-led transition leads to conditions even more regressive than those imposed by a previous BA.

Let us move on to a third sector of the camp opposed to the BA—the moderate opposition. First, the moderate opposition is a true opposition; moreover, it is a democratic one. That is to say, the moderates' goal is not only to put the BA and any authoritarian alternative to an end; their goal is to establish a political democracy, which they consider valuable in and of itself. This opposition is not homogeneous; some of its members do not want to go further than the achievement of a regime of political democracy while others (on its left wing) are committed to an expansion of democracy on other levels, economic and social. Yet the democratic goal that is shared by all members of this opposition distances them, on the one side, from the opportunists in their own camp and, on the other, from the BA's hardliners. Their pursuit of democracy also distinguishes the moderate opposition from those softliners whose aims are limited to a liberalizing transformation of the BA and do not extend to what would be, properly speaking, a political democracy. On the other hand, this is a moderate opposition, in the sense that its members are prepared to extend a serious and reasonable guarantee that, to the extent that the transition remains within their control, the fundamental interests of the BA coalition will not be violated in the process of establishing a democratic regime. The willingness of the moderates to provide such a guarantee places them in direct conflict with the maximalists, who, to say the least, find it difficult to distinguish between the moderate and the opportunistic opposition; the maximalists may even regard the moderates as their "main enemy."

On the basis of the preceding analysis, we can see that as soon as the liberalization is initiated a complex game begins, consisting both of confrontations between former allies and of potential alliances between actors previously located in sharply opposed camps. I argue that the outcome of the transition basically depends upon the moderate opposition and its conflictive and fluctuating coalitions with the softliners. In addition, if the outcome is to be a reasonably viable political democracy, the moderate opposition must comply with several requirements.

The first of these is that it put to use its condition as a true opposition, extracting from the BA alliance decisions that move the process ever closer to political democracy and, therefore, preventing the softliners from stalling the transition in a stage of tempered authoritarianism. In this respect, the basic issues are, first, the characteristics of the regime to be established (fundamentally, the legal-institutional rules in which such a regime would be formally embodied) and, second, the already mentioned redefinition of the fundamental interests of the BA alliance. Typically, at the beginning of the process, the definitions of these interests are very broad, so broad as to interfere with the democratizing goal of the moderate opposition. It is through very complex processes—what I am trying to describe is anything but linear—that the moderates elicit successive concessions not foreseen in the original decisions of the softliners. In fact, these "concessions" are important opposition victories; they involve successive redefinitions of the fundamental interests of the BA alliance, interests that the softliners have pledged themselves—before the hardliners and the undecided—to safeguard. I already mentioned the limits of these redefinitions when discussing the opposition maximalists. That these limits shall not be transposed, the moderates are prepared to guarantee; at the same time, in a complex process, they exercise their condition as a true opposition, impelling the entire BA alliance to accept a degree of democratization (political, at least) greater than that which the softliners envisaged at the beginning of the process.

The second requirement is that the moderate opposition succeed in becoming the dominant voice in its camp; that is, it must politically defeat its two wings, the opportunists and the maximalists. Were it not to do so, consequences that I have already examined would ensue. In the wake of the BA, a long list of unsatisfied demands and grievances will be brewing in many sectors of the population. The moderate opposition must take up a large part of these claims and transform them into issues with potential electoral resonance; their ability to do this successfully greatly affects the moderates' chances of becoming the dominant voice in the opposition camp. On the other hand, given that to take up such demands and grievances may threaten interests that the members of the BA alliance consider fundamental at any particular stage of the process, and given the fact that the moderate opposition should both be and appear to be an authentic opposition—the role of which cannot but be bringing to the fore a good many of such issues—the moderates tread a very narrow path. On one hand, excessive caution in taking up these long-suppressed claims would bring the moderates into a position too similar to that of their opportunistic counterparts; on the other hand, if they "exaggerate" such demands—especially during the initial stages of the process, when the BA alliance defines its interests more broadly and controls the process more tightly—the moderates run the risk of provoking a coup that would annul the transition.

The third requirement that the moderate opposition must meet is to behave in a reasonably predictable fashion; the commitments its leaders give to the BA alliance must be perceived as binding on the organizations they claim to control. For the latter purpose, the most adequate organizational form is probably a party (or a coalition of parties), disciplined enough for the moderates' interlocutors to safely assume the viability the commitments given to them. Even if the moderate opposition meets the two requirements already stated, if it fails to meet the present one, in not controlling the political organizations that it claims to speak for, it runs the risk of being defeated in its own camp by opportunists or maximalists. Were this to occur, the game that the moderates and the softliners are engaged in would change. The requirement of plausibility of the commitments made by the moderates during the transition highlights the advantages of a historical legacy that reemerges in the shape of political parties capable not only of becoming the dominant voice of the opposition but of guaranteeing to other actors the continuity of their leadership. Spain and, in the future, Chile are cases in point. Alternatively, the creation of an "official opposition party"—Brazil's MDB, for example—may also satisfy this requirement. At least, in the crucial initial stages of the transition presently under way, this party has fulfilled the important role of opening up room for the moderate opposition and assuring the continuity of its leadership. The most unfavorable situation appears to be that faced in present day Argentina and Uruguay where, on one hand (in contrast with Brazil), the entire former institutional system has been devastated by the respective BAs and where, on the other hand (in contrast with Spain and Chile), there do not appear to be parties that are both potentially majoritarian in the opposition camp and disciplined enough to plausibly guarantee continuity in their demands and commitments.[23]

The fourth requirement is that the moderate opposition enter into coalition—conflictively and tacitly, but very truly—with the softliners. On the one hand—as the case of Spain suggests and as that of Brazil begins to—if the transition advances sufficiently it is between these two actors that electoral supremacy in the incipient democracy will be decided. In order for such a coalition to be possible, the softliners must acknowledge their underlying continuity with the BA of which they have been part; at the same time, and to the fury of the hardliners among the hardliners, the softliners must abjure the most sinister aspects of that same BA. For its part, the moderate opposition will continually proclaim its credentials as an authentic opposition as against the whole BA alliance; but at the same time it will metabolize existing grievances so that they are not expressed (either in themselves or in the policies demanded) in ways that could lead to the moderates being mistaken for their maximalist counterparts. While the present observations point to areas of real disagreements between the softliners and the moderates, both are strongly interested in neutralizing the hardliners and the maximalists. Depending on the initial intentions of the softliners regarding the extent of the transition—whether it is to be limited to the cosmetic legitimization of their rule (as in Brazil) or extend to the establishment of a political democracy (as in Spain)—the opportunists will present a greater or lesser problem for the moderates and, especially, the more or less severe will be the conflicts between moderates and softliners regarding the point at which the transition should stop. Yet, in both kinds of cases, hardliners and maximalists create lines of conflict against softliners and moderates that are more acute than those that separate these last two from each other. In this sense, one may speak of a liberalizing coalition that—tacit and limited, but nonetheless operative—becomes the axis of the transition; BA softliners and opposition moderates join in a coalition that, mixing real conflicts and common interests, becomes the axis of the transition. Evidently, the game is subtle and complicated, above all for the moderate opposition. Working from an initial position of limited power, at each juncture the moderates must correctly ascertain the extent to which the softliners can be pushed toward democratization; the moderates must also remember the interest they share with the softliners in the ongoing viability of the transition itself. To these subtleties (and to the consequent advances and setbacks in the process that are not always easy to explain to a rapidly repoliticizing citizenry), hardliners and maximalists oppose the simplism of their positions and their indignation about the "betrayals" of their former allies.

It is evident that, under such conditions, the demands placed on the quality of political leadership are extraordinarily severe, when the repressive and depoliticizing characteristics of the BA have tended to impair the development of high quality political leadership. For the moderate opposition, it is not only a question of identifying the basic issues and chief adversaries at each juncture of the process; the moderates must also convince both followers and antagonists that their tactical flexibility is but an instrument in the service of a firm sense of direction in the journey toward democracy. But we should still consider matters that render the situation under discussion even more complex and dynamic.

III

In the period during which the BA appears firmly entrenched, civil society remains profoundly depoliticized. Apathy, "tacit consent," the corporativization of various class organizations and the reduction of others to mere mouth-pieces for official decisions and ceremonies, the fear of rousing the repressive pathos of the BA, censorship and self-censorship, and cultural stultification: these are typical of the periods in which the BA appears able to impose its domination indefinitely. One aspect of such a situation is that, while political activity hardly ceases, it is hidden behind a technocratic and "apolitical" cloak. The main arenas of politics are the bureaucratic arenas of the state; typically, these are entered only by those ensconced at the apex of other bureaucracies—public and private—for the opaque articulation of their interests. These same bureaucratic arenas and the silence imposed by the political exclusion of a large part of the population discourage such actors from even attempting to dress their interests in arguments that appeal to some sort of general interest. The gray, opaque politics of the BA, a politics of bureaucracies and bureaucrats, public and private, is difficult to render in detail, but in the narrowness of its arenas and of the interests therein articulated, it is transparently simple.

The first steps of political liberalization usher in the resurrection, the intense repoliticization, of society—a process that soon outpaces liberalization itself. The resurrection of society is fundamental: it determines the rhythm of the transition no less than the events within the state apparatus and in the renewed political party arena that occupied us in the preceding sections; without reference to the resurrection of society it is impossible to understand the real force of the opposition.

Whatever might have triggered liberalization (but especially when the termination of the BA is extrinsically provoked), people suddenly lose their paralyzing fear of the coercive capacity of the state apparatus. Recently feared figures are now publicly ridiculed. After years of censorship, avid readers find themselves swamped in a flood of publications that—even from an apparently apolitical standpoint—antagonize the existing powers. Various artistic expressions symbolically distill long-festering grievances and demands. In other words, civil society, until lately flat, fearful, and "apolitical," reemerges with extraordinary energy.

Shortly beforehand, from the heights of the state apparatus it seemed possible to control most class organizations. Quite suddenly these organizations begin to move in their own orbits, pulling themselves out of the suffocating control of the state and again becoming voices with something to say about the general guidelines of the organization of the state, the economy, and society. This implies that many organizations of civil society have resuscitated as such. For this very reason, they become camps of struggle over who is to speak on their behalf and in support of what. In this way, politics reaches these organizations, not only because of the claims they begin to make, but also because they become arenas of competition among groups that are often tied to the game that other actors are contesting at the level of parties and elections.

In addition, as we have seen in the transitions that have already occurred or are underway, together with those "old" organizations there emerge new associative forms bearing witness to the social dynamism that, appearances to the contrary, the BA is unable to suppress. Neighborhood committees, self-help organizations, grassroots and other social movements, popular institutions of the Catholic Church and other religions are some of the entries on a long list of organizational forms in which the popular sector distills the lessons of the harsh period of BA rule.

Old and new organizations within civil society, more or less informal and radicalized, in tandem with a generalized revaluation of politics, create from out of civil society an exultant atmosphere of expectant triumph over the BA—even though it may not yet be clear who will capitalize electorally on this anticipated but as yet uncertain victory. It is precisely this resurrection of civil society that sustains the opposition; in the absence of such a resurrection, or were the support that it affords not embraced by the opposition, the latter would be too weak to withstand the pressures and threats mounted by the various forces within the BA alliance.

In other words, if the political arena during BA was narrow and simple, liberalization widens and complicates it enormously: first, it involves the reentry of political parties onto the scene, which presupposes an electoral system that is, at the least—although the extent of liberalization may fall short of political democracy—a point of departure for the reconstruction of the institutions of a democratic regime; second—and, I think, more importantly, because it is here that the central dynamics of the process arguably lie—liberalization broadens and complicates the political arena because it triggers the politicized resurrection of civil society. Analytically speaking, these two developments signal that the system of exclusion that the BA is has ceased to exist. At this point, even though the state and the regime might remain authoritarian, it is no longer a BA but one with characteristics that continually oscillate until a resting point is found: either in an authoritarian relapse or in some form of democracy. The problem for hardliners, softliners, opportunists, maximalists, and moderates, then, is not simply centered around the distribution of forces within the state apparatus (which, for its part, is also penetrated by reverberations of the repoliticization of society) and the arena of party politics; a no less important problem, now, concerns the manner in which these actors articulate their relations with that immense arena of politics that civil society becomes.

The resurrection of civil society is also manifest in an explosion of long-postponed demands. Some demands that are of an economic nature, especially those made by the salaried sectors, function as bridgeheads for further

claims that aim at resecuring control over unions or reorienting their activities; as a result, significant strike activity is unleashed. In addition—sometimes in combination with such economic demands, sometimes expressing
themselves directly—middle-class movements and marginalized popular sectors vigorously present various demands (which are typically more difficult
to negotiate than those made by unions) for autonomy over against the state
and the dominant classes.[24]

While they generate the jubilant, springlike mood characteristic of such
thaws, developments of this kind are found disturbing by the many (not only
the hardliners of the now-defunct BA) who, nostalgic for the "discipline" and
"respect for hierarchy" that epitomized the triumphant moments of the BA,
experience this atmosphere as one of profound disorder. One result is the appearance of hardline promoters of a coup, who spread their message amongst
potentially repeat backers of a BA—the upper bourgeoisie, some segments of
the middle class, and, of course, the armed forces. The success of such attempts, as we have seen, depends on several factors that in part remain beyond the control of coup advocates, but the risk of a coup looms throughout
most of the transition. As we also saw, this same risk is the card with which
the softliners attempt to regulate the pace of the transition. They also use this
card for sometimes applying (although now with a bad conscience) harsh repression, and to support their pretension to be the institutionalized heirs of
the transition and, as such, the only real guarantee against the excesses of the
hardliners and the maximalists.

The role played in all of this by the working class is fundamental. We have
already seen that the BA emerges in the context of extensive but unbalanced
and dependent industrialization. In the large urban centers this lends considerable weight to the working class; on the other hand, the economy becomes
fragile during the transition, due to the concerns of a bourgeoisie that is
weaker than those at the capitalist centers and has become too accustomed to
exploiting a working class silenced by BA repression. The consequent uncertainties—amplified by the repoliticization of middle-class employees that
runs parallel to that of the working class—provoke sharp increases in inflation, swelling fiscal deficits, difficulties with the balance of payments, and, at
least, strong fluctuations in public and private investment, both local and
transnational. These are symptoms, on one hand, of the renewed capacity of
the popular sector to press for some of its demands and, on the other, of what
is at least the acute concern of the bourgeoisie about where the transition
might finally lead. As the case of Spain shows, such tensions need not extend
to a truly deep economic crisis; but the experience of Argentina in 1971–72—
not to mention later events in that country—makes it clear that this possibility
is very real. The emergence of a profound economic crisis is related to the tenuous control of economic and social policy that the softliners characteristi-

cally exercise when, as in Argentina, they attempt liberalization as a last re-sort in the face of an opposition explosion. This scenario differs from cases in which the softliners retain more real power, as in Spain and in the current Brazilian transition. Whether or not the economy will plunge into acute crisis is also contingent upon the degree to which the maximalists succeed in occu-pying the dominant position in the opposition camp. In the Argentine case of 1969–73, it was clearly and openly a matter of the terror of a bourgeoisie that not only saw the "political solution" offered by the softliners shipwrecked but, even more worryingly, was directly challenged at the level of its cellular domination. The fears of the bourgeoisie resulted from the confluence of a working class motivated by militant economism that was also challenging the control of the workplace, and a violent maximalist opposition that the state apparatus (itself shot through by these tensions) was unable to contain. In Argentina, the result of the combination of these factors was, among other things, the severe economic crisis of 1971–72 and a dramatic increase in vio-lence; in these events, both hardliners and maximalists saw the irrefutable confirmation of their respective positions.

When compared with the Argentine case I have just mentioned, the distin-guishing characteristic of Spain and Brazil is that the maximalist opposition has not taken the lead, nor, despite its concerns, has the bourgeoisie felt that a true social eruption of the popular sector, especially of the working class, is likely to occur. Furthermore, the case of Spain illustrates the possibility that an articulate and militant working class may express itself politically through parties of the left (especially, the PSOE and the PCE) committed to the camp of the moderate opposition. In Brazil, on the other hand, it is much more a question of the political weakness of the working class than of any politically metabolized presence of the working class in parties such as the Spanish ones. In effect—reflecting the social structure of Brazil and, in particular, the history of its working class and trade unions—the opposition is mainly based on the middle class and certain segments of bourgeoisie in large urban cen-ters. Although the Brazilian working class is overwhelmingly concentrated in such centers, until 1978 (and, thus, only after the initial years of a transition that began with the elections of 1974 had passed) it mobilized itself little, whether in support of the transition or of more tangible interests such as wages and the control of its unions.[25] Only now[26]—with the transition at a more advanced stage and more difficult to reverse—the engagement of vari-ous layers of the working class in pressing such demands is beginning to shake up and render more dynamic the process of Brazilian democratization.

The fears of the bourgeoisie and the hardliners were allayed in each case: in Brazil, in the earliest and most fragile stage of the transition, the working class was virtually absent from the political process; in Spain, the political represen-tation of the working class has been undertaken by parties historically rooted in it that have identified themselves unequivocally with the moderate opposition. Similar developments are foreseeable in the future of Chile. By contrast, Argentina (and, to a lesser extent, due to the smaller relative and absolute weight of its working class, Uruguay) contains a working class of considerable weight that has been an important actor in national politics but that, at the same time, is not tied to parties such as those of Spain and Chile. Moreover, the Argentine unions cannot substitute for parties as actors in the overall political process or in the political representation of the working class and of middle-class employees. The very logic of the unions' role in society makes it extremely difficult for them to go beyond economic claims, and demands for corporatist participation in the state apparatus. Consequently, in all these respects the Argentine transition of 1969–73 did not enjoy the conditions relatively favorable to the progress of democratization that I have identified in other cases. In the future, this combination of factors may again emerge as a serious problem, unless there have been changes at the party level (peronist or otherwise) that the current "prohibition against politics" momentarily veils.

For the most part, what certain cases demonstrate positively, while others do so negatively, is that the fundamental issue for a viable democratization (that is, a democratization that is neither mortally wounded from the beginning nor merely the cosmetic liberalization of an authoritarian state) is the extent to which the moderates control the opposition camp; that they do so is essential, not only at the political-electoral level but also, to a considerable extent, with respect to the manifold expressions of the resurrection of civil society that is an integral part—and an especially dynamic one—of the transition.[27] These observations underscore the magnitude and the subtlety of the tasks of this opposition.

Notes

1. See chapter 2 of this volume and the author's "Reflections on the Patterns of Change in the BureaucraticAuthoritarian State," *Latin American Research Review* 13 (no. 1, 1978). See also *Bureaucratic Authoritarianism: Argentina, 1966–1973, in Comparative Perspective* (Berkeley: University of California Press, 1988).—*Ed.*

2. See chapter 2 of this volume.—*Ed.*

3. As part of an effort to distinguish the BA from other authoritarian forms (especially, traditional or oligarchic, populist, and fascist), I propose these and other specific characteristics of the BA in several works. See, especially, "Reflections," and *Modernization and Bureaucratic-Authoritarianism*, Institute of International Studies (Berkeley: University of California Press, 1972). See also the discussions and conceptual advances contained in David Collier, ed., *The New Authoritarianism in Latin America* (Princeton: Princeton University Press, 1979).

4. The following attributes are derived from the definition of the BA proposed in my previous works [See n. 3 above.—*Ed*.] with a view to the issues that concern us here.

5. In these processes, as we shall see, the struggle to achieve what could be properly called political democracy—the fight against those who would like to limit the transition to a "decompression" of selected characteristics of BA—is one of the main axes around which the political game is constituted.

6. It is important to adequately distinguish between state, government, and regime. On the first of these, see my "Apuntes para una teoría del Estado," Documentos CEDES/CLACSO 9, Buenos Aires, 1978. By "regime," I understand the set of patterns actually effective (though not necessarily legally or formally established) that determine the following: (1) modalities of recruitment and access to governmental roles, and (2) criteria of representation on the basis of which are formulated expectations regarding access to those roles and expectations regarding influence over their incumbents. By "government," I understand the higher positions in the state apparatus, access to which is determined by the existing regime and from which may be mobilized, by the respective national state, its coercive supremacy over the territory it delimits.

7. At the regime level, the BA is characterized by restriction of access to governmental roles to those at the pinnacle of complex bureaucratic organizations (both public and private), who are—according to a pilarized and/or corporatist vision of society—considered to be, if not representative, entitled to speak for their "respective" social sectors; these criteria obstruct channels of access and exclude demands for the representation of popular interests and aspirations, apart from those that each leadership group claims to embody in a corporatist fashion.

8. Whether or not a regime is formalized—and, if so, the extent to which it is—depends upon the degree to which that regime is crystallized and institutionalized in a constitution and other legal instruments.

9. I will use the term "liberalization" to refer to decisions that, while they imply a significant opening of the BA (such as the restitution of effective judicial guarantees for certain individual rights or the establishment of parliamentary forms not based on free electoral competition), nevertheless fall short of effecting what we might properly call a political democracy. As I have suggested, such liberalization warrants that, analytically, we consider the BA to have disappeared, but it does not eliminate the authoritarian nature of the overall situation.

10. With the apparent exception of Spain (where the initial decisions of the softliners appear to indicate an intention to establish a political democracy), it is typical of the beginning of transitions from BA that the purposes of the softliners do not extend beyond certain liberalizing measures.

11. Hardline opposition may also be based on the view that the proper response to events is not liberalization but an accentuation of existing repressive features of the BA; this was the case in Argentina, as it was in Greece after the riots of Córdoba.

12. In "Tensions in the Bureaucratic-Authoritarian State and the Question of Democracy," [chapter 2 in this volume—*Ed*.] I argue that, whatever degree of success a BA might have achieved, its undeniably antipopular origins and its obstruction of electoral channels pose to this type of rule an insoluble problem: a lack of mechanisms

of legitimation and succession. With the characteristics proper to each case, what we have observed above about Brazil and Spain is an expression of this Achilles heel that afflicts even the most "successful" BAs.

13. As I have mentioned, here I will not deal with the internal tensions of BA, which include the ideological malaise—diffuse but operative—that continuist inclinations typically generate among the most sophisticated sectors of the ruling alliance. To the extent that they interact with such factors, circumstances and developments within the international context must also be taken into account.

14. In the works referred to above, I speak of the upper bourgeoisie as the principal social base of the BA. With this term, I designate the more concentrated, oligopolized, transnationalized layers of industrial, financial, and commercial capital.

15. Non-negotiable points for the upper bourgeoisie apparently do not include a significant redistribution of income or an increase in the political sway of unions. However, neither one of these outcomes would make most of the bourgeoisie happy.

16. At this stage, it is convenient to point out that these categories and those that I will specify in discussing the opposition camp are analytical; as such, they should not be regarded as fixed attributes of concrete actors. One of the features of the transition's fluidity is the displacement of actors from one position to another, as well as the reconstitution of actors' identities; it is precisely for the analysis of such matters that the categories I propose might prove heuristically useful.

17. The term "negotiations" implies that the softliners have found interlocutors in an opposition that is not maximalist; this is an issue that I will discuss shortly.

18. For a detailed analysis of this kind of process, see the author's *Bureaucratic Authoritarianism: Argentina.—Ed.*

19. In general, the maximalist opposition will accord little value to political democracy (except to the extent that it becomes a tactical necessity). At the beginning of the transition, this is so because the maximalist opposition views political democracy as a trap set by the BA alliance. Later on, when the BA has eventually collapsed and this opposition has imposed itself in its stead, the maximalists view political democracy as an unnecessary constraint on the pursuit of their own goals.

20. The author refers to the regime instituted in Portugal in 1979.—*Ed.*

21. This assertion follows from the view that the state is primarily a condensation of relations of social domination, and is to be understood only secondarily as a set of bureaucratic institutions, as I argue in "Apuntes." [See also chapter 2 in this volume.—*Ed.*]

22. This marks an important difference from those transitions, such as the current one in Nicaragua, where the correlates of a neosultanistic regime are a weaker bourgeoisie and less professionalized armed forces.

23. The Argentine case, especially during the period 1971–73, is a rather extreme example of this problem. The voice of the opposition was overwhelmingly captured by peronism. A highly heterogeneous movement, peronism included the most extreme forms of opportunism and maximalism, together with the seed of what might have been a triumphant moderate opposition. Such heterogeneity aside, a central problem was that no peronist leader could offer a plausible guarantee that his commitments in relation to other actors in the transition would bind his party in the future; peronism lacked (and, thanks to the current "freezing of politics," continues to lack) minimally

institutionalized mechanisms of authority. This deficiency was mainly the result of the personalistic leadership of Perón and his strategy of rotating support among the most diverse elements of peronism.

24. I especially refer to various types of religious movements, demands for participation in the governance of unions, public and private enterprises, and universities, as well as the previously mentioned grassroots movements that are based in the poorest sectors of the population.

25. Nor have there been important movements of rural organizations and peasant demands. In cases of BA that have large peasant populations, were there to arise significant challenges to agrarian class domination in combination with the political reactivation of urban workers, a situation eliciting the greatest fears of the dominant class would arise and, with it, the higher likelihood of a coup.

26. 1979.—*Ed.*

27. One theme that I am unable address here, but which should be studied as an important part of the transition, is that of the medium-term consequences that appear to flow from the success of the moderate opposition in controlling its own camp. At least in Spain, and with not a few symptoms already visible in Brazil, the to and for of process, the various tactical concessions (necessary or not, depending on one's view of the matter), and the bureaucratization of the parties involved because of the broadening of their electoral bases and their access to governmental positions, among other reasons, tend to separate the moderates from not a few of the most dynamic opposition movements and militants within civil society. From this results a certain mood of disenchantment and cynicism regarding the sometimes less than brilliant realities of democratic politics, for whose advent these actors struggled so much and so effectively.

PART IV
Perspectives

7

On the State, Democratization, and Some Conceptual Problems: A Latin American View with Glances at Some Postcommunist Countries

I. The State and New Democracies

In the last two decades, the breakdown of various kinds of authoritarian systems has led to the emergence of a number of democracies. These *are* democracies: they are political democracies or, more precisely, following the classic formulation of Robert Dahl,[1] they are polyarchies. Several contributions have shown that there are various types of polyarchies. They differ, as Lijphart first showed,[2] even in such important dimensions as whether they are based on majoritarian or on more consensual rules for the access to and for the exercise of public authority. But they share one crucial characteristic: they are all representative, institutionalized democracies. In contrast, most of the newly democratized countries are not moving toward a representative, institutionalized democratic regime nor seem likely to do so in the foreseeable

First published in *World Development* 21 (no. 8, August 1993): 1355–69. The ideas presented here owe much to the meetings and various intellectual exchanges of the project "East-South System Transformation," supported by the MacArthur Foundation. I am particularly grateful to the director and intellectual leader of this project, Adam Przeworski, for his many extremely helpful criticisms and suggestions. I presented a previous version of this paper at the meeting on "Democracy, Markets and Structural Reforms in Latin America," sponsored by the North-South Center and CEDES, held in Buenos Aires, March 1992, and at the meeting on "Economic Liberalization and Democratic Consolidation," sponsored by the Social Science Research Council, for the project "Democratization and Economic Reform," held at Bologna-Forlí, April 1992. I owe very special thanks to Laurence Whitehead, director of the SSRC project, not only for his helpful criticisms and suggestions but also for his generous efforts to make the present text a reasonably readable one.

future. They are polyarchies, but of a type not yet theorized. The present text is a preliminary attempt to contribute to that theorizing.[3] This exercise may be warranted for two reasons. First, a sufficient theory of polyarchy should encompass all existing (political) democracies, not only the representative, institutionalized ones. Second, since many of the new democracies have a peculiar political dynamic, one should not assume that their societal impacts will be similar to those of present and past representative, institutionalized polyarchies.[4]

On the other hand, recent typologies of the new democracies based on characteristics of the preceding authoritarian regime and/or on the modalities of the first transition have little predictive power concerning what happens after the first democratically elected government has been installed. In regard to the countries of central concern here—Argentina, Brazil, and Peru—the first was an instance of transition by collapse while the second was the most protracted and probably the most negotiated (although not formally pacted) transition we know of; on the other hand, Argentina and Brazil were exclusionary bureaucratic-authoritarian regimes, while Peru was a case of incorporating military-authoritarian populism. In spite of these and other differences, today it seems clear that in the period after a democratic installation, these countries (as well as Ecuador, Bolivia, the Dominican Republic, the Philippines, all the democratizing or liberalizing East Asian and African countries, and most postcommunist ones) share important characteristics, all of them pointing toward their "noninstitutionalized" situation.[5]

In relation to those countries, the existing literature has not gone much beyond indicating what attributes (representativeness, institutionalization, and the like) they do not have, along with a descriptive narration of their various political and economic misadventures. These contributions are valuable, but they are not deemed to yield the theoretical clues we need. Furthermore, the characterization of these cases by the absence of certain attributes may imply a teleology which would hinder adequate conceptualization of the varied types of democracies that have been emerging. Other more policy and "elite" oriented streams of the literature offer useful advice for democratizing political leaders, but the practicality of such prescriptions is contingent on the contextual situation in which those leaders find themselves.

Although for "normal" liberal democracies, or polyarchies, the conceptual baggage of political science may be satisfactory, to analyze the present situation and prospects of most new democracies in Asia, Africa, Latin America, and Eastern/Central Europe, we must go back and do some basic work in political and legal sociology. The discussion in this text will have as its main referents Argentina, Brazil, and Peru, but many of the points have wider applicability.

The analysis that follows is premised on one point: states are interwoven in complex and different ways with their respective societies. This embeddedness means that the characteristics of each state and of each society heavily influence whether the democracy will be likely (if at all) to consolidate—or merely endure or eventually break down. These statements are rather obvious, but we have not pursued sufficiently their implications in terms of the *problématique* of democratization. Part of the reason is that we handle concepts (especially that of the state) which, as they are formulated by most of the contemporary literature, are not very helpful for our theme.

It is a mistake to conflate the state with the state apparatus, the public sector, or the aggregation of public bureaucracies. These, unquestionably, are part of the state, but are not all of it. The state is also, and no less primarily, a set of social relations that establishes a certain order, and ultimately backs it with a centralized coercive guarantee, over a given territory. Many of those relations are formalized in a legal system issued and backed by the state. The legal system is a constitutive dimension of the state and of the order that it establishes and guarantees over a given territory. That order is not an equal, socially impartial order; both under capitalism and bureaucratic socialism it backs, and helps to reproduce, systematically asymmetric power relationships. It is, however, an order, in the sense that manifold social relationships are engaged on the basis of stable (if not necessarily approved) norms and expectations. In one of those moments when ordinary language expresses the power relationships in which it is embedded, when decisions are made at the political center (the "orders given") those decisions usually "give order," in the sense that those commands are regularly obeyed. This acquiescence affirms and reproduces the existing social order. Social relations, including those of daily, preconscious acquiescence to political authority, can be based, as Weber argued, on tradition, fear of punishment, pragmatic calculation, habituation, legitimacy, and/or the effectiveness of the law. The effectiveness of the law over a given territory consists of innumerable habituated behaviors that (consciously or not) are usually consistent with the prescriptions of the law.[6] That effectiveness is based on the widely held expectation, borne out by exemplary evidence, that the law will be, if necessary, enforced by a central authority endowed with the pertinent powers. This is the supporting texture of the order established and guaranteed by the contemporary nation state. We see that the law (including the habituation patterns that the expectation of its regular enforcement leads to) is a constitutive element of the state: it is the "part" of the state which provides the regular, underlying texturing of the social order existing over a given territory.

In both the continental and the Anglo-Saxon traditions the law is, ultimately, a codified dimension, subject to the interpretations of professionalized knowledge. The law has its own organizational expressions, highly ritualized and institutionalized in contemporary democracies. Congress is supposed to be the place of debate and enactment of the main laws of the land, and the judiciary is the place where conflicts of interest and, ultimately, disputes about the very meaning of the political community, are argued and decided. As also occurs with other aspects of the state, congress and the judiciary are the perceivable organizational embodiments of the broader phenomenon consisting of the social effectiveness of the law.

The recognition of the law as a constitutive dimension of the state has been hindered by the various approaches that have dominated Anglo-Saxon political science since the "behavioral revolution." On the other hand, in spite of the contributions by authors such as Max Weber and Herman Heller, the approaches that prevailed in continental Europe were narrowly legalistic; they were based on a formalistic analysis of the written law, with scant attention to its sociological and political aspects. One way or the other, these two great traditions have been colorblind to the state as the complex reality entailed by its organizational/bureaucratic *and* legal dimensions.

There is still another dimension of the state—ideological—that must be considered. The state (more precisely, the state apparatus) claims to be and is normally believed to be a state-for-the-nation. The state claims, from explicit discourses up to the recurrent invocation of the symbols of nationhood, that it is the creator of the order discussed above as well as—in contemporary democracies—of the individual and associational rights that underlie this order. We saw that in all societies order is unequal, even if from the apex of the state it is claimed that such order is an equal one for everyone *qua* member of the nation. But this concealment (which is supported by the law, which structures the inequalities entailed by that order) does not preclude the reality of two fundamental aspects. First, as already noted, this order is actually the supreme collective good: it furnishes generalized social predictability backed by eventually decisive actions of pertinent public bureaucracies. Second, even though it does not extend to other social relations, the equality guaranteed to all members of the nation in terms of citizenship is crucial for the exercise of the political rights entailed by the workings of democracy and, also, for the effectiveness of the individual guarantees consecrated in the liberal tradition.

From the perspective I am proposing, citizenship does not stay within the (narrowly defined, as in most of the contemporary literature) confines of the political. For example, citizenship is at stake when, after entering a contractual relationship, a party which feels it has a legitimate grievance may call upon a legally competent public agency, from which it can expect fair treatment, to intervene and adjudicate the issue. Even in the apparently more private realms of the private (or common) law, the legal system imposes the *public* dimension entailed by the virtual remission of that relationship for legal adjudication by a properly authorized agency of the state. This inherently public dimension of private relationships (or, equivalently, this texturing by the state-as-law of those relationships) is violated when, for example, a peasant is de facto denied access to the judiciary against the landowner. This "private" right must be seen as no less constitutive of citizenship than the "public" right of voting without coercion.

Argentina, Brazil, and Peru (as well as other countries in Latin America and other regions) are not only going through a most serious social and economic crisis. Although with different timing and intensity, these countries are also suffering a profound crisis of their states. This crisis exists in the three dimensions just discussed: of the state as bureaucracies capable of discharging their duties with reasonable efficacy; of the effectiveness of its law; and of the plausibility of the claim that the state agencies normally orient their decisions in terms of some conception of the public good.[7] These countries are living the protracted crisis of a state-centered and inward-oriented pattern of capital accumulation, and of the position of the state in such a pattern. By contrast, some countries—Spain, Portugal, South Korea, Taiwan, and Chile, among the recently democratized or liberalizing ones—under circumstances that do not concern us here, were able to evade that generalized crisis. They emerged as export-oriented economies actively integrated into the world economy. For this task they counted (with variations I cannot discuss here) with a lean but powerful and activist state apparatus.

Too often contemporary discussions confound two different dimensions. One pertains to the size and relative weight of the state apparatus. There is no question that in most newly democratized countries the state is too big, and that this leads to numerous negative consequences. But, in this context, the antonym of big is not small but lean: i.e., an effective and less weighty set of public organizations that is capable of creating solid roots for democracy, for progressively solving the main issues of social equity, and for generating conditions for rates of economic growth suitable for sustaining the advances in the areas of both democracy and social equity. The second dimension refers to the strength or weakness of the state as a whole: i.e., not limited to but including the state apparatus. A "big" or "small" state apparatus may or may not effectively establish its legality over its territory: according to the view I am proposing, a strong state, irrespective of the size of its bureaucracies, is one that effectively establishes that legality and that is not perceived by most of the population as just an arena for the pursuit of particularistic interests. I argue below that current attempts at reducing the size and deficits of the state-as-bureaucracy, mostly unknowingly but with nefarious consequences of all sorts (including for the long-run success of the economic policies that inspire those attempts, to say nothing of the achievement of institutionalized democracy), are *also* destroying the state-as-law and the ideological legitimation of the state.

Current theories of the state often make an assumption which recurs in current theories of democracy: that of a high degree of homogeneity in the scope, both territorial and functional, of the state and of the social order it supports. It is not asked (and, if it is, seldom is problematized) if such order, and the orders issued by the state organizations, have similar effectiveness throughout the national territory and across the existing social stratification.[8] The ideal of "equality before the law" has not fully been achieved in any country; see, for example, the universal finding of class biases in the administration of justice. But the Scandinavian countries come quite close to full homogeneity, while the United States, both territorially and functionally, is close to the lower limit among contemporary institutionalized democracies.

In Latin America the countries of relatively high homogeneity (especially territorial) are the ones which have an older and more solid democratic tradition—Costa Rica, Chile, and Uruguay. Peru is the opposite, recently further accentuated by *Sendero Luminoso* and its sequels. Bolivia and Ecuador are close to the pole of extreme heterogeneity. Brazil and Mexico, in spite of decades of centralizing authoritarian rule, are also cases of high territorial and functional heterogeneity. Argentina, together with Venezuela and Colombia—two rather old but presently troubled democracies—lie somewhere along the middle of this continuum.

What happens when the effectiveness of the law extends very irregularly (it does not altogether disappear) across the territory and the functional relations (including class, ethnic, and gender relations) it supposedly regulates? What kind of state (and society) is this? What influences may this have on what kind of democracy may emerge?

Here I will limit myself to discussing some themes that relate to the crisis of the state in the three dimensions I identified. In these situations, ineffective states coexist with autonomous, also territorially based, spheres of power. States become ostensibly unable to enact effective regulations of social life across their territories and their stratification systems. Provinces or districts peripheral to the national center (which are usually hardest hit by economic crises and are already endowed with weaker bureaucracies than the center) create (or reinforce) systems of local power which tend to reach extremes of violent, personalistic rule—patrimonial, even sultanistic—open to all sorts of violent and arbitrary practices. In many emerging democracies, the effectiveness of a national order embodied in the law and the authority of the state fades off as soon as we leave the national urban centers. But even there the functional and territorial evaporation of the public dimension of the state shows up. The increase in crime, the unlawful interventions of the police in poor neighborhoods, the widespread practice of torture and even summary execution of criminal suspects from poor or otherwise stigmatized sectors, the actual denial of rights to women and various minorities, the impunity of the drug trade, and the great numbers of abandoned children in the streets (all of which mark scant progress in relation to the preceding authoritarian period) reflect not only a severe process of urban decay, they also express the increasing inability of the state to implement its own regulations.[9] Many public spaces disappear, both because of its invasion by the desperate misery of many and because of the dangers entailed in using them. Fear, insecurity, the seclusion of rich neighborhoods, and the ordeals of public transportation shrink the public spaces and lead to a perverse kind of privatization that, as we shall see, has close correlates in other spheres. To be sure, these and other ills are not new, and some of them are more acute in a given country than another. But, not only in Latin America, they have become worse with the superimposition of a huge crisis upon a feeble process of democratization.

Consider those regions where the local powers (both formal and de facto) establish power circuits that operate according to rules which are inconsistent, if not antagonistic, with the law that supposedly regulates the national territory. These are systems of private power (or, better, of privatized power, since some of the main actors hold state positions), where some rights and guarantees of democratic legality have almost no effectiveness. This extends to numerous private relationships which are usually decided, even by the judiciary of those regions, on the basis of the naked power asymmetries that exist among the parties. These neofeudalized regions contain state organizations, national, provincial, and municipal. But the obliteration of legality deprives the regional power circuits, including those state agencies, of the *public*, lawful dimension without which the national state and the order it supports vanish. The mistake of reifying the state may not be evident when theorizing about homogeneous countries, but it becomes apparent when the obliteration of their public dimension makes some state organizations part of circuits of power which are perversely privatized.[10] Parts of the northeast and the whole of Amazonia in Brazil, the highlands in Peru, and various provinces in the center and northwest of Argentina are examples of the evaporation of the public dimension of the state and, consequently, of the odd "reification" of the state as exclusively consisting of organizations that, in those regions, are part of privatized, often sultanistic, circuits of power.

Although these characteristics of Latin America are well known, to my knowledge no attempt has been made to link them with the kinds of democracy that have emerged in Argentina, Brazil, Peru, and similar countries in Latin America and elsewhere. Let us imagine a map of each country in which the areas covered by blue would designate those where there is a high degree of state presence (in terms of a set of reasonably effective bureaucracies and of the effectiveness of properly sanctioned legality), both functionally and territorially; the green color indicates a high degree of territorial penetration and a significantly lower presence in functional/class terms; and the brown color a very low or nil level in both dimensions. In this sense, say, the map of Norway would be dominated by blue; the United States would show a combination of blue and green, with important brown spots in the South and in its big cities; Brazil and Peru would be dominated by brown, and in Argentina the extensiveness of brown would be smaller—but, if we had a temporal series of maps, we could see that those brown sections have grown lately.[11]

In these areas there are elections, governors, and national and state legislators (in addition, in many cases those regions are heavily overrepresented in the national legislatures). The parties operating there, even if they are nominally members of national parties, are no more than personalistic machines anxiously dependent on the prebends they can extract from the national and the local state agencies. Those parties and the local governments function on the basis of phenomena such as personalism, familism, prebendalism, clientelism, and the like. As anthropologists know, this is a world that functions according to an elaborate, if unwritten, set of rules, where—in contrast to "traditional" societies—there exist state bureaucracies, some of them big and complex, and where under extremely politicized and poorly paid bureaucracies the very meaning of the term "corruption" becomes fuzzy.

These circuits of power are represented at the center of national politics, beginning with the congress, the institution that is supposedly the source of the existing, nationally encompassing legality. In general, the interests of the "brown" legislators are quite limited: to sustain the system of privatized domination that has elected them, and to channel toward that system as many state resources as possible. The tendency of their vote is, thus, conservative and opportunistic. For their success they depend on the exchange of "favors" with the executive and various state bureaucracies and, under weakened executives that need some kind of congressional support, they often obtain the control of the state agencies that furnish those resources. This increases the fragmentation (and the deficits) of the state—the brown spots invade even the bureaucratic apex of the state. Furthermore, the game that these individuals play (both in and out of congress) benefits from the existence of parties which are not only of very low ideological content (which per se is not necessarily bad), but are also totally opportunistic in their positions, have no discipline, and where changing parties or creating new ones can be done at virtually no cost—extreme *transformismo* is the rule. Some recent studies have pointed out the deleterious consequences that this has, among other areas, on the functioning of congress and on the emergence of a reasonably stable party system[12]—hardly a good prospect for institutionalizing democracy. For obvious reasons these politicians, too, converge with the delegative, caesaristic orientations of the executive in their hostility to any form of horizontal accountability; even though sometimes they have acute conflicts with the executive, they work together with the latter in preventing the emergence of solid representative institutions.

In a sense the regime that results from this is very representative. It is consistent with the reality of countries whose patterns of political representation further heterogenize them. The problem, of course, is that this representativeness entails the interjection of authoritarianism—understood here as the denial of the publicness and of the effective legality of a democratic state and, hence, of citizenship—at the very center of political power of these countries.[13]

Some important issues, none of which I fully address here, are raised by our mapping exercise. What type of state are those of countries where the brown areas dominate? What kind, if any, of democratic regime can be established over such heterogeneity? To what extent can we extrapolate to those cases theories of the state and of democracy which assume far more homogeneous countries? In their more general terms these questions have been central to the comparative endeavors of the social sciences. But they have to be recalled and specified when the generalized feeling of a universal victory of capitalism, and maybe of democracy, has led to their neglect. We may be going back to some mistakes of the 1960s, when many theories and comparisons were flat, if not ethnocentric: they consisted of the application of supposedly universally valid paradigms which ignored the structured variation to be found outside of the developed world. Today, mainstream economics is a clear case of this problem, but sociologists and political scientists are not exempt from it.

We should remember that in a properly functioning democratic order, its legality is universalistic: it can be successfully invoked by anyone, irrespective of his or her position in society. Coming back to a rather old discussion, can the attributes "democratic" and "authoritarian" be applied to the state or should they be exclusively reserved for the regime? This, of course, depends on how we define state and regime. In respect to the latter, I will repeat my proposed definition:

> the ensemble of patterns, explicit or not, that determines the forms and channels of access to principal governmental positions, the characteristics of the actors who are admitted and excluded from such access, and the resources [and] strategies that they can use to gain access.[14]

With some variations, this kind of definition is noncontroversial in the literature. Instead, as we saw, the definition of the state is problematic. Against the prevailing view, what I am arguing leads to the conclusion that attributes such as "democratic" or "authoritarian" do not only correspond to the regime but also to the state.

This can be seen reasoning *a contrario*. An authoritarian context has a fundamental characteristic: there does not exist (or, if it exists, it does not have real effectiveness, or can be annulled ad hoc, or is subordinate to secret rules and/or to the whim of the rulers) a legal system that guarantees the effectiveness of rights and guarantees that individuals and groups can uphold against the rulers, the state apparatus, and others at the top of the existing social or political hierarchy. This is a truncated legality: even in the case of institutionalized authoritarianism, it does not contain the guarantee of its own enforcement against the rulers and other higher powers. This affects a constitutive dimension of the state: the type of legality (which may entail, in extreme cases, almost absolute arbitrariness) that textures the particular order that is enforced over a territory. From this point of view I do not see how we can evade the conclusion that the state may also be authoritarian.

The converse seems to me no less clear. As long as a legal system includes the rights and guarantees of Western constitutionalism and that there exist public powers which are capable and willing to enforce—according to properly established procedures—such rights and guarantees even against other public powers, that state and the order it helps to implant and reproduce, are democratic. Against the truncated legality of the authoritarian state, that of the democratic state, as Kelsen argued in a somewhat different context, is complete; it "closes" its own circuits by the universalistic application of its rules even against other state organizations. This is what happens in the blue areas and what does not happen in the extensive (and increasing) brown areas of many new democracies.

In countries with extensive "brown" areas, democracies are based on a schizophrenic state: it complexly mixes, functionally and territorially, important democratic and authoritarian characteristics. It is a state in which its components of democratic legality and, hence, of publicness and citizenship, fade away at the frontiers of various regions and class, gender, and ethnic relations.

As a political form effective over a given territory, democracy is necessarily connected with citizenship, and the latter can exist only within the legality of a democratic state. The complete universalization of citizenship is an ideal which existing democracies approximate more or less closely. But the big (and growing) brown areas in many new democracies should not be written off as irrelevant to our theories of state and democracy. Nor should we assume that there is some inherent virtuous effect of political democracy and/or of economic change that will eliminate those areas. It is not the case, as it is in institutionalized democracies, of some authoritarian components in a state which can still be considered democratic: in the countries that concern us here, the authoritarian dimension intermixes complexly and powerfully with the democratic one. This mixing demands reconceptualization of the very state and the peculiar democracy (and regime) that exists there.

A state that is unable to enforce its legality supports a democracy of low intensity citizenship. In most of the brown areas of the newly democratized countries, the *political* rights of polyarchy are respected. Usually, individuals are not subject to direct coercion when voting, their votes are counted fairly, in principle they can create almost any sort of organization, they can express their opinions without censorship, and they can move freely within and outside the national territory. These and other attributes of polyarchy are met in those regions. This is the difference between say, Poland and Argentina on one side, and Romania and Guatemala on the other: whatever their constitutions say, the actual workings of political life disqualify the latter as polyarchies. But countries with extensive brown areas which actually meet the attributes of polyarchy—arguably, the universal core of democracy—are democracies.

Among the countries that meet the criteria of polyarchy, different degrees and dimensions of "democraticness" can be distinguished. This refers to issues of equity and equality in various societal spheres (or, equivalently, to social and economic democratization).[15] But the concept of low intensity citizenship does not refer to those—admittedly very important—issues. It refers specifically to the political sphere, to the *political* theory of political democracy, or polyarchy. As noted above, in the brown areas of new democracies, usually the specifically political conditions for the existence of polyarchy are met. But peasants, slum dwellers, indigenous peoples, women, etc., often are unable to receive fair treatment in the courts, or to obtain from state agencies services to which they are entitled, or to be safe from police violence, etc. These are "extrapolyarchical" but still politically relevant restrictions; they entail the ineffectiveness of the state-as-law, the abating of some rights and guarantees that, as much as voting without coercion, are constitutive of citizenship. From this results a curious disjuncture: in many brown areas the democratic, participatory rights of polyarchy are respected. But the liberal component of democracy is systematically violated. A situation in which one can vote freely and have one's vote counted fairly, but cannot expect proper treatment from the police or the courts, puts into serious question the liberal component of that democracy and severely curtails citizenship.[16] This disjuncture is the other side of the coin of the powerful mix of democratic and authoritarian components of these states.

The denial of liberal rights to (mostly but not exclusively) the poor or otherwise deprived sectors is analytically distinct from, and bears no necessary relation to various degrees of social and economic democratization. But, empirically, various forms of discrimination and extensive poverty and their correlate, extreme disparity in the distribution of (not only economic) resources, go hand in hand with low intensity citizenship.[17] This is the essence of the social conditions necessary for the exercise of citizenship; how can the weaker and the poorer, even if they remain poor, be empowered in terms consistent with democratic legality and, thus, gain their full, democratic and liberal, citizenship? Even a political definition of democracy (such as that recommended by most contemporary authors, and to which I adhere) should not neglect posing the question of the extent to which citizenship is really exercised in a given country. This—let me insist on a point which lends itself to misunder-standings—is not *per se* how much one regrets inequalities and would like to redress them; the argument refers to the consequences of those social condi-tions on the type of polyarchy and on the extent of citizenship with which we are dealing in each case.

In the following sections I discuss, in the highly stylized way that space permits, some themes that relate, first, to the crisis of the state and, second, to a certain kind of economic crisis. These discussions will allow us to gain a more concrete perspective on some of the issues raised in the present section.

II. On Some Aspects of the Crisis of the State

There is abundant evidence that the extraordinarily severe socioeconomic cri-sis most newly democratized countries are suffering furthers the spread of brown regions. These impacts derive not only from various processes of so-cial and economic disintegration; they also result from the profound crisis of the state—as effective legality, as a set of bureaucracies, and as a legitimized agent of the common interest. But those impacts also result from the strong antistatism of neoliberal ideas and policies,[18] especially the commitment to di-minish at all costs the size of the state bureaucracies and its deficit.

Many efforts are being made to reduce the fiscal deficit. On the expenditure side, the main features have been privatizations and attempts to get rid of "ex-cess personnel." The latter has not been easy, in part because in most cases the tenure of those employees is legally protected, and in part because strenuous opposition from the latter's unions has proven costly for shaky governments. More effective for reducing the fiscal deficit have been policies that resulted in the precipitous decline of the salaries of most public employees.

In addition to sharply falling salaries, there are many indications of a se-vere degradation of the functioning and of the very idea of a public service. Many of the more capable officials have left the public for the private sector. For those that have remained, their status has declined no less sharply than their salaries: prevailing antistatist ideologies view their jobs at best with mis-trust, and the news as well as public lore are replete with anecdotes of their (too often true) idleness, lack of competence and interest in their jobs, and corruption. If some time ago to be a state official was a symbol of high status, nowadays it is almost the opposite.

Probably worse still, to be a public official before the present crisis was to be installed in a career. This meant to work in a setting which provided a predictable path toward promotions, and to receive a monthly income and various fringe benefits which allowed a solid middle-class lifestyle (which usually included good housing and affording the university education of their children). Except for some privileged pockets (typically the central banks) this is no longer true in the countries affected by the present crisis. The bleak picture results from the decapitation of the top and more specialized bureaucracies due to the exodus of the more qualified individuals, the politicization of those positions, numerous and always failed "rationalizations" and "reorganizations," and the spectacular decay of the physical plant (perhaps nothing is more discouraging than hammering at a wornout mechanical typewriter in an office the painting and furniture of which have not been renewed for many years). This is extremely propitious for the existence of a poorly motivated and unskilled bureaucracy. This feeds back into the innumerable anecdotes that support the all-out assault on the state, and erodes the political support that would be necessary for effecting a better balanced policy of the government toward its own bureaucracy.

Furthermore, under conditions of high and erratic inflation, in one month state employees may lose 30, 40, and even 50 percent of their real income. Under these circumstances they cannot but despair and demand immediate redress. They go on strike and demonstrate, at times violently. The result is frequent paralysis of essential public services. The consequences of these protests hit the largest cities hardest, the center of power and politics. These protests make a large contribution to the feeling that democratic governments and politicians are unable, and for demagogic reasons even unwilling, to prevent "chaos" and further general economic deterioration. Furthermore, the rational—and desperate—behavior of state employees feeds the generalized image of an unruly public bureaucracy that is far more interested in defending its "privileges" than in discharging its duties. Finally, even though the evidence on this matter is impressionistic, the public employees' strikes and other protests, as they paralyze and further degrade essential public services, antagonize the public, including many middle-class segments. The anger of these sectors, which are more dependent on most public services than the higher classes, adds weight to the antistatist offensive and mixes up the (necessary) task of achieving a leaner state apparatus with the (suicidal) weakening of the state in all its dimensions.

Shrinking personal income, dwindling career prospects, bad working conditions, a hostile political environment, and, at the same time, the countless interventions that the state undertakes are perfect soil for an enormous growth of corruption. In many bureaus few things work without graft that is petty for the rich but which heavily taxes the poor. At the top and even middle levels of the bureaucracy, corruption entails huge amounts of money which plunder the slender public resources. In addition, when some of those acts become public scandals, they undermine trust, not only in the workings and role of the state but also in governments which appear incapable of correcting this situation, if not active participants in it.

For governments desperate for funds, the temporary solution has been to increase indirect taxes and the prices of public services. But this feeds inflation and has deleterious distributional consequences. In terms of an income tax, it can only be easily applied as withholdings on the salaries of the formal sector of the economy (including public employees). If we consider, in addition, that the formally employed are the main contributors to social security, the result is a powerful incentive, both for them and for their employers, to leave the formal sector; in periods of uncertain employment and falling salaries, the sharp deterioration of most social services (observed both in Latin America and in postcommunist countries) adds to the misfortunes of vast segments of the population. Furthermore, the income and the social security taxes imposed on the formally employed entail a burdensome tax rate which very few pay but which is nominally effective for the whole economy—this increases the incentives for tax evasion, and diminishes the cost of bribing. The result is generalized protests about "excessive taxes" at the same time that the overall tax income for the state diminishes, with direct taxes—those that, supposedly, a democratic government would emphasize—dropping even more sharply. The long agony of the state-centered, import substitutive pattern of capital accumulation has left us with a dinosaur incapable even of feeding itself, while the "solutions" undertaken lead toward an anemic entity which may be no less able to support democracy, decent levels of social equity, and economic growth.

III. On Certain Economic Crises

I will discuss here a particular kind of economic crisis: the one suffered by countries—Argentina, Brazil, and Peru—that locked themselves into a pattern of high and recurrent inflation[19] (eventually reaching hyperinflation), punctuated by repeated failed attempts to control inflation and undertake "structural reforms" of the kind presently recommended by international lending organizations. This is, fortunately, a small set of countries, but several postcommunist and African countries seem to have already fallen in, or are at the brink of falling into this pattern. It can be postulated that the longer and the deeper this crisis, and the less the confidence that the government will be able to solve it, the more rational it becomes for everyone to act: (1) at highly disaggregated levels, especially in relation to state agencies that may solve or alleviate the consequences of the crisis for a given firm or sector; (2) with extremely short time horizons; and (3) with assumptions that everyone else will do the same.

A gigantic—national level—prisoner's dilemma holds when a profound and protracted economic crisis teaches every agent the following lessons: (1) inflation will continue to be high, but it is next to impossible to predict in the medium run, to say nothing about the long run, inflation fluctuations; (2) among such fluctuations will probably be periods of extremely high or hyperinflation (say, rates of 50 percent and above per month); (3) at some point the government will make some drastic intervention, aimed at taming inflation, but that intervention is likely to fail; (4) expectations about the future situation of the economy are strongly pessimistic; and (5) predictions about the future economic situation of each agent are contingent on shrewd and timely adaptation to the conditions imposed by the preceding points.

Although there is a dearth of studies at the appropriate microlevel, anyone who has lived under these circumstances knows that this is a harsh, nasty world. Rationally, the dominant strategy is to do whatever is necessary to protect oneself against the losses threatened by high and erratic inflation. Remaining passive and/or not having the power resources for running at the speed of inflation guarantees heavy losses—in extremes, for some bankruptcy and for others falling into abysmal poverty.

This is a world of *sauve qui peut,* and playing this game reinforces the very conditions under which it is played. The first, more basic phenomenon is generalized desolidarization. Every rational agent acts at the level of disaggregation and with the time horizon that she deems most efficacious in her defensive moves. The adequate time horizon is the very short term; what sense would it make to sacrifice short-term gains for the sake of longer-term ones, when the future situation of the world cannot be predicted with any accuracy, and if abstaining from maximizing short-term gains may provoke heavy losses? Some agents, difficult to identify topically with the data available, reap big profits. The ways to achieve this are many, but the chances across classes are extremely skewed. Some of the more important of those ways entail the plundering of the state apparatus. For players of this game, broad, long-run economic policies, negotiated and implemented with the participation of highly aggregated, interest representation associations are not important; as the government also has to dance at the rhythm of the crisis, its capacity to formulate those policies is very limited, and very often their implementation is canceled or captured by the disaggregated strategies just described. What is truly important for defending oneself, and for eventually profiting from the crisis is (basically but not exclusively for capitalists) open and fast access to the state agencies that can deliver the resources hoped for. Privileges and favors of all kinds are procured by the minimum size coalition that is able to obtain the appropriate decisions by a given public agency. Moreover, those advantages must be obtained quickly; if not, continuing inflation would eat them up. Under this situation, the rational strategy consists of a double disaggregation: first, act alone or allied to the minimum possible set of agents that can guarantee the desired outcome; second, colonize the state agencies that can provide the sought after benefits, avoiding more aggregated and/or public arenas that would only complicate the attainment of the topical benefits expected. Various processes noted in the literature, such as the loosening of popular collective identities, the implosion of historically rooted parties, and the decreased importance of capitalists' organizations are expressions of the perverse collective consequences of rational defensive behavior.

Capitalists in Argentina, Brazil, and Peru have an important advantage. This is not a new game for them: only the urgency, the stakes, and the level of disaggregation have increased. Capitalists in those countries, and elsewhere in Latin America, have long experience in living off the largesse of the state, and in colonizing its agencies. They do not have to find many new counterparts inside the public bureaucracies, or to invent new ways to engage them in manifold forms of mutual corruption. But, nowadays, the depth of the crisis has accentuated those ills. First, there is evidence of a great increase in corruption. Second, there is an enormous fragmentation of the state apparatus—or, equivalently, its sharp decline of autonomy—not in relation to "a" capitalist class but in relation to the innumerable segments in which this class has disaggregated itself at the rhythm of the crisis. The problems noted in the preceding section are multiplied by these consequences of the economic crisis, at the same time that the resulting disintegration of the state apparatus makes it even less capable of solving that crisis.

Every spiral of the crisis is unlike the preceding one. Actors learn. Those who were cunning enough to survive and even gain ground can buy at bargain prices assets the losers had. The rapid concentration of capital in these countries reflects the gains of the Darwinian survivors. Agents assume that as the previous stabilization efforts failed (and as the government was further weakened by that failure) the future efforts of the government will also fail. Thus those agents hedge their bets against the high estimated probability of future policy failure, which of course increases the likelihood of that same failure.

On their part, the more spirals occur, the more desperately governments try to find a way out of the crisis. But the accompanying disintegration of the state apparatus, increasing fiscal deficits, a hostile public opinion, political parties that anticipate future electoral gains by harshly criticizing the government (including leaders of the governing party, who see themselves dragged into the abyss of the government's unpopularity), and the anticipatory hedging of powerful economic actors diminish the probability that the next policy attempt will succeed. This also means that, for an economy with increasing levels of immunization, the next stabilization attempt will be a more radical intervention than the preceding one. The stakes of the game become higher at every turn of the wheel.

The repetition of policy failure continues the process of Darwinian selection, at each turn made easier by the decreasing ability of the government to control the distributional consequences of its policies. In particular, since many segments of the middle class are, in relative terms, affected most severely, widespread cries of "the extinction of the middle class" are heard, sometimes with overtones that are not exactly consistent with the foundations of democracy. In this situation, the government projects a curious image that mixes omnipotence with naked impotence. On one hand, every attempt at solving the crisis is resonantly announced as the one that will succeed, and therefore justifies further sacrifices of the population. On the other hand, aside from the welcome relief of a temporary decline in inflation (usually at high cost in terms of economic activity and distribution) it soon becomes evident that the government will not be able to implement other, also necessary, policies. This is another factor in shortening the time horizons and in worsening the expectations that dynamize the overall game.

In these conditions, a society perceives an ugly image of itself. One could collect thousands of expressions of the deep *malaise* that follows. The evidence of widespread opportunism, greed, lack of solidarity, and corruption does not present a positive image. Furthermore, many of those actions entail blatant disregard for the existing laws; when it becomes clear that many violate the law and that the costs of doing so are usually nil, the lesson learned further erodes the predictability of social relations; widespread opportunism and lawlessness increase all sorts of transaction costs, and the texturing of society by the state-as-law weakens at every turn of the spiral.

Bitter denunciations and desperate appeals to overcome the "moral crisis" follow. The media and daily conversations become full of exhortations for "restoring national unity," for the panacea of socioeconomic pacts (that in these conditions no rational actor would enter into in good faith), for "moralizing" public administration and business, and the like. Moralistic criticisms and pious exhortations—however valuable they are as an indication that basic values of public morality somehow survive—ignore the locking in of social action in a colossal prisoner's dilemma.[20] Moreover, such utterances can easily escalate into a full-fledged condemnation of the whole situation, including a democracy that performs poorly in so many respects.

The angry atomization of society is the other side of the same coin of the crisis of the state, not only as a set of bureaucracies but also—and even more—as the lawful source of social predictability. In addition, the crisis leads to the decreasing plausibility of the state as an authoritative agent of the country's interests: rather, it increasingly appears as a burdensome apparatus allowing itself to be plundered by the powerful. The disintegration of the state apparatus and the decreasing effectiveness of the state-as-law makes it incapable of implementing minimally complex policies. It is no easy matter to decide what segments of the state should be given priority for making them more effective; or to implement an industrial policy; or to decide the degree and sequencing of the financial and commercial opening of the economy; or to agree on salaries and employment policies, etc. Without this "restructuring" neither the current neoliberal policies or alternative ones may succeed.

In order for those policies not only to be decided (the easier part, obviously) but to be implemented, three conditions must be met. First, both private and state agents must have at least the medium run as their relevant time horizon. But in the conditions we discussed this is unlikely to be the case. Even government leaders are unlikely to have other than a short-time horizon because the crisis means that they must focus their attention in extinguishing the fires that pop up everywhere, and that their jobs are in perpetual jeopardy. In addition, if stabilization and especially structural policies are going to be something more than a crude translation of whatever interests have access to them, the relevant state agencies must be able to gather and analyze complex information, be sufficiently motivated in the pursuit of some definition of the public interest, and see their role in putting up such policies as a rewarding episode in their careers. As we saw, except for some organizational pockets, these conditions nowadays are nonexistent. Finally, some policies can be successfully implemented only if they go through complex negotiations with the various organized private actors that claim legitimate access to the process. The extreme disaggregation with which it is rational to operate under the crisis, however, erodes the representativeness of most organized interests. Who can *really* speak for someone else in these countries? What *ego* can convince *alter* that what he agreed to with her will be honored by those he claims to represent? The atomization of society mirrors and accentuates the disintegration of the state.[21]

How can this world of actors behaving in extremely disaggregated, opportunistic, and short-term ways be politically represented? Which can be the anchors and links with the institutions (of interest representation and the properly political ones, such as parties and congress) that texture the relationships between state and society in institutionalized democracies? What representativeness and, more broadly, which collective identities can survive these storms? The answer is that very little, if any, progress is made toward achieving institutions of representation and accountability. On the contrary, the atomization of society and state, the spread of brown areas and their peculiar ways of pushing their interests, and the enormous urgency and complexity of the problems to be faced feed the delegative propensities of these democracies, connecting with the deep historical roots of these countries. The pulverization of society into myriad rational/opportunistic actors and their anger about a situation which all—and, hence, apparently nobody—seem to cause has a major culprit: the state and the government. This common sense is, on one hand, fertile ground for simplistic antistatist ideologies; on the other, it propels the abysmal loss of prestige of the democratic government, its shaky institutions, and of all politicians. Of course, these evaluations have good groundings: the policy failures of government, its blunderings and vacillations, its impotent omnipotence, and too often the evidence of its corruption, as well as the dismal spectacles also too often offered by politicians in and out of congress and parties, give the perfect occasion for the projective exculpation of society into the manifold ills of state and government.

The least that can be said about these problems is, first, that they do not help to create a consolidated, institutionalized democracy; second, that they make extremely difficult the implementation of the complex, long-term, multisided negotiated policies that could take these countries out of the muddle; and, third, that (not only in Latin America, indeed) these problems powerfully interact with a tradition of conceiving politics in a caesarist, anti-institutional, and delegative fashion.

At this point an overdue question must be posed: Is there a way out of these downward spirals? Or, more precisely, at what point and under what conditions is there such a way out? We must remember that we are dealing with countries (Argentina, Brazil, and Peru) which unfortunately suffered a pattern of recurrent high inflation, punctuated by periods of hyperinflation or very close to it (depending on definitions I need not argue with here), and which suffered several failed stabilization programs.

One country which recently suffered these problems but that seems to have found a way out is Chile. The policies of the Pinochet government accomplished, with an effectiveness that Lenin would have admired, the destruction of most of what was left (after the Allende government) of the domestic market, import substitution oriented bourgeoisie—which was too grateful to have been rescued as a class to organize any concerted opposition. Of course, the Pinochet government also brutally repressed the labor organizations and the political parties which could have mounted an effective opposition to its policies. In this societal desert, huge social costs were incurred, and although with various changes and accidents, the neoliberal program was mostly implemented. The new democratic government in this country has the still serious but less vexing problem of preserving low inflation, reasonable rates of economic growth, and a favorable international climate. That government is also faced with the problem of how to alleviate the inequalities that were accentuated by the preceding authoritarian regime. But the sober fact is that the distributional consequences of more ambiguous and less harsh policies in countries such as Brazil, Argentina, and Peru have not been better than the ones under Pinochet's government. Furthermore, the resources presently available to the Chilean government for alleviating equity problems are relatively larger than the ones available to Brazil, Peru, and Argentina. Finally, the fact that Chile was some time ago, but is no longer trapped in the spirals depicted here means (although this is not the only reason, there are other historical ones which I cannot elaborate here) that its state is in better shape than in the countries discussed above for dealing with the equity and developmental issues it inherited.

Another such country could be Mexico. But inflation (with its manifold social dislocations) never was as high in Mexico as in Argentina, Brazil, and Peru (or, for that matter, as it is today in most of the former Soviet Union); the PRI provided a more effective instrument for policy implementation than anything available to the latter countries; and the geopolitical interests of the bordering United States are helping the still painful and uncertain but comparatively easier navigation of this country toward the achievement of the long-run goals of its current policies. Another country is Bolivia, where the implementation of policies which were successful in taming inflation and liberalizing trade and finance (but not, at least until now, in restoring growth and investment) was accompanied by a brutal repression which can hardly be seen as consistent with democracy. A more recent candidate for this list is Argentina. Focusing on the South American cases, what do Chile, Bolivia, and Argentina have in common? Quite simply, the crisis in these countries— in the first under authoritarian and in the two latter under democratically elected governments—reached the very bottom. The bottom is the convergence of the following conditions. First, a state that as a principle of order has a tiny hold on the behavior of most actors, and that as a bureaucracy reaches extreme limits of disintegration and ineffectiveness, and at some point becomes unable to support the national currency. Second, a workers' movement is thoroughly defeated, in the sense that it is not any longer able to oppose neoliberal policies except by means of very disaggregated and shortlived protests. Third, a capitalist class has to a large extent devoured itself, with the winners transforming themselves into financially centered and outwardly oriented conglomerates (together with the branches of commerce and the professionals that cater to luxurious consumption). Finally, there is a generalized mood that life under continued high and uncertain inflation is so intolerable that *any* solution is preferable, even if that solution ratifies a more unequal world in which many forms of solidaristic sociability have been lost. At this point whoever tries to control inflation and initiate the "restructuring" advised by neoliberal views does not confront powerful blocking coalitions: the more important fractions of the bourgeoisie no longer have antagonistic interests, the various expressions of popular and middle-class interests are weak and fractionalized, and the state employees that have survived their own ordeal can now hope to improve their situation. The pulverization of society and of the state apparatus, together with the primordial demand to return to an ordered social world, end up eliminating resistances that, unwillingly but effectively, fed the previous turns of the spiral. In Chile this happened through the combined effects of the crisis unleashed under the *Unidad Popular* government and the repressive and determined policies of the Pinochet period. In Bolivia and Argentina it is no small irony that, after hyperinflation, the (apparently, far from clearly achieved yet) end of the spirals came under presidents originating in parties/movements such as MNR and peronism; it was probably incumbent on such presidents, and only to them, to complete the defeat of the respective workers' movement.

Brazil was the last of the countries discussed here to encounter this type of crisis. This was closely related to the larger size of its domestic market and to its more dynamic economic performance which created a more complex and industrialized economy than that of its neighbors. In a "paradox of success," this advantage may turn out to be a severe disadvantage.[22] In Brazil there are more and more powerful agents capable of blocking the more or less orthodox neoliberal policies that, in any case, have been and will be attempted again. Conversely, if there were no alternatives to continuing the downward spiral until a complete collapse, the degree of economic destruction would be much larger. Furthermore, socially, in contrast with the situation of the Southern Cone countries before their own spirals, in Brazil there is already a vast segment of the population that has nowhere lower to fall.

IV. A Partial Conclusion

Are there alternatives to the crisis I have depicted? The prisoner's dilemma has a powerful dynamic: invocations to altruism and national unity, as well as policy proposals that assume wide solidarities and firm identities, will not do. If there is a solution, it probably lies in finding areas which are important in their impacts on the overall situation and in which skilled action (particularly by the government) can lengthen the time horizons (and, consequently, the scope of solidarities) of crucial actors. The best known invention for such achievement is the strengthening of social and political institutions. But under the conditions I have depicted this is indeed a most difficult task. In the contemporary world, the joyful celebration of the advent of democracy must be complemented with the sober recognition of the immense (and, indeed, historically unusual) difficulties its institutionalization and its rooting in society must face. As Haiti, Peru, and Thailand have shown, these experiments are fragile. In addition, there are no immanent historical forces which will guide the new democracies toward an institutionalized and representative form, and to the elimination of their brown areas and the manifold social ills that underlie them. In the long run, the new democracies may split between those that follow this felicitous course and those that regress to all-out authoritarianism. But delegative democracies, weak horizontal accountability, schizophrenic states, brown areas, and low intensity citizenship are part of the foreseeable future of many new democracies.

Notes

1. Robert Dahl, *Polyarchy: Participation and Opposition* (New Haven: Yale University Press, 1971).

2. Arend Lijphart, "Consociational Democracy," *World Politics* 21 (no. 1, January 1968): 207–25, and Lijphart, *Democracies: Patterns of Majoritarian and Consensus Government in Twenty-One Countries* (New Haven: Yale University Press, 1984).

3. In addition to its rather sketchy character, this text has a major limitation: I do not deal directly with international and transnational factors, even though they often enter implicitly in my discussions.

4. One limitation of not dealing with international factors and only very passingly with historical ones is that I will not be able to discuss here an assumption that sometimes creeps into the literature: that new democracies are "only" going through stages that institutionalized democracies passed before.

5. In another work [chapter 8 of the current book. —*Ed.*] I labeled these "delegative democracies," to contrast them with institutionalized (or, equivalently, consolidated or established or representative, or, as we shall see, liberal) democracies. With the term "delegative" I point out to a conception and practice of executive authority as having been electorally delegated the right to do whatever it deems fit for the country. I also argue that delegative democracies are inherently hostile to the patterns of representation normal in established democracies, to the creation and strengthening of political institutions and, especially, to what I term "horizontal accountability." By this I mean the day-by-day control of the validity and lawfulness of the actions of the executive by other public agencies which are reasonably autonomous from the former. Furthermore, as we shall see, the liberal component of these democracies is very weak. Some authors tend to confuse delegative democracy with populism; both, of course, share various important features. But, in Latin America at least, the latter entailed a broadening (even if vertically controlled) of popular political participation and organization, and coexisted with periods of dynamic expansion of the domestic economy. Instead delegative democracy typically attempts to depoliticize the population, except for brief moments in which it demands its plebiscitary support, and presently coexists with periods of severe economic crisis. While my previous text was basically a typo-

logical exercise, this paper examines some societal processes which seem closely related to the emergence and workings of delegative democracies.

6. I am using cautious language because I cannot deal here with the various nuances and qualifications that a more extended treatment of this matter would have to introduce. For a good discussion of these matters see Roger Cotterrell, *The Sociology of Law: An Introduction* (London: Butterworths, 1984).

7. Many postcommunist countries suffer the additional, and enormous, problem that not even their geographical boundaries are beyond dispute and that various ethnic and religious cleavages prevent minimal degrees of allegiance to the respective states. In this sense, while several Latin American countries are undergoing processes of acute erosion of an already existing nation state, several postcommunist ones are facing the even more vexing problem of beginning to build, under very uncongenial economic and social circumstances, a nation state.

8. Truly, "state penetration" was one of the "crises" conceptualized in the famous 1960s series of volumes on "political development" of the Social Science Research Council (see Joseph LaPalombara, "Penetration: A Crisis of Governmental Capacity," in Leonard Binder et al., *Crises and Sequences in Political Development* [Princeton: Princeton University Press, 1971], pp. 205–32). This same issue is central to Samuel Huntington, *Political Order in Changing Societies* (New Haven: Yale University Press, 1968). But while these works are concerned with the spread of any kind of central authority, my discussion here refers to the effectiveness of the type of legality that a democratic state is supposed to implant.

9. Of course, these are matters of degree. For example, the United States stands as a case where in the past some of these problems were pervasive—and they have not been entirely eliminated today. But there (as well as in England before) those problems motivated the creation of a rather effective "apolitical" national civil service. In contrast, underlining some of the tragic but mostly ignored effects of the deep crisis some countries are undergoing and of the economic policies in course, the inverse is what is happening there: the destruction of whatever effective state bureaucracies and notions of a public service existed.

10. One important symptom of this is the degree to which the main operations of the drug trade thrive in these regions, often in coalition with local and national authorities based there. This convergence (and that of numerous other criminal activities) further accentuates the perverse privatization of these regions.

11. It should be noticed that the measures of heterogeneity I am suggesting do not necessarily mean only one nationality under one state (for example, the dominant color of Belgium is blue). The disintegration of supranational empires such as the Soviet Union and Yugoslavia may or may not lead, in the respective emerging units, to states which are homogenous in the sense I am specifying here. For example, the erosion of public authority and the widespread disobedience of legislation issued in Russia mean that, even though this unit may be more "national" in the sense of containing a rather homogeneous population, in terms of the dimensions of "stateness" I have suggested, it would indeed be dominated by brown. For a vivid description of

the fast and extensive "browning" of today's Russia, see Peter Reddaway, "Russia on the Brink," *New York Review of Books,* January 28, 1993, pp. 30–35.

12. See Scott Mainwaring, "Politicians, Parties, and Electoral Systems: Brazil in Comparative Perspective," *Journal of Comparative Politics* 24 (October 1991): 21–43.

13. Consider the present political problems of Italy, which is arguably the most heterogeneous of institutionalized democracies (with the exception of India, if this extremely heterogeneous country can still be considered to belong to that set) but is much more homogenous than most of the countries I am discussing. Those problems are closely connected to Italy's brown areas and to the penetration of legal and illegal representatives of those areas in its national center. In the United States it seems indisputable that in the past decade the brown areas (particularly around large cities) have experienced a worrisome growth. Furthermore, these problems are also appearing in other rich countries, related to a series of global (especially economic) transformations. But in the present text I want to stress some factors, specific to certain countries, that greatly accentuate those problems. Again, and as always, comparisons are a matter of degree.

14. Guillermo O'Donnell and Philippe Schmitter, *Transitions from Authoritarian Rule: Tentative Conclusions about Uncertain Democracies,* vol. IV of Guillermo O'Donnell, Philippe Schmitter, and Laurence Whitehead, eds., *Transitions from Authoritarian Rule: Prospects for Democracy* (Baltimore: Johns Hopkins University Press, 1986), p. 73.

15. See O'Donnell and Schmitter, *Transitions.*

16. As Alan Ware puts it, "The claim of the liberal democracies to be liberal democracies rests on the claim that they have both well established and also accessible procedures for protecting the liberties of individual citizens" (Ware, "Liberal Democracy: One Form or Many?" *Political Studies* 40 [1992]: 130–45).

17. The extensive poverty and high inequality found in most of Latin America and the rest of the Third World (the sediment of a long history, accentuated by the current crisis and economic policies) is different from the process of rapid *unequalization* taking place in postcommunist countries: whichever pattern turns out to be more explosive, the latter points toward democracies which, almost from the moment of their inauguration, are suffering a steep decrease in the intensity of their citizenship.

18. By "neoliberal" policies I mean those advocated by international lending institutions and mainstream neoclassical theories. These policies have undergone some changes, presumably prompted by the very mixed record of their application. But a very strong—and indiscriminate—antistatist bias continues to be at their core. For a critique of these policies, see Przeworski et al., *Sustainable Democracy* (Cambridge and New York: Cambridge University Press, 1995). See also Przeworski, "The Neoliberal Fallacy," *Journal of Democracy* 3 (no. 3, July 1992): 45–59.

19. By this I mean periods of three years or more when monthly inflation averaged above 20 percent per month, with peaks of three digit figures per month.

20. Although I cannot expand on this point here, it should be noted that the situations I am depicting do not have any of the conditions that the literature has identified as conducive to cooperative solutions in the prisoner's dilemma.

21. One should not forget the longer term effects of the crisis and of the indiscriminate antistatist ideology that underlies the current economic policies, on factors crucial

for sustaining economic growth. I refer in particular to education, health, and science and technology policies, and to the modernization of the physical infrastructure. These areas are being grossly neglected, in spite of many warnings and complaints. But to undertake those policies a reasonably lean and effective state apparatus is required.

22. I have discussed Brazil's apparent paradoxes of success in "Transitions, Continuities, and Paradoxes," in O'Donnell, Scott Mainwaring, and Samuel Valenzuela, eds., *Issues in Democratic Consolidation. The New South American Democracies in Comparative Perspective* (Notre Dame, Ind.: University of Notre Dame Press, 1992), pp. 17–56.

8

Delegative Democracy

Here I depict a "new species," a type of existing democracy that has yet to be theorized. As often happens, it has many similarities with other, already recognized species, with cases shading off between the former and some variety of the latter. Still, I believe that the differences are significant enough to warrant an attempt at such a depiction. The drawing of nearer boundaries between these types of democracy depends on empirical research, as well as more refined analytical work that I am now undertaking. But if I really have found a new species (and not a member of an already recognized family, or a form too evanescent to merit conceptualization), it may be worth exploring its main features.

Scholars who have worked on democratic transitions and consolidation have repeatedly said that, since it would be wrong to assume that these processes all culminate in the same result, we need a typology of democracies. Some interesting efforts have been made, focused on the consequences, in terms of types of democracy and policy patterns, of various paths to democratization.[1] My own ongoing research suggests, however, that the more decisive factors for generating various kinds of democracy are not related to the characteristics of the preceding authoritarian regime or to the process of transition. Instead, I believe that we must focus upon various long-term historical factors, as well as the degree of severity of the socioeconomic problems that newly installed democratic governments inherit.

This essay was published in *Journal of Democracy* 5 (no. 1, 1994). Some of the ideas in this essay originated in conversations I had in the 1980s with Luis Pásara concerning the emerging patterns of rule in several Latin American countries. For the preparation of the present version I was privileged to receive detailed comments and suggestions from David Collier.

Let me briefly state the main points of my argument:

1. Existing theories and typologies of democracy refer to *representative* democracy as it exists, with all its variations and subtypes, in highly developed capitalist countries.

2. Some newly installed democracies (Argentina, Brazil, Peru, Ecuador, Bolivia, Philippines, Korea, and many postcommunist countries) *are* democracies, in the sense that they meet Robert Dahl's criteria for the definition of polyarchy.[2]

3. At the same time, these democracies are not—and do not seem to be on the path toward becoming—representative democracies; they present characteristics that prompt me to call them *delegative* democracies (DDs).

4. DDs are not consolidated (i.e., institutionalized) democracies, but they may be *enduring.* In many cases, there is no sign either of any imminent threat of an authoritarian regression, or of advances toward representative democracy.

5. There is an important interaction effect: the deep social and economic crisis that most of these countries inherited from their authoritarian predecessors reinforces certain practices and conceptions about the proper exercise of political authority that lead in the direction of delegative, not representative, democracy.

The following considerations underlie the argument presented above:[3]

1. The installation of a democratically elected government opens the way for a "second transition," often longer and more complex than the initial transition from authoritarian rule.

2. This second transition is supposed to be from a democratically elected *government* to an institutionalized, consolidated democratic *regime.*

3. Nothing guarantees, however, that this second transition will occur. New democracies may regress to authoritarian rule, or they may stall in a feeble, uncertain situation. This situation may endure without opening avenues for institutionalized forms of democracy.

4. The crucial element determining the success of the second transition is the building of institutions that become important decisional points in the flow of political power.

5. For such a successful outcome to occur, governmental policies and the political strategies of various agents must embody the recognition of a paramount shared interest in democratic institution building. The successful cases have featured a decisive coalition of broadly supported political leaders who take great care in creating and strengthening democratic political institutions. These institutions, in turn, have made it easier to cope with the social and economic problems inherited from the authoritarian regime. This was the case in Spain, Portugal (although not immediately after democratic installation), Uruguay, and Chile.

6. In contrast, the cases of delegative democracy mentioned earlier have achieved neither institutional progress nor much governmental effectiveness in dealing with their respective social and economic crises.

Before elaborating on these themes in greater detail, I must make a brief excursus to explain more precisely what I mean by institutions and institutionalization, thereby bringing into sharper focus the patterns that fail to develop under delegative democracy.

II. On Institutions

Institutions are regularized patterns of interaction that are known, practiced, and regularly accepted (if not necessarily normatively approved) by social agents who expect to continue interacting under the rules and norms formally or informally embodied in those patterns. Sometimes, but not necessarily, institutions become formal organizations: they materialize in buildings, seals, rituals, and persons in roles that authorize them to "speak for" the organization.

I am concerned here with a subset: *democratic* institutions. Their definition is elusive, so I will delimit the concept by way of some approximations. To begin with, democratic institutions are political institutions. They have a recognizable, direct relationship with the main themes of politics: the making of decisions that are mandatory within a given territory, the channels of access to decision-making roles, and the shaping of the interests and identities that claim such access. The boundaries between what is and is not a political institution are blurred, and vary across time and countries.

We need a second approximation. Some political institutions are formal organizations belonging to the constitutional network of a polyarchy: these include congress, the judiciary, and political parties. Others, such as fair elections, have an intermittent organizational embodiment but are no less indispensable. The main question about all these institutions is how they work: Are they really important decisional points in the flow of influence, power, and policy? If they are not, what are the consequences for the overall political process?

Other factors indispensable for the workings of democracy in contemporary societies—those that pertain to the formation and representation of collective identities and interests—may or may not be institutionalized, or they may be operative only for a part of the potentially relevant sectors. In representative democracies, those patterns are highly institutionalized and organizationally embodied through pluralist or neocorporatist arrangements.

The characteristics of a functioning institutional setting include the following:

1. *Institutions both incorporate and exclude.* They determine which agents, on the basis of which resources, claims, and procedures, are accepted as valid

participants in their decision-making and implementation processes. These criteria are necessarily selective: they fit (and favor) some agents; they may lead others to reshape themselves in order to meet them; and for various reasons, they may be impossible to meet, or unacceptable, for still others. The scope of an institution is the degree to which it incorporates and excludes its set of potentially relevant agents.

2. *Institutions shape the probability distribution of outcomes.* As Adam Przeworski has noted, institutions "process" only certain actors and resources, and do so under certain rules.[4] This predetermines the range of feasible outcomes, and their likelihood within that range. Democratic institutions, for example, preclude the use or threat of force and the outcomes that this would generate. On the other hand, the subset of democratic institutions based on the universality of the vote, as Philippe Schmitter and Wolfgang Streeck have argued, is not good at processing the intensity of preferences.[5] Institutions of interest representation are better at processing the intensity of preferences, although at the expense of the universalism of voting and citizenship and, often, of the "democraticness" of their decision making.

3. *Institutions tend to aggregate, and to stabilize the aggregation of, the level of action and organization of agents interacting with them.* The rules established by institutions influence strategic decisions by agents as to the degree of aggregation that is more efficacious for them in terms of the likelihood of favorable outcomes. Institutions, or rather the persons who occupy decision-making roles within them, have limited information-processing capabilities and attention spans. Consequently, those persons prefer to interact with relatively few agents and issues at a time.[6] This tendency toward aggregation is another reason for the exclusionary side of every institution.

4. *Institutions induce patterns of representation.* For the same reasons, institutions favor the transformation of the many potential voices of their constituencies into a few that can claim to speak as their representatives. Representation involves, on the one hand, the acknowledged right to speak for some relevant others and, on the other, the ability to deliver the compliance of those others with what the representative decides. Insofar as this capability is demonstrated and the given rules of the game are respected, institutions and their various representatives develop an interest in their mutual coexistence as interacting agents.

5. *Institutions stabilize agents/representatives and their expectations.* Institutional leaders and representatives come to expect behaviors within a relatively narrow range of possibilities from a set of actors that they expect to meet again in the next round of interactions. Certain agents may not like the narrowing of expected behaviors, but they anticipate that deviations from such expectations are likely to be counterproductive. This is the point at which it may be said that an institution (which probably has become a formal

organization) is strong. The institution is in equilibrium; it is in nobody's interest to change it, except in incremental and basically consensual ways.

6. *Institutions lengthen the time horizons of actors.* The stabilization of agents and expectations entails a time dimension: institutionalized interactions are expected to continue into the future among the same (or a slowly and rather predictably changing) set of agents. This, together with a high level of aggregation of representation and of control of their constituencies, is the foundation for the "competitive cooperation" that characterizes institutionalized democracies: one-shot prisoner's dilemmas can be overcome,[7] bargaining (including logrolling) is facilitated, various tradeoffs over time become feasible, and sequential attention to issues makes it possible to accommodate an otherwise unmanageable agenda. The establishment of these practices further strengthens the willingness of all relevant agents to recognize one another as valid interlocutors, and enhances the value that they attach to the institution that shapes their interrelationships. This virtuous circle is completed when most democratic institutions achieve not only reasonable scope and strength but also a high density of multiple and stabilized interrelationships. This makes these institutions important points of decision in the overall political process, and a consolidated, institutionalized democracy thus emerges.

A way to summarize what I have said is that, in the functioning of contemporary, complex societies, democratic political institutions provide a crucial level of mediation and aggregation between, on one side, structural factors and, on the other, not only individuals but also the diverse groupings under which society organizes its multiple interests and identities. This intermediate—i.e., institutional—level has an important impact on the patterns of organization of society, bestowing representation upon some participants in the political process and excluding others. Institutionalization undeniably entails heavy costs—not only exclusion but also the recurring, and all too real, nightmares of bureaucratization and boredom. The alternative, however, submerges social and political life in the hell of a colossal prisoner's dilemma.

This is, of course, an ideal typical description, but I find it useful for tracing, by way of contrast, the peculiarities of a situation where there is a dearth of democratic institutions. A noninstitutionalized democracy is characterized by the restricted scope, the weakness, and the low density of whatever political institutions exist. The place of well-functioning institutions is taken by other nonformalized but strongly operative practices—clientelism, patrimonialism, and corruption.

III. Characterizing Delegative Democracy

Delegative democracies rest on the premise that whoever wins election to the presidency is thereby entitled to govern as he or she sees fit, constrained only by the hard facts of existing power relations and by a constitutionally limited term of office. The president is taken to be the embodiment of the nation and the main custodian and definer of its interests. Governmental policies need bear no resemblance to campaign promises—has not the president been authorized to govern as he (or she) thinks best? Since this paternalistic figure is supposed to take care of the whole nation, his political base must be a movement, the supposedly vibrant overcoming of the factionalism and conflicts associated with parties. Typically, winning presidential candidates in DDs present themselves as above both political parties and organized interests. How could it be otherwise for somebody who claims to embody the whole of the nation? In this view, other institutions—courts and legislatures, for instance—are nuisances that come attached to the domestic and international advantages of being a democratically elected president. Accountability to such institutions appears as a mere impediment to the full authority that the president has been delegated to exercise.

Delegative democracy is not alien to the democratic tradition. It is more democratic, but less liberal, than representative democracy. DD is strongly majoritarian. It consists in constituting, through clean elections, a majority that empowers someone to become, for a given number of years, the embodiment and interpreter of the high interests of the nation. Often, DDs use devices such as runoff elections if the first round of elections does not generate a clear-cut majority.[8] This majority must be created to support the myth of legitimate delegation. Furthermore, DD is strongly individualistic, but more in a Hobbesian than a Lockean way: voters are supposed to choose, irrespective of their identities and affiliations, the individual who is most fit to take responsibility for the destiny of the country. Elections in DDs are a very emotional and highstakes event: candidates compete for a chance to rule virtually free of all constraints save those imposed by naked, noninstitutionalized power relations. After the election, voters/delegators are expected to become a passive but cheering audience of what the president does.

Extreme individualism in constituting executive power combines well with the organicism of the Leviathan. The nation and its "authentic" political expression, the leader and his "Movement," are postulated as living organisms.[9] The leader has to heal the nation by uniting its dispersed fragments into a harmonious whole. Since the body politic is in disarray, and since its existing voices only reproduce its fragmentation, delegation includes the right (and the duty) of administering the unpleasant medicines that will restore the health of the nation. For this view, it seems obvious that only the head really knows: the president and his most trusted advisors are the alpha and the omega of politics. Furthermore, some of the problems of the nation can be solved only by highly technical criteria. *Técnicos*, especially in economic policy, must be politically shielded by the president against the manifold resistance of society. In the meantime, it is "obvious" that resistance—be it from congress, political parties, interest groups, or crowds in the streets—has to be ignored. This organicistic discourse fits poorly with the dry arguments of the technocrats, and the myth of delegation is consummated. The president isolates himself from most political institutions and organized interests, and bears sole responsibility for the successes and failures of "his" policies.

This curious blend of organicistic and technocratic conceptions was present in recent BAs. Although the language (but not the organicistic metaphors) was different, those conceptions were also present in communist regimes. But there are important differences between these regimes and DDs. In DDs, parties, the congress, and the press are generally free to voice their criticisms. Sometimes the courts, citing what the executive typically dismisses as "legalistic, formalistic reasons," block unconstitutional policies. Workers' and capitalists' associations often complain loudly. The party (or coalition) that elected the president despairs about its loss of popularity, and refuses parliamentary support for the policies he has "foisted" on them. This increases the political isolation of the president, his difficulties in forming a stable legislative coalition, and his propensity to sidestep, ignore, or corrupt the congress and other institutions.

Here it is necessary to elaborate on what makes representative democracy different from its delegative cousin. Representation necessarily involves an element of delegation: through some procedure, a collectivity authorizes some individuals to speak for it, and eventually to commit the collectivity to what the representative decides. Consequently, representation and delegation are not polar opposites. It is not always easy to make a sharp distinction between the type of democracy which is organized around "representative delegation" and the type where the delegative element overshadows the representative one.

Representation entails accountability: somehow representatives are held responsible for their actions by those they claim to be entitled to speak for. In institutionalized democracies, accountability runs not only vertically, making elected officials answerable to the ballot box, but also horizontally, across a network of relatively autonomous powers (i.e., other institutions) that can call into question, and eventually punish, improper ways of discharging the responsibilities of a given office. Representation and accountability entail the republican dimension of democracy: the existence and enforcement of a careful distinction between the public and the private interests of office holders. Vertical accountability, along with the freedom to form parties and to try to influence public opinion, exists in both representative and delegative democracies. But the horizontal accountability characteristic of representative democracy is extremely weak or nonexistent in delegative democracies. Furthermore, since the institutions that make horizontal accountability effective are seen by delegative presidents as unnecessary encumbrances to their "mission," they make strenuous efforts to hamper the development of such institutions.

Notice that what matters is not only the values and beliefs of officials (whether elected or not) but also the fact that they are embedded in a network of institutionalized power relations. Since those relations may be mobilized to impose punishment, rational actors will calculate the likely costs when they consider undertaking improper behavior. Of course, the workings of this system of mutual responsibility leave much to be desired everywhere. Still, it seems clear that the rulelike force of certain codes of conduct shapes the behavior of relevant agents in representative democracies much more than in delegative democracies. Institutions do matter, particularly when the comparison is not among different sets of strong institutions but between strong institutions and extremely weak or nonexistent ones.

Because policies are carried out by a series of relatively autonomous powers, decision making in representative democracies tends to be slow and incremental and sometimes prone to gridlock. But, by this same token, those policies are usually vaccinated against gross mistakes, and they have a reasonably good chance of being implemented. Moreover, responsibility for mistakes tends to be widely shared. As noted, DD implies weak institutionalization and, at best, is indifferent toward strengthening it. DD gives the president the apparent advantage of having practically no horizontal accountability. DD has the additional apparent advantage of allowing swift policymaking, but at the expense of a higher likelihood of gross mistakes, of hazardous implementation, and of concentrating responsibility for the outcomes on the president. Not surprisingly, presidents in DDs tend to suffer wild swings in popularity: one day they are acclaimed as providential saviors, and the next they are cursed as only fallen gods can be.

Whether it is due to culture, tradition, or historically structured learning, the plebiscitarian tendencies of delegative democracy were detectable in most Latin American (and, for that matter, many postcommunist, Asian, and African) countries long before the present social and economic crisis. This kind of rule has been analyzed as a chapter in the study of authoritarianism, under such names as caesarism, bonapartism, *caudillismo,* populism, and the like. But it should also be seen as a peculiar type of democracy that overlaps with and differs from those authoritarian forms in interesting ways. Even if DD belongs to the democratic genus, however, it could hardly be less congenial to the building and strengthening of democratic political institutions.

IV. Comparisons with the Past

The great wave of democratization prior to the one we are now witnessing occurred after World War II, as an imposition by the Allied powers on defeated Germany, Italy, Japan, and to some extent Austria. The resulting conditions were remarkably different from the ones faced today by Latin America and the postcommunist countries: in the wake of the destruction wrought by the war, the economic expectations of the people probably were very moderate; there were massive injections of capital, principally but not exclusively (e.g., the forgiving of Germany's foreign debt) through the Marshall Plan; and, as a consequence—and assisted by an expanding world economy—the former Axis powers soon achieved rapid rates of economic growth. These were not the only factors at work, but they greatly aided in the consolidation of democracy in those countries. Furthermore, these same factors contributed to political stability and to stable public policy coalitions: it took about twenty years for a change of the governing party in Germany, and the dominant parties in Italy and Japan held sway for nearly half a century.

In contrast, in the transitions of the 1970s and 1980s, reflecting the much less congenial context in which they occurred, victory in the first election after the demise of the authoritarian regime guaranteed that the winning party would be defeated, if not virtually disappear, in the next election. This happened in Spain, Portugal, Greece, Argentina, Bolivia, Brazil, Ecuador, Peru, Uruguay, Korea, and the Philippines. But this pattern appears together with important variations in the social and economic performance of the new governments. Most of these countries inherited serious socioeconomic difficulties from the preceding authoritarian regimes, and were severely affected by the worldwide economic troubles of the 1970s and early 1980s. In all of them, the socioeconomic problems at some point reached crisis proportions and were seen to require decisive government action. Yet however serious the economic problems of the 1970s in Southern Europe may have been, they appear mild when compared to those besetting the newly democratized postcommunist and Latin American countries (with Chile as a partial exception). Very high inflation, economic stagnation, a severe financial crisis of the state, a huge foreign and domestic public debt, increased inequality, and a sharp deterioration of social policies and welfare provisions are all aspects of this crisis.

Again, however, important differences emerge among the Latin American countries. During its first democratic government under President Sanguinetti, the Uruguayan economy performed quite well: the annual rate of inflation dropped from three to two digits, while GNP, investment, and real wages registered gradual increases. The government pursued incremental economic policies, most of them negotiated with congress and various organized interests. Chile under President Aylwin has followed the same path. By contrast,

Argentina, Brazil, and Peru opted for drastic and surprising economic stabilization "packages": the Austral Plan in Argentina, the Cruzado Plan in Brazil, and the Inti Plan in Peru. Bolivia, too, adopted this kind of stabilization package in the 1980s. Although this program—closer than the previously mentioned ones to the prescriptions of the international financial organizations—has been praised for its success in controlling inflation, GNP and investment growth remain anemic. Moreover, the brutality with which worker protests against the program were suppressed hardly qualifies as democratic.

These "packages" have been disastrous. They did not solve any of the inherited problems; rather, it is difficult to find a single one that they did not worsen. Disagreement lingers about whether these programs were intrinsically flawed, or suffered from corrigible defects, or were sound but undone by "exogenous" political factors. However that may be, it is clear that the experience of these failures reinforced the decision by the democratic leaders of Chile to avoid this ruinous road. This makes Uruguay—a country that inherited from the authoritarian regime a situation that was every bit as bad as Argentina's or Brazil's—a very interesting case. Why did the Uruguayan government not adopt its own stabilization package, especially during the euphoria that followed the first stages of the Austral and the Cruzado plans? Was it because President Sanguinetti and his collaborators were wiser or better informed than their Argentinean, Brazilian, and Peruvian counterparts? Probably not. The difference is that Uruguay is a case of *redemocratization*, where Congress went to work effectively as soon as democracy was restored. Facing a strongly institutionalized legislature and a series of constitutional restrictions and historically embedded practices, no Uruguayan president could have gotten away with decreeing a drastic stabilization package. In Uruguay, for the enactment of many of the policies typically contained in those packages, the president must go through Congress. Furthermore, going through Congress means having to negotiate not only with parties and legislators, but also with various organized interests. Consequently, against the presumed preferences of some of its top members, the economic policies of the Uruguayan government were "condemned" to be incremental and limited to quite modest goals such as achieving the decent performance we have seen. Looking at Uruguay and, more recently, Chile one learns about the difference between having or not having a network of institutionalized powers that gives texture to the policymaking process. Or, in other words, about the difference between representative and delegative democracy.

V. The Cycle of Crisis

Now I will focus on some South American cases of delegative democracy—Argentina, Brazil, and Peru. There is no need to detail the depth of the crisis that these countries inherited from their respective authoritarian regimes. Such a crisis generates a strong sense of urgency and provides fertile terrain for unleashing the delegative propensities that may be present in a given country. Problems and demands mount up before inexperienced governments that must operate through a weak and disarticulated (if not disloyal) bureaucracy. Presidents get elected by promising that they—being strong, courageous, above parties and interests, *machos*—will save the country. Theirs is a "government of saviors" *(salvadores de la patria)*. This leads to a "magical" style of policymaking: the delegative "mandate" supposedly bestowed by the majority, strong political will, and technical knowledge should suffice to fulfill the savior's mission—the "packages" follow as a corollary.

The longer and deeper the crisis, and the less the confidence that the government will be able to solve it, the more rational it becomes for everyone to act: (1) in a highly disaggregated manner, especially in relation to state agencies that may help to alleviate the consequences of the crisis for a given group or sector (thus further weakening and corrupting the state apparatus); (2) with extremely short time horizons; and (3) with the assumption that everyone else will do the same. In short, there is a general scramble for narrow, short-term advantage. This prisoner's dilemma is the exact opposite of the conditions that foster both strong democratic institutions and reasonably effective ways of dealing with pressing national problems.

Once the initial hopes are dashed and the first packages have failed, cynicism about politics, politicians, and government becomes the pervading mood. If such governments wish to retain some popular support, they must both control inflation and implement social policies which show that, even though they cannot rapidly solve most of the underlying problems, they do care about the fate of the poor and (politically more important) of the recently impoverished segments of the middle class. But minimal though it may be, this is a very tall order. These two goals are extremely difficult to harmonize, at least in the short run—and for such flimsy governments little other than the short run counts.

Governments like to enjoy sustained popular support, and politicians want to be reelected. Only if the predicaments described above were solvable within the brief compass of a presidential term would electoral success be a triumph instead of a curse. How does one win election and how, once elected, does one govern in this type of situation? Quite obviously—and most destructively in terms of the building of public trust that helps a democracy to consolidate—by saying one thing during the campaign and doing the contrary when in office. Of course, institutionalized democracies are not immune to this trick, but the consequences are more devastating when there are few and weak institutions and a deep socioeconomic crisis afflicts the country. Presidents have gained election in Argentina, Bolivia, Ecuador, and Peru by promising expansionist economic policies and many other good things to come with them, only to enact severe stabilization packages immediately or shortly after entering office. Whatever the merits of such policies for a given country at a given time, their surprise adoption does nothing to promote public trust, particularly if their immediate and most visible impact further depresses the already low standard of living of most of the population.

Moreover, the virtual exclusion of parties and congress from such momentous decisions has several malign consequences. First, when the executive finally, and inevitably, needs legislative support, he is bound to find a congress that is resentful and feels no responsibility for policies it had no hand in making. Second, the congress is further weakened by its own hostile and aloof attitude, combined with the executive's public condemnations of its slowness and "irresponsibility." Third, these squabbles promote a sharp decline in the prestige of *all* parties and politicians, as opinion polls from many Latin American and postcommunist countries abundantly show. Finally, the resulting institutional weakness makes it ever more difficult to achieve the other magical solution when the packages fail: the socioeconomic pact.

VI. From Omnipotence to Impotence

If we consider that the logic of delegation also means that the executive does nothing to strengthen the judiciary, the resulting dearth of effective and autonomous institutions places immense responsibility on the president. Remember that the typical incumbent in a DD has won election by promising to save the country without much cost to anyone, yet soon gambles the fate of his government on policies that entail substantial costs for many parts of the population. This results in policymaking under conditions of despair: the shift from wide popularity to general vilification can be as rapid as it is dramatic. The result is a curious mixture of governmental omnipotence and impotence. Omnipotence begins with the spectacular enactment of the first policy packages and continues with a flurry of decisions aimed at complementing those packages and, unavoidably, correcting their numerous unwanted consequences. This accentuates the anti-institutional bias of DDs and ratifies traditions of high personalization and concentration of power in the executive. The other side of the coin is extreme weakness in making those decisions into effective long-term regulations of societal life.

As noted above, institutionalized democracies are slow at making decisions. But once those decisions are made, they are relatively more likely to be implemented. In DDs, in contrast, we witness a decision-making frenzy, what in Latin America we call *decretismo*. Because such hasty, unilateral executive orders are likely to offend important and politically mobilized interests, they are unlikely to be implemented. In the midst of a severe crisis and increasing popular impatience, the upshot is usually new flurries of decisions which, because of the experience many sectors have had in resisting the previous ones, are even less likely to be implemented. Furthermore, because of the way those decisions are made, most political, social, and economic agents can disclaim responsibility. Power was delegated to the president, and he did what he deemed best. As failures accumulate, the country finds itself stuck with a widely reviled president whose goal is just to hang on until the end of his term. The resulting period of passivity and disarray of public policy does nothing to help the situation of the country.

Given this scenario, the "natural" outcome in Latin America in the past would have been a successful coup d'etat. Clearly, DDs, because of their institutional weaknesses and erratic patterns of policymaking, are more prone to interruption and breakdown than representative democracies. At the moment, however—for reasons mostly linked to the international context, which I cannot discuss here—DDs exhibit a rather remarkable capacity for endurance. With the partial exception of Peru, where the constitutional breakdown was led by its delegative president, no successful coups d'etat have taken place.

The economic policy undertaken by DDs is not always condemned to be widely perceived as a failure, particularly in the aftermath of hyperinflation or long periods of extremely high inflation.[10] This is the case in Argentina today under President Menem, although it is not clear how sustainable the improved economic situation is. But such economic achievements, as well as the more shortlived ones of Collor (Brazil), Alfonsín (Argentina), and García (Peru) at the height of the apparent successes of their economic packages, can lead a president to give the ultimate proof of the existence of a delegative democracy. As long as their policies are recognized as successful by electorally weighty segments of the population, delegative presidents find it simply abhorrent that their terms should be constitutionally limited; how could these "formal limitations" preclude the continuation of their providential mission? Consequently, they promote by means that further weaken whatever horizontal accountability still exists constitutional reforms that would allow their reelection or, failing this, their continuation at the apex of government as prime ministers in a parliamentary regime. Oddly enough, successful delegative presidents, at least while they believe they are successful, may become proponents of some form of parliamentarism. In contrast, this kind of maneuver was out of the question in the cases of the quite successful President Sanguinetti of Uruguay and the very successful President Aylwin of Chile, however much they might have liked to continue in power. Again, we find a crucial difference between representative and delegative democracy.[11]

As noted, among the recently democratized countries of Latin America only Uruguay and Chile, as soon as they redemocratized, revived earlier political institutions that the other Latin American countries (as well as most postcommunist ones) lack. This is the rub: effective institutions and congenial practices cannot be built in a day. As consolidated democracies show, the emergence, strengthening, and legitimation of these practices and institutions take time, during which a complex process of positive learning occurs. On the other hand, to deal effectively with the tremendous economic and social crises faced by most newly democratized countries would require that such institutions already be in place. Yet the crisis itself severely hinders the arduous task of institutionalization.

This is the drama of countries bereft of a democratic tradition: like all emerging democracies, past and present, they must cope with the manifold negative legacies of their authoritarian past, while wrestling with the kind of extraordinarily severe social and economic problems that few if any of the older democracies faced at their inception.

Although this essay has been confined largely to a typological exercise, I believe that there is some value in identifying a new species, especially since in some crucial dimensions it does not behave as other types of democracy do. Elsewhere I have further elaborated on the relationship between DDs and socioeconomic crisis and on related theoretical issues,[12] and I intend to present more comprehensive views in the future. Here I can only add that an optimist viewing the cycles I have described would find that they possess a degree of predictability, thus supplying some ground on which longer-term perspectives could be built. Such a view, however, begs the question of how long the bulk of the population will be willing to play this sort of game. Another optimistic scenario would have a decisive segment of the political leadership recognizing the self-destructive quality of those cycles, and agreeing to change the terms on which they compete and govern. This seems to me practically the only way out of the problem, but the obstacles to such a roundabout but ultimately happy outcome are many.

Notes

1. Terry Lynn Karl and Philippe C. Schmitter, "Modes of Transition and Types of Democracy in Latin America, Southern and Eastern Europe," *International Social Science Journal* 128 (May 1991): 269–84.

2. See Robert A. Dahl, *Polyarchy: Participation and Opposition* (New Haven: Yale University Press, 1971); and Dahl, *Democracy and its Critics* (New Haven: Yale University Press, 1989). I draw further distinctions concerning various characteristics of polyarchies in "On the State, Democratization and Some Conceptual Problems" [chapter 7 of the current book.—*Ed.*]

3. For a more detailed discussion, see my essay "Transitions, Continuities and Paradoxes," in Scott Mainwaring, Guillermo O'Donnell, and J. Samuel Valenzuela,

eds., *Issues in Democratic Consolidation: The New South American Democracies in Comparative Perspective* (Notre Dame, Ind.: University of Notre Dame Press, 1992), pp. 17–56.

4. Adam Przeworski, "Democracy as a Contingent Outcome of Conflicts," in Jon Elster and Rume Slagstad, eds., *Constitutionalism and Democracy* (Cambridge: Cambridge University Press, 1988), pp. 59–80.

5. Wolfgang Streeck and Philippe C. Schmitter, "Community, Market, State—and Associations? The Prospective Contribution of Interest Governance to Social Order," in Wolfgang Streeck and Philippe C. Schmitter, eds., *Private Interest Government: Beyond Market and State* (London: Sage Publications, 1985), pp. 1–29.

6. See James March and Johan Olsen, *Rediscovering Institutions: The Organizational Basis of Politics* (New York: The Free Press, 1989).

7. A prisoner's dilemma exists when, even if all of the agents involved could make themselves better off by cooperating among themselves, it nonetheless proves rational for each of them, irrespective of what the others decide, not to cooperate. In this sense, institutions may be seen as social inventions that serve to make cooperation the rational preference.

8. Arturo Valenzuela, "Latin America: Presidentialism in Crisis," *Journal of Democracy* 4 (October 1993): 17, notes that "all of the countries (except for Paraguay) that drafted new constitutions in the 1980s and early 1990s (Guatemala, El Salvador, Colombia, Ecuador, Peru, Chile, and Brazil) instituted the French system of a *ballotage,* or second round, for presidential races." Of these countries, Guatemala and El Salvador did not qualify as polyarchies, Chile's constitution was a product of the Pinochet regime, and Ecuador, Peru, and Brazil are among the purest cases of DD.

9. Giorgio Alberti has insisted on the importance of *movimientismo* as a dominant feature of politics in many Latin American countries. See his "Democracy by Default, Economic Crisis, and Social Anomie in Latin America" (paper presented to the Twenty-fifth World Congress of Political Science, Buenos Aires, 1991).

10. I discuss these themes in my essay "On the State, Democratization, and Some Conceptual Problems."

11. I do not ignore the important discussions currently underway about various forms of presidentialism and parliamentarism, of which recent and interesting expressions are Scott Mainwaring and Matthew Shugart, "Juan Linz, Presidentialism, and Democracy: A Critical Appraisal," *Journal of Comparative Politics* 29 (July 1997): 449–71; Alfred Stepan and Cindy Skach, "Constitutional Frameworks and Democratic Consolidation: Parliamentarism versus Presidentialism," *World Politics* 46 (October 1993): 1–22; and Arturo Valenzuela, "Latin America: Presidentialism." In the present text I discuss patterns that are independent of those institutional factors, although they may be convergent in their consequences. Clearly, presidentialism has more affinity with DD than parliamentarism. However, if delegative propensities are strong in a given country, the workings of a parliamentary system could be rather easily subverted or lead to impasses even worse than the ones discussed here.

12. I must refer again to "On the State, Democratization, and Some Conceptual Problems" (chapter 7 of the current book)—*Ed.*

9

Illusions about Consolidation

Democracies used to be few in number, and most were located in the northwestern quarter of the world. Over the last two decades, however, many countries have rid themselves of authoritarian regimes. There are many variations among these countries. Some of them have reverted to new brands of authoritarianism (even if from time to time they hold elections), while others have clearly embraced democracy. Still others seem to inhabit a gray area; they bear a family resemblance to the old established democracies, but either lack or only precariously possess some of their key attributes. The bulk of the contemporary scholarly literature tells us that these "incomplete" democracies are failing to become consolidated, or institutionalized.

This poses two tasks. One is to establish a cutoff point that separates all democracies from all nondemocracies. This point's location depends on the questions we ask, and so is always arbitrary. Many definitions of democracy have been offered.[1] The one that I find particularly useful is Robert Dahl's concept of "polyarchy." Once a reasonably well-delimited set of democracies

This paper was first published in *Journal of Democracy* 7 (no. 2, April 1996): 34–51. It generated a debate, printed in the subsequent issue. See Richard Gunther, P. Nikiforos Diamandouros, and Hans-Jürgen Puhle, "O'Donnell's 'Illusions': A Rejoinder," and Guillermo O'Donnell, "Illusions and Conceptual Flaws," *Journal of Democracy* 7 (no. 4): 151–59 and 160–68, respectively.

An earlier version of this essay was presented at a conference on "Consolidating Third World Democracies: Trends and Challenges," held August 27–30, 1995 in Taipei, Taiwan, under the auspices of the Institute for National Policy Research of Taipei and the International Forum for Democratic Studies of Washington, D.C. The author wishes to thank Michael Coppedge, Gabriela Ippolito-O'Donnell, Scott Mainwaring, Sebastián Mazzuca, Peter Moody, Gerardo Munck, and Adam Przeworski for their comments on the earlier version.

is obtained, the second task is to examine the criteria that a given stream of the literature uses for comparing cases within this set. If the criteria are found wanting, the next step is to propose alternative concepts for these comparisons. This is what I attempt here, albeit in preliminary and schematic fashion.

Contemporary Latin America is my empirical referent, although my discussion probably also applies to various newly democratized countries in other parts of the world. The main argument is that, contrary to what most of current scholarship holds, the problem with many new polyarchies is not that they lack institutionalization. Rather, the way in which political scientists usually conceptualize some institutions prevents us from recognizing that these polyarchies actually have two extremely important institutions. One is highly formalized, but intermittent: elections. The other is informal, permanent, and pervasive: particularism (or clientelism, broadly defined). An important fact is that, in contrast to previous periods of authoritarian rule, particularism now exists in uneasy tension with the formal rules and institutions of what I call the "full institutional package" of polyarchy. These arguments open up a series of issues that in future publications I will analyze with the detail and nuance they deserve. My purpose at present is to furnish some elements of what I believe are needed revisions in the conceptual and comparative agenda for the study of all existing polyarchies, especially those that are *informally institutionalized.*[2]

Polyarchy, as defined by Dahl, has seven attributes: (1) elected officials; (2) free and fair elections; (3) inclusive suffrage; (4) the right to run for office; (5) freedom of expression; (6) alternative information; and (7) associational autonomy.[3] Attributes 1 to 4 tell us that a basic aspect of polyarchy is that elections are inclusive, fair, and competitive. Attributes 5 to 7 refer to political and social freedoms that are minimally necessary not only during but also between elections as a condition for elections to be fair and competitive. According to these criteria, some countries of Latin America currently are not polyarchies: the Dominican Republic, Haiti, and Mexico have recently held elections, but these were marred by serious irregularities before, during, and after the voting.

Other attributes need to be added to Dahl's list. One is that elected (and some appointed) officials should not be arbitrarily terminated before the end of their constitutionally mandated terms (Peru's Alberto Fujimori and Russia's Boris Yeltsin may have been elected in fair elections, but they abolished polyarchy when they forcefully closed their countries' congresses and fired their supreme courts). A second addition is that the elected authorities should not be subject to severe constraints, vetoes, or exclusion from certain policy domains by other, nonelected actors, especially the armed forces.[4] In this sense, Guatemala and Paraguay, as well as probably El Salvador and Honduras, do not qualify as polyarchies.[5] Chile is an odd case, where restrictions of this sort are part of a constitution inherited from the authoritarian regime. But Chile clearly meets Dahl's seven criteria of polyarchy. Peru is another doubtful case, since the 1995 presidential elections were not untarnished, and the armed forces retain tutelary powers over various policy areas. Third, there should be an uncontested national territory that clearly defines the voting population.[6] Finally, an appropriate definition of polyarchy should also include an intertemporal dimension: the generalized expectation that a fair electoral process and its surrounding freedoms will continue into an indefinite future.

These criteria leave us with the three polyarchies—Colombia, Costa Rica, and Venezuela—whose origins date from before the wave of democratization that began in the mid-1970s, and with nine others that resulted from this wave: Argentina, Bolivia, Brazil, Ecuador, Nicaragua, Panama, Uruguay, and, with the caveats noted, Chile and Peru. Only in the oldest Latin American polyarchy (Costa Rica) and in two cases of redemocratization (Chile and Uruguay) do the executive branch, congress, parties, and the judiciary function in a manner that is reasonably close to their formal institutional rules, making them effective institutional knots in the flow of political power and policy. Colombia and Venezuela used to function like this, but do so no longer. These two countries, jointly with Argentina, Bolivia, Brazil, Ecuador, Nicaragua, Panama, and Peru—a set that includes a large majority of the Latin American population and GNP—function in ways that current democratic theory has ill prepared us to understand.

We must go back to the definition of polyarchy. This definition, precise in regard to elections (attributes 1 to 4) and rather generic about contextual freedoms (attributes 5 to 7) is mute with respect to institutional features such as parliamentarism or presidentialism, centralism or federalism, majoritarianism or consensualism, and the presence or absence of a written constitution and judicial review. Also, the definition of polyarchy is silent about important but elusive themes such as if, how, and to what degree governments are responsive or accountable to citizens between elections, and the degree to which the rule of law extends over the country's geographic and social terrain.[7] These silences are appropriate: the definition of polyarchy, let us recall, establishes a crucial cutoff point—one that separates cases where there exist inclusive, fair, and competitive elections and basic accompanying freedoms from all others, including not only unabashed authoritarian regimes but also countries that hold elections but lack some of the characteristics that jointly define polyarchy.

Among polyarchies, however, there are many variations. These differences are empirical, but they can also be normatively evaluated, and their likely effect on the survival prospects of each polyarchy may eventually be assessed. These are important issues that merit some conceptual clarification.

By definition, all the Latin American cases that I have labeled polyarchies are such because of a simple but crucial fact: elections are institutionalized. By an institution I mean a regularized pattern of interaction that is known, practiced, and accepted (if not necessarily approved) by actors who expect to continue interacting under the rules sanctioned and backed by that pattern.[8] Institutions are typically taken for granted, in their existence and continuity, by the actors who interact with and through them. Institutions are "there," usually unquestioned regulators of expectations and behavior. Sometimes, institutions become complex organizations: they are supposed to operate under highly formalized and explicit rules, and materialize in buildings, rituals, and officials. These are the institutions on which both "prebehavioral" and most of contemporary neoinstitutionalist political science focus. An unusual characteristic of elections *qua* institutions is that they are highly formalized by detailed and explicit rules, but function intermittently and do not always have a permanent organizational embodiment.

In all polyarchies, old and new, elections are institutionalized, both in themselves and in the reasonable[9] effectiveness of the surrounding conditions of freedom of expression, access to alternative information, and associational autonomy. Leaders and voters take for granted that in the future, inclusive, fair, and competitive elections will take place as legally scheduled, voters will be properly registered and free from physical coercion, and their votes will be counted fairly. It is also taken for granted that the winners will take office, and will not have their terms arbitrarily terminated. Furthermore, for this electoral process to exist, freedom of opinion and of association (including the freedom to form political parties) and an uncensored media must also exist. Countries where elections do not have these characteristics do not qualify as polyarchies.[10]

Most students of democratization agree that many of the new polyarchies are at best poorly institutionalized. Few seem to have institutionalized anything but elections, at least in terms of what one would expect from looking at older polyarchies. But appearances can be misleading, since other institutions may exist, even though they may not be the ones that most of us would prefer or easily recognize.

I. Theories of "Consolidation"

When elections and their surrounding freedoms are institutionalized, it might be said that polyarchy (or political democracy) is "consolidated," i.e., likely to endure. This, jointly with the proviso of absence of veto powers over elected authorities, is the influential definition of "democratic consolidation" offered by Juan J. Linz, who calls it a state of affairs "in which none of the major political actors, parties, or organized interests, forces, or institutions consider that there is any alternative to democratic processes to gain power, and no political institution or group has a claim to veto the action of democratically elected decisionmakers. To put it simply, democracy must be seen as the 'only game in town.'"[11] This minimalist definition has important advantages. Still, I see little analytical gain in attaching the term "consolidated" to something that will probably though not certainly endure—"democracy" and "consolidation" are terms too polysemic to make a good pair.

Other authors offer more expanded definitions of democratic consolidation, many of them centered on the achievement of a high degree of "institutionalization."[12] Usually these definitions do not see elections as an institution.[13] They focus on complex organizations, basically the executive, parties, congress, and sometimes the judiciary. Many valuable studies have been conducted from this point of view. By the very logic of their assessment of many new polyarchies as noninstitutionalized, however, these studies presuppose, as their comparative yardstick, a generic and somewhat idealized view of the old polyarchies. The meaning of such a yardstick perplexes me: often it is unclear whether it is something like an average of characteristics observed within the set of old polyarchies, or an ideal type generated from some of these characteristics, or a generalization to the whole set of the characteristics of some of its members, or a normative statement of preferred traits. Furthermore, this mode of reasoning carries a strong teleological flavor. Cases that have not "arrived" at full institutionalization, or that do not seem to be moving in this direction, are seen as stunted, frozen, protractedly unconsolidated, and the like. Such a view presupposes that there are, or should be, factors working in favor of increased consolidation or institutionalization, but that countervailing "obstacles" stymie a process of change that otherwise would operate unfettered.[14] That some of these polyarchies have been in a state of "protracted unconsolidation"[15] for some twenty years suggests that there is something extremely odd about this kind of thinking.

A recently published book on democratic consolidation in Southern Europe is a case in point.[16] This is the first in a series of five volumes, resulting from an eight-year project that involved, as coauthors and discussants, many of the most active and distinguished students of democratization. The introduction (pp. 1–32) and the conclusions (pp. 389–413) by the coeditors and codirectors of the project offer an impressively learned distillation of these extensive scholarly exchanges. These texts are also paradigmatic of the views that I am criticizing. The editors use the concept of "*trajectories* of democratic transitions and consolidations," with which, even though they warn that it "should in no way be understood as implying a deterministic conceptual bias," they intend to "capture and highlight the particular combination and interplay of freedom and constraint *at each successive stage of the democratization process*"

(p. xvi, emphasis added). Further on, they state, "We regard *continued move-ment towards the ideal type of democratic consolidation* as very significant" (p. 9, emphasis added). Consistent with this view, most of Latin America—in con-trast to Southern European countries that the authors say became consoli-dated democracies in part because they "leap-frogged" democratization and developmental *stages*—is seen as "*still* struggling with transitional problems of varying, and often major, magnitude and intensity" (p. xiv–xvi, emphasis added). An exception is Chile, where the transition is "*moving to-wards consolidation*" (p. 19, emphasis added), and "seems to be *well on its way to successful completion*" (p. 389, emphasis added). The Southern European countries, after achieving consolidation, are said to be entering yet another stage of "democratic persistence," which is the "end product of a long demo-cratization process" (p. xiii).

One way or the other, polyarchies that are seen as unconsolidated, non-institutionalized, or poorly institutionalized are defined negatively, for what they lack: the type and degree of institutionalization presumably achieved by old polyarchies. Yet negative definitions shift attention away from building typologies of polyarchies on the basis of the specific, positively described traits of each type.[17] Such typologies are needed, among other purposes, for assessing each type's likelihood of endurance, for exploring its patterns of change, and for clarifying the various dimensions on which issues of quality and performance of polyarchy may be discussed and researched. There is no theory that would tell us why and how the new polyarchies that have institu-tionalized elections will "complete" their institutional set, or otherwise be-come "consolidated." All we can say at present is that, as long as elections are institutionalized, polyarchies are likely to endure. We can add the hypothesis that this likelihood is greater for polyarchies that are formally institutional-ized. But this proposition is not terribly interesting unless we take into ac-count other factors that most likely have strong independent effects on the survival chances of polyarchies.[18] Consequently, calling some polyarchies "consolidated" or "highly institutionalized" may be no more than saying that they are institutionalized in ways that one expects and of which one ap-proves. Without a theory of how and why this may happen, it is at best pre-mature to expect that newer polyarchies will or should become "consoli-dated" or "highly institutionalized." In any event, such a theory can only be elaborated on the basis of a positive description of the main traits of the perti-nent cases.

II. The Importance of Informal Rules

Polyarchy is the happy result of centuries-long processes, mostly in countries in the global Northwest. In spite of many variations among these countries, polyarchy is embodied in an institutional package: a set of rules and institutions (many of them complex organizations) that is explicitly formalized in constitutions and auxiliary legislation. Rules are supposed to guide how individuals in institutions, and individuals interacting with institutions, behave. The extent to which behavior and expectations hew to or deviate from formal rules is difficult to gauge empirically. But when the fit is reasonably close, formal rules simplify our task; they are good predictors of behavior and expectations. In this case, one may conclude that all or most of the formal rules and institutions of polyarchy are fully, or close to fully, institutionalized.[19] When the fit is loose or practically nonexistent, we are confronted with the double task of describing actual behavior and discovering the (usually informal) rules that behavior and expectations do follow. Actors are as rational in these settings as in highly formalized ones, but the contours of their rationality cannot be traced without knowing the actual rules, and the common knowledge of these rules, that they follow. One may define this situation negatively, emphasizing the lack of fit between formal rules and observed behavior. As anthropologists have long known, however, this is no substitute for studying the actual rules that are being followed; nor does it authorize the assumption that somehow there is a tendency toward increasing compliance with formal rules. This is especially true when informal rules are widely shared and deeply rooted; in this case, it may be said that these rules (rather than the formal ones) are highly institutionalized.[20]

To some extent this also happens in the old polyarchies. The various laments, from all parts of the ideological spectrum, about the decay of democracy in these countries are largely a consequence of the visible and apparently increasing gap between formal rules and the behavior of all sorts of political actors. But the gap is even larger in many new polyarchies, where the formal rules about how political institutions are supposed to work are often poor guides to what actually happens.

Many new polyarchies do not lack institutionalization, but a fixation on highly formalized and complex organizations prevents us from seeing an extremely influential, informal, and sometimes concealed institution: clientelism and, more generally, particularism. For brevity's sake, I will put details and nuances aside[21] and use these terms to refer broadly to various sorts of nonuniversalistic relationships, ranging from hierarchical particularistic exchanges, patronage, nepotism, and favors to actions that, under the formal rules of the institutional package of polyarchy, would be considered corrupt.[22] Particularism—like its counterparts, neopatrimonial[23] and delegative conceptions and practices of rule—is antagonistic to one of the main aspects of the full institutional package of polyarchy: the behavioral, legal, and normative distinction between a public and a private sphere. This distinction is an important aspect of the formal institutionalization of polyarchy. Individuals performing roles in political and state institutions are supposed to be guided not by particularistic motives but by universalistic orientations to some version of the public good. The boundaries between the public and the private are often blurred in the old polyarchies, but the very notion of the boundary is broadly accepted and, often, vigorously asserted when it seems breached by public officials acting from particularistic motives. Where particularism is pervasive, this notion is weaker, less widely held, and seldom enforced.

But polyarchy matters, even in the institutional spheres that, against their formal rules, are dominated by particularism. In congress, the judiciary, and some actions of the executive, rituals and discourses are performed as if the formal rules were the main guides of behavior. The consequences are twofold. On one side, by paying tribute to the formal rules, these rituals and discourses encourage demands that these rules be truly followed and that public-oriented governmental behavior prevail. On the other side, the blatant hypocrisy of many of these rituals and discourses breeds cynicism about the institutions of polyarchy, their incumbents, and "politicians" in general. As long as this second consequence is highly visible, particularism is taken for granted, and practiced as the main way of gaining and wielding political power. In such polyarchies, particularism is an important part of the regime.[24] Polyarchies are regimes, but not all polyarchies are the same kind of regime.

Here we see the ambiguity of the assertion made by Juan J. Linz, Adam Przeworski,[25] and others who argue that consolidation occurs when democracy becomes "the only game in town." It is clear that these authors are referring to the formal rules of polyarchy. More generally, even though they may not refer to "institutionalization," authors who limit themselves to the term "consolidation" also assert, more or less implicitly, the same close fit between formal rules and actual behavior.[26] For example, Przeworski argues that democratic consolidation occurs "when no one can imagine acting outside the democratic institutions." But this does not preclude the possibility that the games played "inside" the democratic institutions are different from the ones dictated by their formal rules. Przeworski also states: "To put it somewhat more technically, democracy is consolidated when compliance—acting within the institutional framework—constitutes the equilibrium of the decentralized strategies of all the relevant forces."[27] Clearly, Przeworski is assuming that there is only one equilibrium, the one generated by a close fit between formal rules and behavior. Yet however inferior they may be in terms of performances and outcomes that we value, the situations that I am describing may constitute an equilibrium, too.[28]

III. A Theoretical Limbo

If the main criterion for democratic consolidation or institutionalization is more or less explicitly a reasonably close fit between formal rules and actual behavior, then what of countries such as Italy, Japan, and India? These are long-enduring polyarchies where, by all indications, various forms of particularism are rampant. Yet these cases do not appear problematic in the literature I am discussing. That they are listed as "consolidated" (or, at least, not listed as "unconsolidated") suggests the strength—and the inconsistency—of this view. It attaches the label "consolidated" to cases that clearly do not fit its arguments but that have endured for a significantly longer period than the new polyarchies have so far. This is a typical paradigmatic anomaly. It deals with these cases by relegating them to a theoretical limbo,[29] as if, because they are somehow considered to be "consolidated," the big gaps between their formal rules and behavior were irrelevant. This is a pity, because variations that are theoretically and empirically important for the study of the whole set of existing polyarchies are thereby obscured.

Another confusing issue is raised by the requirement of "legitimacy" that some definitions of consolidation add. Who must accept formal democratic rules, and how deep must this acceptance run? Here, the literature oscillates between holding that only certain leaders need adhere to democratic principles and arguing that most of the country's people should be democrats, and between requiring normative acceptance of these principles and resting content with a mere perception that there is no feasible alternative to democracy. The scope of this adherence is also problematic: Is it enough that it refers to the formal institutions of the regime, or should it extend to other areas, such as a broadly shared democratic political culture?

Given these conceptual quandaries, it is not surprising that it is impossible clearly to specify when a democracy has become "consolidated." To illustrate this point, consider the "tests" of democratic consolidation that Gunther et al., propose.[30] These tests supposedly help them to differentiate the consolidated Southern European cases from the unconsolidated Latin American, as well as East European and Asian, ones. The indicators that "may constitute evidence that a regime is consolidated" are: (1) "alternation in power between former rivals";[31] (2) "continued widespread support and stability during times of extreme economic hardship"; (3) "successful defeat and punishment of a handful of strategically placed rebels"; (4) "regime stability in the face of a radical restructuring of the party system"; and (5) "the absence of a politically significant antisystem party or social movement."

With respect to Latin America, it bears commenting in relation to each of these points that: (1) alternations in government through peaceful electoral processes have occurred in Latin America as frequently as in Southern Europe; (2) in the former, support for regime stability has persisted—in Argentina, Brazil, and Bolivia, among other countries—even in the face of far more acute recessions than Southern Europe has seen, and in the midst of quadruple-digit inflation; (3) the record of punishment is poor, albeit with important exceptions in both regions; (4) even when thinking about Italy today, it is hard to imagine party system restructurings more radical than the ones that occurred in Bolivia, Brazil, and Ecuador; and (5) "antisystem" political parties are as absent from the Latin American as from the Southern European polyarchies. The indicators of democratic consolidation invoked by these authors (and shared by many others) suffer from extreme ambiguity.[32] Finally, one might note that their argument points toward a *reductio ad absurdum,* for one could in following its logic argue that Latin America's polyarchies are actually "more consolidated" because they have endured more "severe tests" (p. 12) than their Southern European counterparts.

IV. Polyarchies, Particularism, and Accountability

It almost goes without saying that all actual cases exhibit various combinations of universalism and particularism across various relevant dimensions. This observation, however, should not lead to the Procrustean solution of lumping all cases together; differences in the degree to which each case approximates either pole may justify their separate classification and analysis. Of course, one may for various reasons prefer a political process that adheres quite closely to the formal rules of the full institutional package of polyarchy. Yet there exist polyarchies—some of them as old as Italy, India, and Japan, or in Latin America, Colombia, and Venezuela—that endure even though they do not function as their formal rules dictate. To understand these cases we need to know what games are really being played, and under what rules.

In many countries of the global East and South, there is an old and deep split between the *pays réel* and the *pays légal.* Today, with many of these countries claiming to be democracies and adopting a constitutional framework, the persistence and high visibility of this split may not threaten the survival of their polyarchies—but neither does it facilitate overcoming the split. Institutions are resilient, especially when they have deep historical roots; particularism is no exception. Particularism is a permanent feature of human society; only recently, and only in some places and institutional sites, has it been tempered by universalistic norms and rules. In many new polyarchies, particularism vigorously inhabits most formal political institutions, yet the incumbency of top government posts is decided by the universalistic process of fairly counting each vote as one. This may sound paradoxical but it is not; it means that these are polyarchies, but they are neither the ones that the theory of democracy had in mind as it grew out of reflection on the political regimes of the global Northwest, nor what many studies of democratization assume that a democracy should be or become.

That some polyarchies are informally institutionalized has important consequences. Here I want to stress one that is closely related to the blurring of the boundary between the private and the public spheres: accountability, a crucial aspect of formally institutionalized polyarchy, is seriously hindered. To be sure, the institutionalization of elections means that retrospective electoral accountability exists, and a reasonably free press and various active segments of society see to it that some egregiously unlawful acts of government are exposed (if seldom punished). Polyarchy, even if not formally institutionalized, marks a huge improvement over authoritarian regimes of all kinds. What is largely lacking, however, is another dimension of accountability, which I call "horizontal." By this I mean the controls that state agencies are supposed to exercise over other state agencies. All formally institutionalized polyarchies include various agencies endowed with legally defined authority to sanction unlawful or otherwise inappropriate actions by other state agents. This is an often overlooked expression of the rule of law in one of the areas where it is hardest to implant, i.e., over state agents, especially high-ranking officials. The basic idea is that formal institutions have well-defined, legally established boundaries that delimit the proper exercise of their authority, and that there are state agencies empowered to control and redress trespasses of these boundaries by any official or agency. These boundaries are closely related to the private-public boundary, in that those who perform public roles are supposed to follow universalistic and public-oriented rules, rather than their own particular interests. Even though its actual functioning is far from perfect, this network of boundaries and accountabilities is an important part of the formal institutionalization of the full package of polyarchy.[33]

By contrast, little horizontal accountability exists in most new polyarchies. Furthermore, in many of them the executive makes strenuous, and often successful, efforts to erode whatever horizontal accountability does exist. The combination of institutionalized elections, particularism as a dominant political institution, and a big gap between the formal rules and the way most political institutions actually work makes for a strong affinity with delegative, not representative, notions of political authority. By this I mean a caesaristic, plebiscitarian executive that once elected sees itself as empowered to govern the country as it deems fit. Reinforced by the urgencies of severe socioeconomic crises and consonant with old *volkisch*, nonindividualistic conceptions of politics, delegative practices strive headlong against formal political institutionalization; congress, the judiciary, and various state agencies of control are seen as hindrances placed in the way of the proper discharge of the tasks that the voters have delegated to the executive. The executive's efforts to weaken these institutions, invade their legal authority, and lower their prestige are a logical corollary of this view.[34] On the other hand, as Max Weber warned, institutions deprived of real power and responsibility tend to act in ways that seem to confirm the reasons adduced for this deprivation. In the cases that concern us here, particularism becomes even more rampant in congress and parties, courts ostensibly fail to administer justice, and agencies of control are eliminated or reduced to passivity. This context encourages the further erosion of legally established authority, renders the boundary between public and private even more tenuous, and creates enormous temptations for corruption.

In this sea of particularism and blurred boundaries, why does the universalistic process of fair and competitive elections survive? Governments willing to tamper with laws are hardly solid guarantors of the integrity of electoral processes. Part of the answer, at least with respect to elections to top national positions, is close international attention and wide reporting abroad of electoral irregularities. Fair elections are the main, if not the only, characteristic that certifies countries as democratic before other governments and international opinion. Nowadays this certification has important advantages for countries and for those who govern them. Within the country, elections are a moment when something similar to horizontal accountability operates: parties other than the one in government are present at the polling places, sharing an interest in preventing fraud. Elections create a sharp focus on political matters and on the symbols and rituals that surround the act of voting. At this moment, the citizens' sense of basic fairness manifests itself with special intensity. Violations are likely to be immediately reported. Faced with the protests that might ensue and their repercussions in the international media, and considering the further damage that would come from trying to impose obviously tainted results, most governments are willing to run the risks inherent in fair and competitive elections.

Pervasive particularism, delegative rule, and weak horizontal accountability have at least two serious drawbacks. The first is that the generalized lack of control enables old authoritarian practices to reassert themselves.[35] The second is that, in countries that inaugurated polyarchy under conditions of sharp and increasing inequality, the making and implementing of policy becomes further biased in favor of highly organized and economically powerful interests.

In the countries that occupy us here, the more properly political, *democratic* freedoms are effective: uncoerced voting; freedom of opinion, movement, and association; and others already listed. But for large sections of the population, basic *liberal* freedoms are denied or recurrently trampled. The rights of battered women to sue their husbands and of peasants to obtain a fair trial against their landlords, the inviolability of domiciles in poor neighborhoods, and in general the right of the poor and various minorities to decent treatment and fair access to public agencies and courts are often denied. The effectiveness of the whole ensemble of rights, democratic and liberal, makes for full civil and political citizenship. In many of the new polyarchies, individuals are citizens only in relation to the one institution that functions in a manner close to what its formal rules prescribe—elections. As for full citizenship, only the members of a privileged minority enjoy it.[36] Formally institutionalized polyarchies exhibit various mixes of democracy, liberalism, and republicanism (understood as a view that concurs with liberalism in tracing a clear public-private distinction, but that adds an ennobling and personally demanding conception of participation in the public sphere). Informally institutionalized polyarchies are democratic, in the sense just defined; when they add, as they often do, the plebiscitarian component of delegative rule, they are also strongly majoritarian. But their liberal and republican components are extremely weak.

V. Freeing Ourselves from Some Illusions

I have rapidly covered complicated terrain.[37] Lest there be any misunderstanding, let me insist that I, too, prefer situations that get close to real observance of the formal rules of polyarchy, a citizenry that firmly approves democratic procedures and values, fair application of the law in all social and geographical locations, and low inequality. Precisely because of this preference, I have argued for the need to improve our conceptual tools in the complex task of studying and comparing the whole set of existing polyarchies. It is through a nonteleological and, indeed, nonethnocentric, positive analysis of the main traits of these polyarchies that we scholars can contribute to their much needed improvement. This is especially true of the polyarchies that are institutionalized in ways we dislike and often overlook, even if they do not—and some of them may never—closely resemble the "consolidated democracies" of the Northwest.

For this purpose, we must begin by freeing ourselves from some illusions. As an author who has committed most of the mistakes I criticize here, I suspect that we students of democratization are still swayed by the mood of the times that many countries have more or less recently passed through. We believe that democracy, even in the rather modest guise of polyarchy, is vastly preferable to the assortment of authoritarian regimes that it has replaced. We shared in the joy when those regimes gave way, and some of us participated in these historic events. These were moments of huge enthusiasm and hope. Multitudes demanded democracy, and international opinion supported them. The demand for democracy had many meanings, but in all cases it had a powerful common denominator: "Never Again!"[38] Whatever confused, utopian, or limited ideas anyone held concerning democracy, it was clear that it meant getting rid of the despots once and for all. Democracy, even if—or perhaps precisely because—it had so many different meanings attached to it, was the central mobilizing demand that had to be achieved and preserved forever. Somehow, it was felt, this democracy would soon come to resemble the sort of democracy found in admired countries of the Northwest—admired for their long-enduring regimes and for their wealth, and because both things seemed to go together. As in these countries, after the transition democracy was to be stabilized, or consolidated; the Northwest was seen as the endpoint of a trajectory that would be largely traversed by getting rid of the authoritarian rulers. This illusion was extremely useful during the hard and uncertain times of the transition. Its residue is still strong enough to make democracy and consolidation powerful, and consequently pragmatically valid, terms of political discourse.[39] Their analytical cogency is another matter.

On the other hand, because the values that inspired the demands for democracy are as important as ever, the present text is an effort toward opening more disciplined avenues for the study of a topic—and a concern—I share with most of the authors that I have discussed: the quality, in some cases rather dismal, of the social life that is interwoven with the workings of various types of polyarchy. How this quality might be improved depends in part on how realistically we understand the past and present situation of each case.

Notes

1. Reflecting the lack of clearly established criteria in the literature, David Collier and Steven Levitsky have inventoried and discussed the more than one hundred qualifiers that have been attached to the term "democracy." Many such qualifiers are intended to indicate that the respective cases are in some sense lacking the full attributes of democracy as defined by each author. See Collier and Levitsky, "Democracy 'With Adjectives': Conceptual Innovation in Comparative Research," *World Politics* 49 (no. 3): 430–51.

2. I have tried unsuccessfully to find terms appropriate to what the literature refers to as highly versus noninstitutionalized (or poorly institutionalized), or as consolidated versus unconsolidated democracies, with most of the old polyarchies belonging to the first terms of these pairs, and most of the new ones to the second. For reasons that will be clear below, I have opted for labeling the first group "formally institutionalized" and the second "informally institutionalized," but not without misgivings: in the first set of countries, many things happen outside formally prescribed institutional rules, while the second set includes one highly formalized institution, elections.

3. This list is from Robert Dahl, *Democracy and Its Critics* (New Haven: Yale University Press, 1989), p. 221; the reader may want to examine further details of these attributes, discussed by Dahl in this book.

4. See, especially, J. Samuel Valenzuela, "Democratic Consolidation in Post-Transitional Settings: Notion, Process, and Facilitating Conditions," in Scott Mainwaring, Guillermo O'Donnell, and J. Samuel Valenzuela, eds., *Issues in Democratic*

Consolidation: The New South American Democracies in Comparative Perspective (Notre Dame, Ind.: University of Notre Dame Press, 1992), pp. 57–104; and Philippe C. Schmitter and Terry Lynn Karl, "What Democracy Is and Is Not," *Journal of Democracy* 2 (1991): 75–88.

5. See Terry Lynn Karl, "The Hybrid Regimes of Central America," *Journal of Democracy* 6 (1995): 73–86; and "Imposing Consent? Electoralism vs. Democratization in El Salvador," in Paul Drake and Eduardo Silva, eds., *Elections and Democratization in Latin America, 1980–1985* (San Diego: Center for Iberian and Latin American Studies, 1986), pp. 9–36.

6. See, especially, Juan J. Linz and Alfred Stepan, *Problems of Democratic Transition and Consolidation: Southern Europe, South America, and Postcommunist Europe* (Baltimore: Johns Hopkins University Press, 1996); and Philippe Schmitter, "Dangers and Dilemmas of Democracy," *Journal of Democracy* 5 (April 1994): 57–74.

7. For a useful listing of these institutional variations, see Schmitter and Karl, "What Democracy Is and Is Not."

8. For a more detailed discussion of institutions, see Guillermo O'Donnell, "Delegative Democracy," *Journal of Democracy* 5 (January 1994): 56–69 [chapter 8 in the current book.—*Ed.*]

9. The term "reasonable" is admittedly ambiguous. Nowhere are these freedoms completely uncurtailed, if by nothing else than the political consequences of social inequality. By "reasonable" I mean that there are neither de jure prohibitions on these freedoms nor systematic and usually successful efforts by the government or private actors to annul them.

10. On the other hand, elections can be made more authentically competitive by, say, measures that diminish the advantages of incumbents or of economically powerful parties. These are, of course, important issues. But the point I want to make at the moment is that these differences obtain among countries that already qualify as polyarchies.

11. Juan J. Linz, "Transitions to Democracy," *Washington Quarterly* 13 (1990): p. 156. The assertion about "the only game in town" entails some ambiguities that I discuss later in the text.

12. Even though most definitions of democratic consolidation are centered around "institutionalization" (whether explicitly or implicitly, by asserting acceptance or approval of democratic institutions and their formal rules), they offer a wide variety of additional criteria. My own count in a recent review of the literature is twelve; see Doh Chull Shin, "On the Third Wave of Democratization: A Synthesis and Evaluation of Recent Theory and Research," *World Politics* 47 (October 1994): 137–70.

13. Even though he does not use this language, an exception is the definition of democratic consolidation offered by J. Samuel Valenzuela, which is centered in what I call here the institutionalization of elections and the absence of veto powers; see his "Democratic Consolidation in Post-Transitional Settings," p. 69.

14. It is high time for self-criticism. The term "stunted" I used jointly with Scott Mainwaring and J. Samuel Valenzuela in the introduction to our *Issues in Democratic Consolidation*, p. 11. Furthermore, in my chapter in the same volume (pp. 17–56), I offer a nonminimalist definition of democratic consolidation, and propose the concept of a "second transition" from a democratically elected government to a consolidated

democratic regime. These concepts partake of the telelogy I criticize here. This teleological view is homologous to the one used by many modernization studies in the 1950s and 1960s; it was abundantly, but evidently not decisively, criticized at the time. For a critique of the concept of "democratic consolidation" that is convergent with mine, see Ben Ross Schneider, "Democratic Consolidations: Some Broad Comparisons and Sweeping Arguments," *Latin American Research Review* 30 (1995): 215–34; Schneider concludes by warning against "the fallacy of excessive universalism" (p. 231).

15. Philippe C. Schmitter with Terry Lynn Karl, "The Conceptual Travels of Transitologists and Consolidologists: How Far to the East Should They Attempt to Go?" *Slavic Review* 63 (spring 1994): 173–85.

16. Richard Gunther, P. Nikiforos Diamandouros, and Hans-Jürgen Puhle, eds., *The Politics of Democratic Consolidation: Southern Europe in Comparative Perspective* (Baltimore: Johns Hopkins University Press, 1995).

17. We should remember that several typologies have been proposed for formally institutionalized polyarchies; see, especially, Arend Lijphart, *Democracies: Patterns of Majoritarian and Consensus Government in Twenty-One Countries* (New Haven: Yale University Press, 1984). This work has been extremely useful in advancing knowledge about those polyarchies, which underscores the need for similar efforts on the now greatly expanded whole set of polyarchies. For an attempt in this direction see Carlos Acuña and William Smith, "Future Politico-Economic Scenarios for Latin America," in William Smith, Carlos Acuña, and Eduardo Gamarra, eds., *Democracy, Markets, and Structural Reform in Latin America* (New Brunswick: Transaction, 1993), pp. 1–28.

18. Adam Przeworski and his collaborators found that higher economic development and a parliamentary regime increase the average survival rate of polyarchies. These are important findings, but the authors have not tested the impacts of socioeconomic inequality and of the kind of informal institutionalization that I discuss below. Pending further research, it is impossible to assess the causal direction and weight of all these variables. I suspect that high socioeconomic inequality has a close relationship with informal institutionalization. But we do not know if either or both, directly or indirectly, affect the chances of survival of polyarchy, or if they might cancel the effect of economic development that Przeworski et al. found. See Adam Przeworski, Michael Alvarez, José Antonio Cheibub, and Fernando Limongi, "What Makes Democracies Endure?" *Journal of Democracy* 7 (January 1996): 39–55.

19. A topic that does not concern me here is the extent to which formal rules are institutionalized across various old polyarchies and, within them, across various issue areas, though the variations seem quite important on both counts.

20. The lore of many countries is filled with jokes about the naive foreigner or the native sucker who gets in trouble by following the formal rules of a given situation. I have explored some of these issues with reference to Brazil and Argentina in "Democracia en la Argentina: Micro y macro," in Oscar Oszlak, ed., *El "Proceso," crisis y transición democrática* (Buenos Aires: Centro Editor de América Latina, Biblioteca de Política Argentina, 1984) [chapter 3 of the current book—*Ed.*]; in "'And Why Should I Give a Shit?' Notes on Sociability and Politics in Argentina and Brazil" [chapter 5 of the current book—*Ed.*]; and in "Micro-escenas de la privatización de lo público en

Brasil," with commentaries by Roberto DaMatta and J. Samuel Valenzuela (University of Notre Dame, Kellogg Institute Working Paper no. 21, 1989).

21. For the purposes of the generic argument presented in this essay, and not without hesitation because of its vagueness, from now on I will use the term "particularism" to refer to these phenomena. On the contemporary relevance of clientelism, see Luis Roniger and Ayse Gunes-Ayata, eds., *Democracy, Clientelism, and Civil Society* (Boulder: Lynne Rienner, 1994). For studies focused on Latin America that are germane to my argument, see especially Roberto DaMatta, *A casa e a rua: espaco, cidadania, mulher e morte no Brasil* (São Paulo: Editora Brasiliense, 1985); Jonathan Fox, "The Difficult Transition from Clientelism to Citizenship," *World Politics* 46 (January 1994): 151–84; Francis Hagopian, "The Compromised Transition: The Political Class in the Brazilian Transition," in Mainwaring et al., *Issues in Democratic Consolidation*, pp. 243–93; and Scott Mainwaring, "Brazilian Party Underdevelopment in Comparative Perspective," *Political Science Quarterly* 107 (winter 1992–93): 677–707. These and other studies show that particularism and its concomitants are not ignored by good field researchers. But, attesting to the paradigmatic force of the prevalent views on democratization, in this literature the rich data and findings emerging from such case studies are not conceptually processed as an intrinsic part of the *problématique* of democratization, or are seen as just "obstacles" interposed in the way of its presumed direction of change.

22. Particularistic relationships can be found in formally institutionalized polyarchies, of course. I am pointing here to differences of degree that seem large enough to require conceptual recognition. One important indication of these differences is the extraordinary leniency with which, in informally institutionalized polyarchies, political leaders, most of public opinion, and even courts treat situations that in the other polyarchies would be considered as entailing very severe conflicts of interest.

23. For a discussion of neopatrimonialism, see my "Transitions, Continuities, and Paradoxes," in Mainwaring et al., *Issues in Democratic Consolidation*, pp. 17–56. An interesting recent discussion of neopatrimonialism is Jonathan Hartlyn's "Crisis-Ridden Elections (Again) in the Dominican Republic: Neopatrimonialism, Presidentialism, and Weak Electoral Oversight," *Journal of Interamerican and World Affairs* 34 (winter 1994): 91–144.

24. By "regime" I mean "the set of effectively prevailing patterns (not necessarily legally formalized) that establish the modalities of recruitment and access to governmental roles, and the permissible resources that form the basis for expectations of access to such roles," as defined in my *Bureaucratic Authoritarianism: Argentina, 1966–1973, in Comparative Perspective* (Berkeley: University of California Press, 1988), p. 6.

25. Adam Przeworski, *Democracy and the Market: Political and Economic Reforms in Eastern Europe and Latin America* (Cambridge: Cambridge University Press, 1991).

26. See, among many others that could be cited (some transcribed in Shin, "On the Third Wave of Democratization"), the definition of democratic consolidation proposed by Gunther, Diamandouros, and Puhle in *Politics of Democratic Consolidation*, p. 3: "The achievement of substantial attitudinal support for and behavioral compliance with the new democratic institutions and the rules which they establish." A broader but equivalent definition is offered four pages later.

27. Przeworski, *Democracy and the Market*, p. 26.

28. In another influential discussion, Philippe C. Schmitter, although he does not use this language, expresses a similar view of democratic consolidation; see his "Dangers and Dilemmas of Democracy." Schmitter begins by asserting, "In South America, Eastern Europe, and Asia the specter haunting the transition is 'nonconsolidation.' These countries are 'doomed' to remain democratic almost by default." He acknowledges that the attributes of polyarchy may hold in these countries—but these "patterns never quite crystallize" (pp. 60–61). To say that democracy exists "almost by default" (i.e., is negatively defined) and is not "crystallized" (i.e., not formally institutionalized) is another way of stating the generalized view that I am discussing.

29. An exception is Gunther et al., *Politics of Democratic Consolidation*, where Italy is one of the four cases studied. But the way they deal with recent events in Italy is exemplary of the conceptual problems I am discussing. They assert that in Italy "several important partial regimes were challenged, became deconsolidated, and entered into a significant process of restructuring beginning in 1991" (p. 19). On the same page, the reader learns that these partial regimes include nothing less than "the electoral system, party system, and the structure of the state itself." Added to this list later on is "the basic nature of executive-legislative relations" (p. 394). Yet the "Italian democracy remains strong and resilient"—after practically every important aspect of its regime, and even of the state, became 'deconsolidated'" (p. 412). If the authors mean that, in spite of a severe crisis, the Italian polyarchy is likely to endure, I agree.

30. Gunther et al., *The Politics of Democratic Consolidation*, pp. 12–73.

31. Actually, the authors are ambiguous about this first "test." Just before articulating their list of tests with this one at its head, they assert that they "reject [peaceful alternation in government between parties that were once bitterly opposed] as a *prerequisite* for regarding a regime as consolidated." See Gunther et al., *Politics of Democratic Consolidation*, p. 12 (emphasis added).

32. In the text on which I am commenting, the problem is further compounded by the use of categories such as "partial consolidation" and "sufficient consolidation" (which the authors say preceded "full consolidation" in some Southern European cases). They even speak of a stage of "democratic persistence" that is supposed to follow the achievement of "full [democratic] consolidation."

33. I may have sounded naive in my earlier comments about how individuals performing public roles are supposed to be guided by universalistic orientations to some version of the public good. Now I can add that, as the authors of the *Federalist Papers* knew, this is not only, or even mostly, a matter of the subjective intentions of these individuals. It is to a large extent contingent on institutional arrangements of control and accountability, and on expectations built around these arrangements, that furnish incentives (including the threats of severe sanctions and public discredit) for that kind of behavior. That these incentives are often insufficient should not be allowed to blur the difference with cases where the institutional arrangements are nonexistent or ineffective; these situations freely invite the enormous temptations that always come with holding political power. I wish to thank Adam Przeworski and Michael Coppedge for raising this point in private communications.

34. The reader has surely noticed that I am referring to countries that have presi-

dentialist regimes and that, consequently, I am glossing over the arguments, initiated by Juan J. Linz and followed up by a number of other scholars, about the advantages of parliamentarism over the presidentialist regimes that characterize Latin America. Although these arguments convince me in the abstract, because of the very character- istics I am depicting I am skeptical about the practical consequences of attempting to implant parliamentarism in these countries.

35. For analyses of some of these situations, see Paulo Sérgio Pinheiro, "The Legacy of Authoritarianism in Democratic Brazil," in Stuart S. Nagel, ed., *Latin American Development and Public Policy* (New York: St. Martin's Press, 1995), pp. 237–53; and Martha K. Huggins, ed., *Vigilantism and the State in Modern Latin America: Essays on Extralegal Violence* (New York: Praeger, 1991). See also the worrisome analysis, based on Freedom House data, that Larry Diamond presents in his "Democracy in Latin America: Degrees, Illusions, and Directions for Consolidation," in Tom Farer, ed., *Beyond Sovereignty: Collectively Defending Democracy in the Americas* (Baltimore: Johns Hopkins University Press, 1995). In recent years, the Freedom House indices reveal, more Latin American countries have regressed rather than advanced. For a discussion of various aspects of the resulting obliteration of the rule of law and weakening of citizenship, see Guillermo O'Donnell, "On the State, Democratization, and Some Conceptual Problems" [chapter 7 of the current book.—*Ed*].

36. There is a huge adjacent theme that I will not discuss here: the linkage of these problems with widespread poverty and, even more, with deep inequalities of various sorts [see chapter 10 of the current book.—*Ed*].

37. Obviously, we need analyses that are more nuanced, comprehensive, and dy- namic than the one that I have undertaken here. My own list of topics meriting much further study includes: the opportunities that may be entailed by demands for more universalistic and public-oriented governmental behavior; the odd coexistence of per- vasive particularism with highly technocratic modes of decision making in economic policy; the effects of international demands (especially regarding corruption and un- certainty in legislation and adjudication) that the behavior of public officials should conform more closely to the formal rules; and the disaggregation of various kinds and institutional sites of clientelism and particularism. Another major issue that I overlook here, raised by Larry Diamond in a personal communication, is locating the point at which violations of liberal rights should be construed as canceling, or making ineffec- tive, the political freedoms surrounding elections. Finally, Philippe C. Schmitter makes an argument worth exploring when he urges that polyarchies be disaggregated into various "partial regimes"; most of these would surely look quite different when comparing formally versus informally institutionalized cases. See Schmitter, "The Consolidation of Democracy and Representation of Social Groups," *American Behavioral Scientist,* 35 (March–June, 1992): 422–49.

38. This is the title of the reports of the commissions that investigated human rights violations in Argentina and Brazil. For further discussion of what I call a dominant antiauthoritarian mood in the transitions, see my "Transitions, Continuities, and Paradoxes," in Mainwaring et al., *Issues in Democratic Consolidation,* pp. 17–56; and Nancy Bermeo, "Democracy and the Lessons of Dictatorship," *Comparative Politics* 24 (April 1992): 273–91.

39. Symptomatically illustrating the residues of the language and the hopes of the transition as well as the mutual influences between political and academic discourses, on several occasions the governments of the countries that I know more closely (Argentina, Brazil, Chile, and Uruguay) triumphantly proclaimed that their democracies had become "consolidated."

10

Poverty and Inequality in Latin America: Some Political Reflections

The social situation of Latin America is a scandal. In 1990 about 46 percent of Latin Americans lived in poverty. Close to half of these are indigents who lack the means to satisfy very basic human needs. Today there are more poor than in the early 1970s: a total, in 1990, of 195 million, 76 million more than in 1970. These appalling numbers include 93 million indigents, 28 million more than in 1970.[1] The problem is not just *poverty*. Equally important is the sharp increase of *inequality* in most of the region during the 1970s and/or the 1980s;[2] rapid economic growth in some countries in the late 1980s and/or early 1990s has not reversed this trend.[3] The rich are richer, the poor and indigent[4] have increased, and the middle sectors have split between those who have successfully navigated economic crises and stabilization plans and those who have fallen into poverty or are lingering close to the poverty line.

Furthermore, since around 1970 countries that were partial exceptions to the general pattern (Chile and Argentina) have greatly increased their poverty and inequality, in spite of recent years of rapid economic growth. Costa Rica and, to a lesser extent, Uruguay have held their own; only Colombia has improved, but marginally and with higher levels of poverty than the previously mentioned countries. Looking at this matter from another angle, indicators of literacy, infant mortality, and life expectancy have improved.[5] But even in countries that by the 1960s had developed the rudiments of a welfare state

This chapter was first published in Guillermo O'Donnell and Víctor Tokman, eds., *Poverty and Inequality in Latin America* (Notre Dame, Ind.: University of Notre Dame Press, 1998).

The author thanks Vilmar Faria, Gabriela Ippolito-O'Donnell, and Víctor Tokman for their useful commentaries on earlier versions of this text.

(Argentina, Brazil, Chile),[6] the access to, and quality of, social services for the poor have deteriorated. These include health, housing, and the real value of pensions; education is more ambiguous—overall increases in enrollment have been accompanied by numerous indications of the deterioration of the quality of public education, the only one that the poor may hope to access. Of the "welfare pioneer" countries, only Uruguay has escaped the general decay.[7] In Latin America as a whole, the informal sector has grown from 25.6 percent in 1980 to 31.9 percent in the 1990s as a proportion of the nonagrarian work force, while the per capita and family incomes of the informal sector have fallen and its internal segmentation has increased.[8] Finally, but certainly not least, women and children have been and continue to be the most victimized by poverty and impoverishment.[9]

Here I do not deal in any detail with the relevant data.[10] I am a generalist, a political scientist interested in processes of democratization in Latin America and elsewhere. I will limit myself to presenting some broad issues and to proposing some criteria that might contribute, from a political perspective, to the emerging debates on poverty and inequality in Latin America.

Extensive poverty and deep social inequality are characteristics of Latin America that go back to the colonial period. We have not overcome these conditions; we have aggravated them.

One may point out that some problems in some countries did not turn out so badly, especially among those that have registered high rates of economic growth in recent years; but even these countries' present poverty and inequality data look bad indeed when compared with data from the 1960s and early 1970s.[11] Or, as the dominant mood in the 1980s dictated, one may argue that the current increases in poverty and inequality are the unavoidable consequence of correcting past errors. Or one may simply ignore these trends, availing oneself of some of the many mechanisms that human beings invent for justifying their callousness toward others. One way or the other, these stances naturalize poverty and inequality: although different from arguments of centuries past, they still cast poverty and inequality as inevitable consequences of the natural ordering of things. From this point of view, while one may regret some of the visible manifestations of such ordering, it would be senseless, if not worse, to try to change it.[12]

We should begin by recognizing some hard facts:

1. Poverty-generated needs are so many and so vital that one is morally and professionally impelled to alleviate them. But these efforts, and the highly specialized knowledge required, should not detract one from attempting to grasp the overall picture and forging alliances that are premised on broad agreements about a non-naturalized vision of what poverty and inequality are and what might done about them. Of course, remedial action should be praised: in terms of actual human beings it does make a lot of dif-

ference. Also praiseworthy is moral indignation leading to energetic condemnations of the situation and proposals for a much better world—but too often we are not told how to get from here to there, and in the meantime these invocations often include a disparaging tone toward "mere" remedial actions.

2. Somewhere in the middle there are various policy prescriptions, typical of reports of various commissions and international organizations, with which in most cases I agree.[13] These include improving tax collection and making the tax system less regressive; investing more resources in social policies and finding more creative means of cooperation between the state and nongovernmental organizations (NGOs), churches, and business; correctly targeting some social policies; promoting popular participation; and other good ideas that I need not detail here. Although some progress in some policy areas has been registered in some countries, an obvious question is why so little of so much good advice has been actually implemented.

3. The third hard fact is that the poor are politically weak. Their permanent struggle for survival is not conducive, excepting very specific (and usually short-lived) situations and some remarkable individuals, to their organization and mobilization. Furthermore, this weakness opens ample opportunity for manifold tactics of cooptation, selective repression, and political isolation. Democracy makes a difference, in that the poor may use their votes to support parties that are seriously committed to improving their lot. But, if elected, these parties face severe economic constraints. In addition, they must take into account that determined pro-poor policies will mobilize concerns not only among the privileged but also among important segments of the middle class who, after their own sufferings through economic crises and adjustments, feel that it is they who deserve preferential treatment.[14] These concerns, to which I will return, may coagulate in a veto coalition that threatens not only the policy goals of those governments but also whatever economic stability or growth has been achieved.

I. What Can Be Done?

Good intentions and good advice are necessary but not sufficient to redress the appalling problems of poverty and inequality in our countries. The overall political and economic conditions are not congenial to giving top priority to the eradication of poverty and to a significant diminution of inequality. What, then, can be done? There are three time-honored tactics of would-be reformers:

1. *Appeal to the fears of the privileged:* Instead of exit or voice,[15] the all-too-human situation of the poor, particularly the poorest, is silent suffering. But sometimes they angrily rebel. Chiapas is the most spectacular but not the

only recent reminder. Even though nowadays nobody seriously believes in the possibility of a social revolution (which diminishes the effectiveness of this kind of appeal), these episodes give some credence to arguments that the winners should make some "sacrifices" if "everything" is not to explode. This allows at least for the rebellious regions to obtain some new resources from domestic and international agencies. But it is a hard law of policy that these problems disappear from the national agenda soon after the regions in question return to silent suffering. Furthermore, the way these problems are usually dealt with include, in addition to providing some resources, measures such as repression, attempts at coopting (if not murdering) the leaders, splitting the rank and file of the movements, and other niceties.

2. *Appeal to the enlightened self-interest of the privileged:* This consists in arguing that in the medium or long run the privileged themselves will be worse off if they do not begin to address at least some aspects of a given problem right now. A prominent example is the argument (which I believe is correct) that the future growth of the country is severely jeopardized by a work force that lacks the skills to be competitive in the world economy.[16] Except for its effect on altruistic individuals among the privileged, as a general appeal this one tends to get locked into a collective action problem: Why should I sacrifice part of my personal or corporate income for an outcome to which I cannot be sure that others will contribute sufficiently to make it come about?[17] Furthermore, if I am convinced that the grim prognosis of economic stagnation is correct, would not this be a good reason to become wary about keeping my present and future savings or investments in such a country?

Thus, both kinds of appeal may produce some beneficial results, but their overall consequences are deemed to be limited and ambivalent. Notice that both are appeals to the *private* interests of the privileged. Neither is a substitute for the recognition that in redressing poverty and inequality there is a *public* interest that goes well beyond any private interest. The assertion of such a public interest can only be based on the conviction that all human beings share in the same dignity and that they are entitled to freedoms and resources that are denied by the kind of poverty I am discussing here.[18]

II. The Need for a Strong State

I admit that this kind of language is alien to the mood of the present times, not only in Latin America. Worse still, my argument leads toward sharply devalued currencies: politics, politicians, and the state. It is only through politics, in its dialogues and conflicts, that a persuasive and effective argument about the public interest can be built. And it is through the state that such interest can be mobilized and made effective, by its own policies and by the stimulation of concurrent actions by private agents (beginning by extricating them from collective action problems such as the one I depicted above). This means building the kind of state that, with few and partial exceptions, we do not have after the hurricanes of socioeconomic crises, stabilization programs, and various strands of *enragé* antistatism: a strong state. "Strong" does not mean big. By "strong" I mean several interrelated features: a reasonably well-motivated, noncorrupt, and skilled civil service; capacity to formulate and implement policies; openness to, but not colonization by, society; at least some transparency and accountability; and responsiveness to goals and priorities formulated through a democratic political process.[19]

Moisés Naim[20] correctly argues that after the application of economic stabilization policies—which did not demand extensive bureaucratic capabilities—more and more difficult tasks for the state have emerged. Now the challenges of resuming economic growth, especially of putting growth on a sustainable path, require complex and well-calibrated actions by the state. As a consequence, Naim persuasively stresses the need for greatly enhancing the state institutions directly linked with economic policies.

Everything indicates that this need is even greater in relation to the social policies' area of the state. Those who can afford it have extricated themselves from dependence on the state by means of private transportation, private or privatized health and education services, and in some cases private pension plans. On the other hand, the salaries, working conditions, and career prospects of the "street bureaucrats" who typically deliver services to the poor (health workers, teachers, *asistentes sociales*) have greatly deteriorated. The same is true of officials in the central bureaucracies, national and especially local, of the social policy apparatus. Admittedly these areas of the state have often been bastions of clientelism and inefficiency. But the *blitzkrieg* conducted against them for deficit-reducing purposes or out of sheer antistatism has done nothing to improve their performance.[21] To the contrary, in several countries this offensive has practically amputated the arm of the state that is most needed for implementing reasonably effective social policies. The problem is compounded by the high motivation and varied skills that are required for effective performance by state agents in the delivery of these services.[22]

It says a lot about actual policy priorities that, while in several countries efforts have been recently made to enhance the economic policymaking area of the state, to my knowledge no effort, except for Chile, has been made in relation to the social policy area of the state. Despite overwhelming evidence to the contrary, the belief that the market will take good care of everything, including the poor, still seems to hold the upper hand.

I finish this section with a piece of advice similar to the policy prescriptions I mentioned above: devote serious attention and necessary resources to strengthening the social area of the state; this will have beneficial effects in itself and may generate new and more effective paths of cooperation between the state and private agents.

Anyone driving around a large city in the United States realizes how difficult it is, in spite of more favorable conditions than in Latin America, to eradicate poverty.[23] Also, since the 1980s inequality has increased in most Organization for Economic Cooperation and Development (OECD) countries, especially in those, such as Great Britain, New Zealand, and the United States, that followed neoliberal economies policies, akin to the ones most of Latin America has adopted since that same period.[24] Even without considering how much deeper and more ingrained poverty and inequality are in Latin America, these are sobering references. What can we really hope for, and in what time span?

As noted above, the sheer dimension and complexity of raising our countries to decent levels of social welfare, encourage—with important help from conservative ideologies, some of them dressed as scientific economic arguments—the naturalization of these problems. In view of this, it is tempting to adopt the posture of an unflagging optimist: because it is too unwieldy, forget the overall picture; concentrate, in policy and academic circles, on topical policies and their eventual successes and dismiss as "pessimists" those who insist on also looking at the overall picture. This "optimism" is helpful, because it stimulates and lends broader justification to the remedial actions I praised above. But I would like to insist that we need to keep the overall situation very much in mind. Whatever optimism we feel has to be filtered through the highly structured situation of poverty and inequality that, both for historical and contemporary reasons, we are facing.

III. A Dualistic Scenario

I have just begged a huge question: What is this "overall picture"? Here I will limit myself to sketchily mentioning some characteristics that seem to me particularly relevant. They are the expression of what Altimir[25] calls a historical pattern of development that is "structurally disequilibrated and socially exclusionary." This may be summarized by an image that has been frequently used by students of Latin America: dualism. Many countries have been dualist since colonial times; others that were not, such as Argentina and Chile, became dualist in the last two decades; only Costa Rica and Uruguay do not fit this category. The idea of dualism points to the coexistence of two worlds within the same national boundaries. One is the world of the rich, as well as of the segments of the middle class and the working class that have been able to attain reasonable levels of income, education, housing, personal security, and related goods. The other is the world of the dispossessed, composed predominantly, but not exclusively, of the poor as classified by the studies to which I have referred. These are not worlds apart. They are closely inter-linked. They cannot be understood without taking into account these link-ages—among others, the relationships between the formal and the informal sectors studied by the authors already cited and the massive presence of indi-gents in the cities that the rich also inhabit are two among many other possi-ble examples.

The numbers of the poor have increased. Also, although we do not know the exact numbers, many others hover above the low line that defines the up-per limit of poverty. These are segments of the middle class or of the old working class at risk of falling into a category that the social disasters of the last two decades invited sociologists to invent: the "new poor." This is well known. Perhaps less notorious is that the privileged are, so to speak, moving away. The contrast between the amount and the quality of the goods and ser-vices they enjoy and those of the poor is bigger and more evident than ever. Furthermore, in a world that is rapidly globalizing, the poor cannot do much more than contemplate consumption booms that, following a Latin American tradition, make our rich even more ostentatious than those in the countries of origin of the goods and services that our rich enjoy. Aside from this contem-plation, what the poor receive from globalization, and from the way require-ments for national competitiveness in a global economy are usually read, are damaging fiscal policies and labor reforms whose likely effect on them is far from clearly beneficial. To what extent this situation will lead to popular rebellions based on unmet expectations or will reinforce patterns of social ex-clusion and individual anomie is a moot question that I do not have the ele-ments, theoretical and empirical, to answer here.

As Tokman argues,[26] actions that seriously tackle poverty and inequality can only be based on an effective solidarity. This, in turn, can only be based on recognizing the basic duty of, to name it somehow, human decency toward all individuals. The sharp, and deepening, dualism of our countries severely hinders the emergence of broad and effective solidarity. Social distances have increased, and the rich tend to isolate themselves from the strange and dis-quieting world of the dispossessed. The fortified ghettos of the rich and the secluded schools of their children bear witness to their incorporation into the transnationalized networks of modernity, as well as of the gulf that separates them from large segments of the national population.[27]

IV. Room for Improvement

So, what can be done? Not much, I am afraid, in terms of changing the overall situation, at least in the short and medium term. A lot in terms of concrete

remedial actions, not only because of how much difference they make to concrete individuals but also because they are a source of learning that, with
proper precautions, can be usefully disseminated. And we should not underestimate what can be achieved by stubbornly hammering away with policy
proposals and with data about the overall situation.

There are some things we could arguably do better.

1. Analyze more systematically and comparatively public and private social policies (including some of the many that, one may suspect, have as yet
gone unregistered) to increase learning and potential for dissemination.

2. As noted above, one puzzling question is why so much good general
policy advice is not being heeded. I believe that this is in part because we
have not sufficiently worked out potential tradeoffs between those policies
and, especially, the extent to which their implementation may require changes
in the content and general orientation of current economic policies. This is a
very important intellectual task. At this moment I would offer a general sug-
gestion: it is high time that social policy regain some autonomy in relation to
economic policy. No reasonable person disputes today that responsible and
skilled economic policymaking is needed, even for effectiveness in social areas. But in recent times economic policy has completely ignored the social
dimension or has addressed this dimension exclusively in terms of its (narrowly defined) economic implications. At best, economic policy has paid attention to social issues when they seemed to threaten the achievement of economic goals. No decent society was ever built on such a unilateral basis. In
particular, after the depths of economic crises have been (one hopes) left behind, there is no reason to keep treating the social dimension as the *pariente
pobre* [poor relation] of the economic one. Of course, this plea will be dis-
missed by some as an excuse for "economic irresponsibility." Persuading
them that this is not the case, and that in the medium and long run a socially
more balanced situation will be helpful even for economic growth, is a very
important political task.

3. Since *lo mejor es enemigo de lo bueno* [the best is the enemy of the good]
and since economic and political constraints do exist, I do not argue for an immediate and full-fledged enhancement of the state's social policy apparatus.
Through a political process that is open to many voices, the poor somehow
included, some policy areas should be chosen because of their particular importance or urgency and because they seem amenable both to effective results
and to learning-disseminating consequences. Among these it would be a
good idea to include programs that promise fruitful interactions with private
agents—NGOs, churches, foundations, and business, especially. In all cases, it
is necessary to invest in the enhancement of the bureaucratic agencies that
will be involved and in finding out what the intended beneficiaries really ex-

pect and want. The designers of these policies should make sure to create op-portunities for exchanging experiences with participants in similar or conver-gent programs and for truly independent and skilled evaluations.

Enormous social energy, political skill, and intellectual clarity are needed for progress in these directions. Altruistic individuals find in themselves the main resource and motivation for these actions. As we saw, their efforts may find support from appeals to fear and/or to enlightened self-interest. This is a lot but it most likely falls short of getting us, *antes de las Calendas griegas*,[*] to the eradication of indigence and most[28] poverty and to reasonable[29] levels of social (in)equality.

V. Linking Poverty and Democracy

There may be still another possibility. By itself it will not take us to the promised land but, combined with the ones I have discussed (and others that escape me), it may get us closer. I am referring to another typical maneuver of the would-be reformer:[30] *causally link your preferred issue to another one that is likely to attract more support than the former.* Actually this is not new in this pa-per: appealing to fears and to enlightened self-interest are instances of the general rule I have just transcribed. But fear does not appeal to the noblest of human predispositions, and the effectiveness of the appeal is not likely to en-dure after the specific motive has disappeared. Furthermore, insofar as the appeal to self-interest refers to private interests, the consequences are likely to be limited and ambivalent. What I am going to suggest is linking poverty and inequality to something that is, arguably, a public and general interest: democracy.

This, I hasten to add, is rather tricky. To begin with, even if the causal links are carefully worked out (a tall order, indeed), for the argument to be persua-sive one has to really care about democracy. Why should the privileged *really* care? Several answers have been given, none of them guaranteeing that this should be the case:

1. The privileged sectors, particularly but not exclusively business, should care because the demise of democracy will likely lead to a military regime, and the military have proved that they are unreliable allies in supporting, im-plementing, and maintaining "market-oriented" policies.[31] In extreme cases, these regimes may go berserk, terrorizing the whole population and even en-tering into crazy wars.

2. By and large, the present democratic governments are supporting,

---

[*] *Before the Greek Calends*: The Greeks did not reckon time by calends, so to plan to settle one's bills at the Greek Calends means that one will pay at a time that will never arrive.—*Ed.*

implementing, and maintaining policies under which the privileged sectors are faring very well. This includes, for these sectors, better access to policy-making than was the rule under military regimes.[32]

3. There are not, nowadays, serious threats that parties determined to produce a radical overhaul of society will win elections.

4. The present international climate of opinion would make it costlier than it was decades ago to undertake and support the adventure of an authoritarian regression.[33]

5. As I found out watching even strong supporters of our past authoritarian regimes, it is rather embarrassing when abroad to be asked questions such as: "Your country is under some kind of dictatorship, isn't it?" Individuals, particularly those who are members of transnationalized networks, prefer not to be put into the category of belonging to some primitive tribe. Furthermore, part of the international climate of opinion is that international business and political leaders have also learned the scant reliability of armed forces' governments and are at least as satisfied as their domestic counterparts with the current policies of most Latin American governments—more rigorous payments of the external debt, fewer obstacles to profit remittances, financial and commercial liberalization, high domestic interest rates, and privatizations *mediante.*

These are pragmatic reasons, subject to reversal if the contextual conditions that support them change. This is not insignificant, but we should do better, hoping for a more principled commitment to democracy. In this sense one should make the moral and political argument that democracy is grounded on values that dictate a respectful attitude toward the dignity and autonomy of every human being. To the obvious retort that respect for these attributes is not exactly paramount in our new democracies, one can answer that, however deeply imperfect today, since democracy *is* based on those values, it offers better chances than any other regime to make them effective some day.[34] Some contemporary authors, following Schumpeter,[35] define democracy in narrow terms as a mechanism that, through competitive elections, decides who will govern for a given period. I do not agree: if democracy were not also a wager on the dignity and autonomy of individuals, it would lack the extraordinary moral force that it has evinced many times in modern history.

In contemporary Latin America the gap between those values and their effectiveness is extraordinarily wide. But one cannot jump to the conclusion that, per se, this gap will eliminate democracy.[36] India shows that democracy can long survive in the midst of enormous poverty and inequality,[37] and some of our new democracies have endured crises (including rapid impoverishment of broad sectors of the population) that not too long ago would have immediately provoked military coups and/or revolutionary upheavals.

The real issue is the quality of democracy. Citizens are the individual counterparts of a democratic regime. Citizens are supposed to be protected and empowered by the clusters of rights sanctioned by modern constitutionalism. The basis of citizenship is the assumption of the autonomy and, consequently, of the basic equality, of all individuals. Without this assumption even the narrowest definitions of democracy would be senseless: autonomy and equality are presupposed in the act of choosing among competing candidates and in fairly counting each vote as one, irrespective of the social condition of the voter. Effective citizenship is not only uncoerced voting; it is also a mode of relationship between citizens and the state and among citizens themselves. It is a continuing mode of relationship, during, before, and after elections, among individuals protected and empowered by their citizenship. Citizenship is no less encroached upon when voting is coerced than when a battered woman or a peasant cannot hope to obtain redress in court or when the home of a poor family is illegally invaded by the police. In these and related senses, ours are democracies of truncated, or low-intensity, citizenship. In many regions and cities, and for large parts of the population, it is the same old story: *La ley se acata pero no se cumple* [the law is acknowledged but not obeyed]. A corollary of citizenship and a central component of democracy, the rule of law, extends only intermittently across our countries.[38] Widespread violence, weak and unpredictable courts, and unpunished abuses of all sorts of powers, public and private, compound in many parts of Latin America a sense of unpredictability and ugliness in daily life, especially for the losers but also for the winners.[39]

Admittedly, as noted before, many of the rich opt for exit: living in fortified ghettos, sending their children to well-guarded schools where they meet only the children of people like them, moving their offices out of downtown or other dangerous areas, mistrusting the inefficient and often corrupt police and hiring private guards,[40] and making transnational society the frame of reference of as many of their activities as possible. This process is also observable in the United States, but it is my distinct impression that it has advanced much more in Latin America. On the other hand, as suggested by the data of endnote 39 and numerous journalistic reports, the realities of an extremely impoverished and unequal society inexorably filter into the lives of the privileged: fear while going back and forth to work and school, manifold horrors highlighted on TV, the pervasive threats of the drug trade, the fear of kidnapping, and the like invade even the most secluded lives.

Literary talent is needed for depicting these situations. Here I want to point out their profound ambivalence. On one hand, they may lead to further exit, as the privileged sometimes seek added protection by supporting repressive measures against the *classes dangereuses*. This support entails indifference toward the gulf that separates winners and losers and further deterioration of values of solidarity and shared human dignity. Also, despite its many inconveniences, the present situation has important advantages, especially cheap and abundant labor, both at work and at home.[41] There are many, albeit unsystematic, indications that this mix of exit with support for repression may be the direction being taken. In this scenario democracy, narrowly understood as a reasonably competitive and clean electoral process, may survive; but its quality would be dismal.[42]

On the other hand, perception of this bleak scenario may mobilize values and solidarities that could reverse the overall situation. Because nobody can completely extricate him- or herself from the consequences of extended poverty and deep inequality, and because these characteristics deeply offend the values on which democracy is grounded, a general argument for committing oneself to enhancing the quality of these democracies can be derived. As noted above, this argument can be made, through politics, a *public* one only if it is embraced by a broad coalition of social and political forces.

I have noted some of the difficulties that, if created, this coalition is likely to face. For thinking a bit further about this matter, it is useful to note that the image of dualism, like every dichotomy, is a simplification of limited value. It serves to underline the sad fact that there are in our countries two poles and they have been getting farther apart. But this image ignores the layers of the population that do not properly belong at either pole. "Middle sectors" is too diffuse a category for designating these layers, but for want of a better concept I will use it here. The term itself alludes to those who are somewhere in between the truly rich and the truly poor.

Unfortunately, we know too little about these layers, especially after the changes provoked by the economic crises and adjustment programs of the last couple of decades.[43] Assorted indications,[44] however, plausibly suggest that, just as with the rest of society, a strong differentiation has occurred within the middle sectors themselves. Considerable decreases in pensions and in the salaries of public employees, particularly the lower ranking ones, unemployment resulting from privatizations and various "rationalization" programs, high rates of bankruptcy of small enterprises during economic crises and at least during the first phases of economic stabilization, and the deterioration (or disappearance) of various social services to which these sectors had good access have combined to bring about a sharp fall of the income and the standard of living of significant numbers of people in the middle sectors.[45] On the other hand, various indications suggest that some layers, especially those composed by individuals who cater to the rich—highly educated professionals and owners of firms dedicated to luxury goods and services—have notably improved their situation throughout these years. It seems, consequently, that "the middle" has significantly differentiated itself, with some moving toward the poor and some toward the rich poles, while the "middle of the middle" has become thinner. Thus, despite the simplification it entails, the image of dualism still fits Latin America—now better than ever.

Some time ago the Latin American middle sectors were supposed to be the main carriers of social modernization, economic development, and democracy.[46] For reasons I will not delve into here, these hopes were dispelled. I am not aiming at resurrecting these expectations here, but I believe that some layers of the contemporary middle sectors will have to play a pivotal role in any political alliances that effectively attack poverty and inequality. Because poverty entails that the poor are poor in many resources, not only economic, they are unlikely to organize autonomously and, especially, to sustain collective actions appropriate for overcoming their condition. On the other hand, I surmise that the exit option is likely to be preferred by most of the rich. Toward the other pole of the middle, those whose income and welfare have sharply diminished and/or who linger dangerously close to poverty probably are, at best, as likely to support as to oppose policies aimed at improving the situation of the poor.[47]

This leaves us basically with the middle of the middle sectors. Many of the individuals belonging to this category are socially active, politically aware, highly educated, reasonably well informed about the world in which they live, and with strong aspirations of ascending social mobility. Particularly among the young, lack of employment (or of reasonably good employment) and the extremes of poverty and affluence they confront every day may thoroughly alienate them. But, still, those who have the aforementioned characteristics and, consequently, enjoy many of the advantages of modern life but—in terms of housing, transportation, education, health services, and the like—cannot exit as the rich can, seem the more likely to be mobilized by, and mobilize, the kind of political coalition I postulated above.

The structural position of other segments of the middle sectors generates, as I have argued, serious constraints for collectively playing an active role in efforts to redress poverty and, even more so, inequality. But constraints are not impossibilities. They can be partially overcome[48] with clear-headed actions, imaginative policies, persuasive arguments, good examples, and, underlying and reinforcing all this, the emergence of an adequate political coalition. This coalition should have as its dynamic core the valuable if often intermittent collective efforts of the poor, the middle layers referred to above, and the altruists who exist at all levels of the social structure. As soon as it eventually emerges, the coalition will face some hard tests. One will be how to further link itself with the poor with a minimum of clientelism and paternalism. Another test will be to persuade a majority of public opinion, not only the privileged, that the policy orientations of the coalition are not inimical to the stability of basic macroeconomic parameters. A third test relates to the relations of this coalition with the unions. This is a topic in which generalizations across countries, and even across economic sectors and regions, are particularly risky.

With this caveat in mind, it seems clear that, if they were willing to voice the interests of workers in general (i.e., including those who are unemployed and not formally employed), the unions would become a weighty component of the coalition. On the other hand, I fear that, given the social and economic conditions prevailing in Latin America, most of the unions are likely to limit themselves to the defense of the interests of workers employed in the formal sector. In this case the relations between the aforementioned coalition and the unions will be punctuated by serious (albeit, hopefully, not mutually self-destructive) conflicts.

Clearly, the creation and the successful development of the kind of coalition I have sketched is a very tall order.[49] Ultimately the glue of this coalition can only be a moral argument: the decent treatment that is due to every human being. An additional argument is one of public interest: the improvement of the quality of our democracies is tantamount to advancing toward such decency. On the other hand, if the polarizing tendencies I have registered in this text continue unabated, what I have said here may well be a futile exercise in wishful thinking.

Notes

1. Data from CEPAL (Comisión Económica Para América Latina y el Caribe), *Panorama social de América Latina* (Santiago de Chile, 1994), p. 157. Concerning the operational definition of these categories, see Juan Carlos Feres and Arturo León, "The Magnitude of Poverty in Latin America," *CEPAL Review* 41 (August 1990): 133–51, and Oscar Altimir, "Cambios en la desigualdad y la pobreza en la América Latina," *El Trimestre Económico* 241 (1994): 85–134.

2. See Víctor Tokman, "Pobreza y homogenización social: Tareas para los 90," *Pensamiento Iberoamericano* 19 (1991): 81–104, and Tokman, "Pobreza y equidad: Dos objetivos relacionados" (Lima: ILO, 1995, multicopied).

3. As a publication of the International Monetary Fund puts it: "Not only is poverty widespread in Latin America and the Caribbean, it has increased during the past decade. The unequal distribution of income is generally seen to be at the heart of poverty in the region—the bottom 20 percent of the population receive less than 4 percent of total income." See Javed Shahid Burki and Sebastián Edwards, "Consolidating Economic Reforms in Latin America and the Caribbean," *Finance and Development* 32 (no. 1, March 1995): 8.

4. From now on, except when the context requires otherwise, I will apply the generic label of "poor" to both categories. It should be noted that in the CEPAL methodology developed by Altimir and his associates those placed at the upper limit of the operational definition of poverty barely satisfy basic needs. This is even more

true of studies by the World Bank, which established an even lower cutting point of U.S. $60 (1985 U.S. $) per person per month, corrected by a purchasing power parity exchange rate index for each country (World Bank, *World Development Report 1990. Poverty: World Development Indicators* [Washington, D.C.: Oxford University Press, 1990] and World Bank, *Social Indicators of Development 1994* [Baltimore: Johns Hopkins University Press, 1994]). For a useful discussion of these indicators, see Samuel Morley, *Poverty and Inequality in Latin America: Past Evidence, Future Prospects* (Washington, D.C.: Overseas Development Council, 1994).

5. See, among other sources, Eliana Cardoso and Ann Helwege, "Below the Line: Poverty in Latin America," *World Development* 20 (no. 1, January 1992): 19–37; CEPAL, *Panorama social*, and World Bank, *Social Indicators*.

6. See Carmelo Mesa-Lago's classic study, *Social Security in Latin America: Pressure Groups, Stratification, and Inequality* (Pittsburgh: University of Pittsburgh Press, 1978).

7. See CEPAL, *Panorama social*, and CEPAL, *Informe de la Comisión Latinoamericana y del Caribe sobre el desarrollo social* (Santiago de Chile, IDB/CEPAL/UNPD, 1995). Valuable studies of some important social policy areas are found in the following works by Carmelo Mesa-Lago: *Ascent to Bankruptcy: Financing Social Security in Latin America* (Pittsburgh: University of Pittsburgh Press, 1989); *Social Security and Prospects*; and *Health Care for the Poor in Latin America and the Caribbean* (Washington, D.C.: Panamerican Health Organization, 1992).

8. See these works by Víctor Tokman: "Policies for a Heterogeneous Informal Sector in Latin America," *World Development* 17 (no. 37, 1989): 1067–76; "Economic Development and Labor Markets: Segmentation in the Latin American Periphery," *Journal of Interamerican Studies and World Affairs* 31 (1989): 23–47; "Pobreza y homogenización social"; "Informalidad y pobreza: Progreso social y modernización productiva," *El Trimestre Económico* 61 (1994): 177–99. See, in general, the important work of PREALC, an institution that this author led for many years. See also Carlos Filgueira, "América Latina: Tendencias e incertidumbres del desarrollo social" (CIESU, 1993, multicopied), and Cathy A. Rakowski, ed., *Contrapunto: The Informal Sector Debate in Latin America* (Albany: New York University Press, 1994), especially the chapters by Frank, Márquez, de Oliveira and Roberts, and Portes.

9. See, especially, CEPAL, *Panorama social*, and the more general assessments in UNICEF, *The Progress of Nations: The Nations of the World Ranked According to Their Achievements in Health, Nutrition, Education, Family Planning, and Progress for Women* (New York: UNICEF, 1993); UNRISD (United Nations Research Institute for Social Development), *The Crisis of Social Development in the 1990s: Preparing for the World Social Summit* (Geneva: UNRISD, February, 1994); and UNRISD, *States of Disarray: The Social Effects of Globalization* (London: UNRISD, 1995). An analysis of several important issues on this matter is in María de los Angeles Crummet and Marya Buvinic, Symposium on "Women and the Transition to Democracy: The Impact of Political and Economic Reform in Latin America" (Washington, D.C.: Woodrow Wilson International Center for Scholars, Latin American Program, Working Paper 211, 1994).

10. Within a large and diverse literature, in addition to the sources already cited I have found particularly useful the following works by Oscar Altimir: "Development, Crisis and Equity," *CEPAL Review* 41 (August 1990): 7–27; "Income Distribution and

Poverty through Crisis and Adjustment," CEPAL/United Nations Working Paper 15, September 1993; "Cambios en la desigualdad," and "Distribución del ingreso e incidencia de la pobreza a lo largo del ajuste," *Revista de la CEPAL* 42 (April 1994), as well as works by CEPAL, *Informe de la Comisión Latinoamericana*; Louis Emmerij, "Social Tensions and Social Reform in Latin America" (IDB, August 1994, draft, multicopied); Rubén M. Lo Vuolo and Alberto C. Barbeito, *La nueva oscuridad de la política social: del estado populista al neoconservador* (Argentina: Miño and Dávila, 1993); Nora Lustig, "Poverty and Inequality in Latin America: Facts, Issues, and Dilemmas," *Inter-American Dialogue*, 1992; and Lustig, "Coping with Austerity: Poverty and Inequality in Latin America" (Washington, D.C.: Brookings Institute Press, March 1994).

For more detailed studies on Argentina, Brazil, Chile, and Uruguay, I refer to the studies resulting from the Kellogg/CEBRAP "Social Policies" project and printed as special *Democracy and Social Policy Series* working papers by the Kellogg Institute, University of Notre Dame: Juarez R. Brandão Lopes, "Brazil, 1989: A Socioeconomic Study of Indigence and Urban Poverty," Working Paper 7, 1994; Sonia M. Draibe, Maria Helena Guimarães de Castro, and Beatriz Azaredo, "The System of Social Protection in Brazil," Working Paper 3, 1995; Vilmar Faría, "The Current Social Situation in Brazil: Dilemmas and Perspectives," Working Paper 1, 1994; Carlos Filgueira, "Heterogeneity and Urban Poverty in Uruguay," Working Paper 9, 1994; Fernando Filgueira, "A Century of Social Welfare in Uruguay: Growth to the Limit of the Battlista Social State," Working Paper 5, 1995; Laura Golbert and Emilio Tenti Fanfani, "Poverty and Social Structure in Argentina: Outlook for the 1990s," Working Paper 6, 1994; Arturo León Batista, "Urban Poverty in Chile: Its Extent and Diversity," Working Paper 8, 1994; Rubén Lo Vuolo, "The Welfare State in Contemporary Argentina: An Overview," Working Paper 2, 1995; and Dagmar Raczynski, "Social Policies in Chile: Origin, Transformation, and Perspectives," Working Paper 4, 1994.

For overviews of the economics of the period, among others see Albert Fishlow, "Latin American Failure against the Backdrop of Asian Success," *The Annals of the American Academy* 505 (September 1989): 117–28, and Jaime Ros, ed., *La edad de plomo del desarrollo latinoamericano* (Mexico: Instituto Latinoamericano de Estudios Transnacionales/Fondo de Cultura Económica, 1993).

11. The authors cited in the preceding notes disagree as to how effective economic growth per se would be in diminishing poverty—assuming that economic growth may be achieved and sustained for a reasonably long period. But whatever the answer to this question, it is hard to imagine that, even if it is a necessary condition for effectively addressing poverty (not to say anything of inequality, a much harder problem) economic growth will in itself be sufficient without criteria and policies that specifically focus on poverty and inequality. Persuasive arguments along these lines are made by Altimir, "Development, Crisis and Equality"; Atilio Borón, "La pobreza de las naciones: La economía política del neoliberalismo en la Argentina" (Buenos Aires: EURAL, multicopied, 1992); Emmerij, "Social Tensions"; Tokman, "Informalidad y pobreza"; and Tokman, "Pobreza y equidad."

12. For an interesting analysis of the repertoire of arguments supporting the status quo, see Albert O. Hirschman, *The Rhetoric of Reaction* (Cambridge, Mass.: Belknap Press of Harvard University Press, 1991) and Hirschman, "The Rhetoric of Reaction—Two Years Later," *Government and Opposition* 28 (no. 3, 1993): 282–314.

13. With some exceptions, there seems to be widespread agreement that "decentralization" is a good thing. In abstract I agree. But transferring resources to highly inefficient, utterly clientelistic, and often corrupt local administrations reinforces circuits of power that worsen the problems that decentralization is supposed to address. On the other hand, "decentralization" by way of transferring responsibilities to local administrations without the necessary resources has been an effective, if somewhat cynical and in the medium run counterproductive, way of showing "progress" in the reduction of national fiscal deficits.

14. For a discussion of this scenario, see Joan Nelson, "Poverty, Equity, and the Politics of Adjustment," in Haggard and Kaufman, eds., *Politics of Economic Adjustment* (Princeton: Princeton University Press, 1992), pp. 221–69.

15. Albert O. Hirschman, *Exit, Voice, and Loyalty: Responses to Decline in Firms, Organizations, and States* (Cambridge, Mass.: Harvard University Press, 1970).

16. Although the results are open to methodological dispute, there is some evidence that inequality is inimical to economic growth (e.g., Edward N. Muller, "Democracy, Economic Development, and Income Inequality," *American Sociological Review* 53 (no. 1, February 1988): 50–68. This theme has attracted the attention of mainstream economists in view of the economic successes of the rather egalitarian "East Asian Tigers," especially after the report on these countries by the World Bank (World Bank, *The East Asian Miracle: Economic Growth and Public Policy* [New York: Oxford University Press, 1993]). Among the discussions that this report has provoked, see Albert Fishlow, Catherine Gwin, Stephan Haggard, Dani Rodrik, and Robert Wade, *Miracle or Design? Lessons from the East Asian Experience* (Washington, D.C.: Overseas Development Council, 1994) and, from a different angle, Paul Streeten, *Strategies for Human Development* (Copenhagen: Handelshojkolens Forlag, 1994), and Cynthia Hewitt de Alcántara, ed., *Real Markets: Social and Political Issues of Food Policy Reform* (Geneva: UNRISD, 1993). But it is very difficult to assess the impact of equality independently from other facts that seem just as likely to have fostered those economic successes.

17. This remark does not ignore the fact that, whether out of altruism, enlightened self-interest, technological need, or a combination of these, some enterprises do take care of adequately training, and retaining, some of their workers. This is excellent for both these enterprises and workers, but it includes only a small proportion of the work force.

18. For recent discussions on this matter by economists who would not usually be classified as "soft-headed" (as moralists and the present author may be argued to be), see Amartya Sen, *Inequality Reexamined* (Cambridge, Mass.: Harvard University Press, 1992); and Partha Dasgupta, *An Inquiry into Well-Being and Destitution* (Oxford: Clarendon Press, 1993). In Sen's terms, poverty does not only matter by itself but also because it curtails capabilities that are essential for the choice of functionings compatible with the human condition. For a convergent philosophical discussion, see Charles Taylor, "What's Wrong with Negative Liberty?" *Philosophy and the Human Sciences: Philosophical Papers 2* (Cambridge: Cambridge University Press, 1985), pp. 211–29.

19. For recent discussion of these aspects, see Colin I. Bradford, Jr., ed., *Redefining the State in Latin America* (Paris: OECD, 1994), and Peter Evans, *Embedded Autonomy:*

States and Industrial Transformation (Princeton: Princeton University Press, 1995). [See also chapter 7 of the current book.—*Ed.*]

20. Moisés Naim, "Latin America: The Second Stage of Reform," *Journal of Democracy* 5 (no. 4, October 1994): 32–48.

21. Commenting on the sharp and generalized fall of social expenditures by the state in the 1980s, Cominetti says: ". . . by the end of the decade, the social expenditure indicators evinced a generalized deterioration, particularly in real per capita terms as well as in relation to GNP, showing that the deterioration did not correspond only to the fall in the level of economic activity but also to the orientation of the policies implemented" (Rosella Cominetti, "Gasto social y ajuste fiscal en América Latina" [Santiago de Chile: CEPAL, Proyecto Regional de Política Pública, 1994], p. 35) (translation by O'Donnell). For a more general picture on state employment, see Adriana Marshall, ed., *El empleo público frente a la crisis* (Geneva: Instituto Internacional de Estudios Laborales, 1990).

22. The classic study of these workers is Michael Lipsky, *Street-Level Bureaucracy: Dilemmas of the Individual in Public Services* (New York: Russell Sage Foundation, 1980), to whom the term italicized in the main text belongs. The concerns I express in the text do not preclude the possibility that, as Tendler and Freedheim show in the case of health policies in Ceará, Brazil, some successful programs may be devised and implemented (Judith Tendler and Sara Freedham, "Trust in a Rent-Seeking World: Health and Government Transformed in Northeast Brazil," *World Development* 22 (no. 12, December 1994): 1771–91. But this and other similar cases are, at least for the time being, no more than encouraging exceptions.

23. Or, for that matter, several cities in Britain, France, Italy, and Spain, even though poverty there is more recent and less extensive. For thoughtful discussions about the United States, see Isabel V. Sawhill, "Poverty in the US: Why Is It So Persistent?" *Journal of Economic Literature* 26 (no. 3, September 1988): pp. 1073–119, and Sheldon Danzinger and Peter Gottschalk, eds., *Uneven Tides: Rising Inequality in America* (New York: Russell Sage Foundation, 1993). William Julius Wilson stirred interesting controversies on this topic with *The Truly Disadvantaged: The Inner City, the Underclass, and Public Policy* (Chicago: University of Chicago Press, 1987) which are recapitulated in Wilson, "Another Look at 'The Truly Disadvantaged,'" *Political Science Quarterly* 106 (no. 4, 1991–92): pp. 639–56.

24. A recent assessment of the welfare state in OECD countries is in Gosta Esping-Andersen, "After the Golden Age: The Future of the Welfare State in the New Global Area" (Geneva: UNRISD Occasional Paper 7, 1994).

25. Altimir, "Development, Crisis and Equity."

26. Tokman, "Pobreza y homogenización," and Tokman, "Pobreza y equidad."

27. Others, like myself, have migrated to the center, not just partially, as in these ghettos, but entirely. From here we observe a situation of which we arguably are the worst example.

28. I write "most" because, after numerous studies in the highly developed countries, it seems clear that everywhere some pockets of permanent poverty remain, requiring specific interventions for alleviating its more damaging consequences, especially for children. But the Latin American rates of poverty and indigence go much beyond the small numbers and proportions implied by the metaphor of the 'pocket.'

29. The term "reasonable" is admittedly ambiguous. There is no way of establishing an objective and indisputable criterion of what would be an acceptable, or fair, degree of equality nor of deciding which of the various dimensions of equality should be given priority. See Douglas Rae, *Equalities* (Cambridge, Mass.: Harvard University Press, 1981).

30. As will be obvious to the reader, the source here is Albert O. Hirschman, *Journeys toward Progress: Studies of Economic Policy-Making in Latin America* (New York: Twentieth-Century Fund, 1963).

31. In this respect Chile is a notorious exception. But nothing guarantees that it would be so again, if unfortunately the occasion should arise.

32. For studies supporting the conditions stated in paragraphs 1 and 2, see, especially, Carlos H. Acuña and William C. Smith, "The Political Economy of Structural Adjustment: The Logic of Support and Opposition to Neoliberal Reform," in William C. Smith, Carlos H. Acuña, and Eduardo A. Gamarra, eds., *Latin American Political Economy in the Age of Neoliberal Reform: Theoretical and Comparative Perspectives for the 1990s* (London: Transaction Publishers, 1994), pp. 17–66; Catherine Conaghan and James Malloy, *Unsettling Statecraft: Democracy and Neoliberalism in the Central Andes* (Pittsburgh: University of Pittsburgh Press, 1994); and Albert Stepan, *Rethinking Military Politics: Brazil and the Southern Cone* (Princeton: Princeton University Press, 1988).

33. Caveat: in Peru Fujimori seems to have found a solution. If you carry out a coup that is openly supported by the military but still keep an elected president at the top, if the economic policies of the government are blessed by the domestic and international agents who matter, if you defeat one of the ugliest guerrilla movements in history, if the economy begins to grow at a fast pace, and if the same coup-president is reelected, then you can get away with the coup, even if congress and the judiciary are utterly subordinated to the executive, gross human violations continue, and the elections were not exactly immaculate (see the election reports in *LASA Forum* 26 [no. 2, 1995]: 9–20). In a similar, if bloodier, coup in a larger and geopolitically much more important country, Yeltsin got away with less than Fujimori.

34. To which the "Singapore argument" (or, until sometime ago, the oddly similar "Cuban argument") will hasten to retort that, with no constitutional democracy whatsoever, some populations enjoy much higher and widespread welfare than our democracies. Since our countries are far more likely to produce predatory authoritarian regimes than Singapore (and since the Pinochet regime is not a very good example in terms of poverty and inequality), this argument does not concern me here.

35. Joseph Schumpeter, *Capitalism, Socialism, and Democracy* (New York: Harper & Row, 1975 [1942]).

36. Although, admittedly, such an assertion can be, in certain contexts, a rhetorically persuasive argument.

37. But it should be noted that some comparative quantitative studies have found that income inequality (Muller, "Democracy, Economic Development") or poverty (Adam Przeworski and Fernando Limongi, "Modernization: Theories and Facts," Chicago Center for Democracy, University of Chicago, Working Paper 4, November 1994, multicopied) tend to negatively affect the likelihood of survival of democratic regimes.

38. The rule of law in our countries (or, rather its absence for vast sectors of the population) is a complicated and extremely important topic, which I cannot elaborate here. Interesting and eloquent analyses of some of these matters can be found in Sérgio Pinheiro and Malak El-Chichini Poppovic, "Poverty, Marginalization, Violence, and the Realization of Human Rights" (Geneva: United Nations World Conference on Human Rights, April 1993, multicopied) and Pinheiro, Poppovic, and Túlio Khan, "Pobreza, violência e direitos humanos," *Novos Estudos CEBRAP* 39 (July 1994): 189–208. For another, convergent, perspective, see Jonathan Fox, "The Difficult Transition from Clientelism to Citizenship," *World Politics* 46 (no. 2, January 1994): 151–84.

39. As one indication of these problems, a recent survey applied to 320 persons in top private and public positions in Brazil asked the following question: "In your opinion, what is the most important negative consequence of the increase in poverty in the large Brazilian cities?" (translation by O'Donnell). Of the interviewees, 65.3 percent gave answers that reflect how these problems impinge on their own lives: violence, crime, insecurity (51.4 percent); possibilities of social chaos (8.4 percent); and diminution of the quality of life for all (5.5 percent) (Elisa Reis and Zairo Cheibub, "Valores políticos das elites e consolidação democrática," *Dados* 38 [no. 1, 1995]: 31–56; see also Maria Regina Soares de Lima and Renato R. Boschi, "Democracia e reforma econômica: A visão das elites brasileiras," *Dados* 38 [no. 1, 1995]: 7–30).

40. In addition to the texts already cited, see Teresa Pires do Rio Caldeira, "City of Walls: Crime, Segregation, and Citizenship in São Paulo," Ph.D. Dissertation, Department of Anthropology, University of California, Berkeley, 1992.

41. An interesting thought experiment is to imagine the incredible disruptions that would be caused in well-to-do families by the disappearance of domestic laborers.

42. It is thought provoking, if disquieting, that in a comparative quantitative study Muller and Seligson found that inequality is the strongest negative factor in changes in the level (or quality, as I call it here) of democracy (Edward N. Muller and Mitchell A. Seligson, "Civic Culture and Democracy: The Question of Causal Relations," *American Political Science Review* 88 [no. 3, September 1994]: 635–52).

43. I concur with Carlos Filgueira ("América Latina: Tendencias") in his plea for devoting more attention and resources to basic studies of the present social structure of our countries. Various recent projects would have greatly benefited from the knowledge generated by the type of research C. Filgueira advocates. In particular, studies on the political correlates of adjustment programs that speculate about the classes or social sectors that are likely to support or oppose these programs make assumptions based on a social structure that is dated or about which they have no information (see, e.g., relevant chapters in John Williamson, ed., *The Political Economy of Policy Reform* [Washington, D.C.: Institute for International Economics, 1994]).

44. Among others, CEPAL, *Panorama social*; Diane Davis, "With Capital, Labor, or on Their Own? Middle Classes in the Economic Development of Latin America and East Asia" (New School for Social Research, Graduate Faculty of Political and Social Science, 1994, multicopied); Alvaro Díaz, "Tendencias en la reestructuración económica y social en América Latina," *Revista Mexicana de Sociología* 6 (no. 4, 1994): 3–35; Filgueira, "América Latina: Tendencias"; International Labor Organization, *World Employment 1995* (Geneva: ILO, 1995); Tokman, "Informalidad y pobreza"; and

Susana Torrado, *Estructura social de la Argentina 1945–1983* (Buenos Aires: Ediciones de la Flor, 1992).

45. For recent data on and discussion of this matter, see Tokman, "Pobreza y equidad."

46. John J. Johnson, *Political Change in Latin America: The Emergence of the Middle Sectors* (Stanford: Stanford University Press, 1958) is the classic statement. It may be worth noting that these conceptions strongly influenced the Alliance for Progress.

47. We saw that the social expenditures that, in general and often against stated policy goals, have benefited these layers more than the poor (education, housing, urban services, and some health services) have lately deteriorated in many of our countries. In addition to their loss of income, this diminution in their welfare goes a long way in making understandable the demands of these layers to receive preferential treatment from the state—and their, at least implicit, opposition to diverting resources to the poor (for a discussion of these issues, see Nelson, "Poverty"). Here lies another major political and intellectual challenge: devising pro-poor policies that would overcome or sidestep these obstacles. One clear but politically difficult way to advance in this direction would be to decrease the present reliance on regressive indirect taxes (especially value added ones) and emphasize direct taxes on income and wealth; see, especially, Borón, "La pobreza de las naciones."

48. I write "partially" because it would be a serious mistake to expect some kind of angelic consensus around these issues. Politics means both consensus and conflict; democratic politics peacefully processes, but does not cancel, conflict.

49. Given the high level of generality at which I placed myself in this paper, I cannot go further in the present discussion. In each country the possibilities as well as the modalities of the eventual emergence of such a coalition will be contingent on the pre-existing political allegiances of the popular and middle sectors and on the configuration of the respective party systems.

Books and Other Publications
by the Author

Books

Modernization and Bureaucratic-Authoritarianism. Institute of International Studies. Berkeley: University of California, 1972. Second edition, with new Postscript, 1979. Third edition, with new Preface, 1998.

Dependencia y Autonomía, with Delfina Linck. Buenos Aires: Amorrortu Editores, 1973.

Capitalism and Bureaucratic-Authoritarianism. (Korean), a selection of the author's writings by Sang Jin Han. Seoul: National University of Seoul, 1985.

Transitions from Authoritarian Rule: Prospects for Democracy, edited with Philippe Schmitter and Laurence Whitehead. 4 volumes. Baltimore and London: Johns Hopkins University Press, 1986.

Co-authored with Philippe Schmitter. *Tentative Conclusions about Uncertain Democracies.* Volume 4 of *Transitions from Authoritarian Rule.* Baltimore and London: Johns Hopkins University Press, 1986.

Development, Democracy, and the Art of Trespassing: Essays in Honor of Albert O. Hirschman, edited with Alejandro Foxley and Michael S. McPherson. Notre Dame, Ind.: University of Notre Dame Press, 1986.

Reflexões sobre os Estados Burocrático-Autoritários. São Paulo: Ed. Vértice, 1987.

A Democracia no Brasil: Dilemas e Perspectivas, edited with Fábio Wanderley Reis. São Paulo: Ed. Vértice, 1988.

Bureaucratic Authoritarianism: Argentina, 1966–1973, in Comparative Perspective. Berkeley: University of California Press, 1988.

Issues in Democratic Consolidation: The New South American Democracies in Comparative Perspective, edited with Scott Mainwaring and J. Samuel Valenzuela. Notre Dame, Ind.: University of Notre Dame Press, 1992.

Contributor to Adam Przeworski, editor and main author. *Sustainable Democracy*. New York: Cambridge University Press, 1995.

Poverty and Inequality in Latin America, edited with Víctor Tokman. Notre Dame, Ind.: University of Notre Dame Press, 1998.

The (Un)Rule of Law and the Underprivileged in Latin America, edited with Juan Méndez and Paulo Sérgio Pinheiro. Notre Dame, Ind.: University of Notre Dame Press, 1999.

Papers in Professional Journals and Chapters in Edited Books

"Integración latinoamericana: Un enfoque macropolítico." *La Ley* 2. Buenos Aires, 1965.

"Argentina, en crisis?" *Estudios CEDES* 3. Buenos Aires, 1966.

"Un juego imposible: Competición y coaliciones entre partidos en la Argentina." *Revista Latinoamericana de Sociología*. Buenos Aires, 1972.

"Democracia y desarrollo social." In Cándido Mendes, ed., *Indicadores del desarrollo social en Latinoamérica*. México, D.F.: Fondo de Cultura Económica, 1974.

"Modernization and Military Coups: Theory, Comparison, and the Argentine Case." In Abraham Lowenthal, ed., *Armies and Parties in Latin America*. New York: Holmes & Meier, 1976.

"Reflections on the Patterns of Change in the Bureaucratic-Authoritarian State." *Latin American Research Review* 13, no. 1, 1978.

"Corporatism and the Question of the State." In James Malloy, ed., *Authoritarianism and Corporatism in Latin America*. Pittsburgh: University of Pittsburgh Press, 1977. Second printing, 1979.

Co-authored with Oscar Oszlak. "Estado y políticas estatales en América Latina: Hacia una estrategia de investigación." *Documentos CEDES/CLACSO* 4. Buenos Aires, 1976.

Entries "Modernización" and "Populismo" for the *Diccionario de Ciencias Sociales*. UNESCO, Paris, 1977.

"Apuntes para una teoría del Estado." *Revista Mexicana de Sociología* 40, no. 4, 1978.

"Permanent Crisis and the Failure to Create a Democratic Regime: Argentina 1955–1966." In Juan Linz and Alfred Stepan, eds., *The Breakdown of Democratic Regimes: Latin America*. Baltimore and London: Johns Hopkins University Press, 1978.

"Notas para el estudio de la burguesía local, con especial referencia a sus vinculaciones con el capital transnacional y el aparato estatal." *Estudios CEDES* 12. Buenos Aires, 1978.

"State and Alliances in Argentina, 1956–1976." *Journal of Development Studies* 15, no. 1, 1979. [Chapter 1 in the current book—*Ed.*]

Co-authored with Roberto Frenkel. "The Stabilization Programs of the IMF and Their Internal Effects." In Richard Fagen, ed., *Capitalism and the State in the US-Latin American Relations.* Stanford: Stanford University Press, 1979.

"Tensions in the Bureaucratic-Authoritarian State and the Question of Democracy." In David Collier, ed., *The New Authoritarianism in Latin America.* Princeton: Princeton University Press, 1979. [Chapter 2 in the current book—*Ed.*]

"Notas para el estudio de procesos de democratización a partir del estado burocrático-autoritario." *Estudios CEDES* 2, no. 5. Buenos Aires, 1979. [Chapter 6 in the current book—*Ed.*]

"Desenvolvimento Político ou Mudança Política?" In Paulo Sérgio Pinheiro, ed., *O Estado Autoritário e os Movimentos Populares.* Rio de Janeiro: Ed. Paz e Terra, 1980.

"Comparative Historical Formations of the State Apparatus and Socio-Economic Change in the Third World." *International Social Science Journal* 32, no. 4. Paris, 1980.

"A Argentina Antes e um Pouco Depois das Malvinas." *Novos Estudos CEBRAP* 1, no. 4. São Paulo, 1982.

"La derecha sin votos, la paranoia del poder y el suicidio de la democracia." Buenos Aires, *El Porteño* 1, no. 12, December 1982.

"Argentina: La cosecha del miedo." *Nexos* 6, no. 61. México, D.F., 1983.

"Democracia en la Argentina: Micro y macro." In Oscar Oszlak, ed., *El "Proceso," crisis y transición democrática.* Buenos Aires: Centro Editor de América Latina, Biblioteca de Politica Argentina, 1984. [Chapter 3 in the current book—*Ed.*]

"Y a mí, qué me importa? Notas sobre sociabilidad y política en Argentina y Brasil." *Estudios CEDES,* Buenos Aires, 1984. [Chapter 5 in the current book—*Ed.*]

"External Debt: Why Don't Our Governments Do the Obvious?" *CEPAL Review* no. 27. Santiago, 1985.

"Latin America, The United States, and Democracy: Variations on a Very Old Theme." In Carlos Rico and Kevin Middlebrook, eds., *The United States and Latin America in the 1980s: Contending Perspectives on a Decade of Crisis.* Pittsburgh: University of Pittsburgh Press, 1986.

"On the Fruitful Convergences of Hirschman's *Exit, Voice, and Loyalty* and *Shifting Involvements.* Reflections from the Recent Argentine Experience." In Alejandro Foxley, Michael McPherson, and Guillermo O'Donnell, eds.,

Development, Democracy, and the Art of Trespassing. Notre Dame, Ind.: University of Notre Dame Press, 1986. [Chapter 4 in the current book—*Ed.*]

"Os Atores do Pacto Democratizante. Reflexões Sobre a Transição Brasileira." *A Transição Política. Necessidade e Limites da Negociação.* São Paulo: University of São Paulo, 1987.

"Brazil's Failure: What Future for Debtor's Cartels?" *Third World Quarterly* 9, no. 4, October 1987.

"Challenges to Democratization in Brazil: The Threat of a Slow Death." *World Policy Journal* 5, no. 2, Spring 1988.

"Situações: Microcenas da Privatização do Público em São Paulo." *Novos Estudos CEBRAP,* 22, October 1988.

"Hiatos, Instituições e Perspectivas Democráticas." In Guillermo O'Donnell and Fábio W. Reis, eds., *A Democracia no Brasil: Dilemas e Perspectivas.* São Paulo: Ed. Vértice, 1988.

"Transitions to Democracy: Some Navigation Instruments." In Robert A. Pastor, ed., *Democracy in the Americas: Stopping the Pendulum.* New York: Holmes & Meier, 1989.

"Argentina, de nuevo." *Novos Estudos CEBRAP,* no. 24, July 1989.

"Reflexões Comparativas sobre Políticas Públicas e Consolidação Democrática." In Alexandrina Sobreira de Moura, ed., *O Estado e as Políticas Públicas,* São Paulo: Ed. Vértice, 1989.

"East and South: Uncertain Democracies." In *Resurgence of Democracy and Market Economy.* Chicago: The Chicago Council of Foreign Relations, 1991.

"Transitions, Continuities, and Paradoxes." In Scott Mainwaring, Guillermo O'Donnell, and J. Samuel Valenzuela, eds., *Issues in Democratic Consolidation: The New South American Democracies in Comparative Perspective.* Notre Dame, Ind.: University of Notre Dame Press, 1992.

"Substantive or Procedural Consensus? Notes on the Latin American Bourgeoisie." In Douglas A. Chalmers, Maria do Carmo Campello de Souza, and Atilio A. Boron, eds., *The Right and Democracy in Latin America.* New York: Praeger, 1992.

"On the State, Democratization and Some Conceptual Problems: A Latin American View with Glances at Some Postcommunist Countries." *World Development* 21, no. 8, 1993, pp. 1355–69. [Chapter 7 in the current book—*Ed.*]

"Some Reflections on Redefining the Role of the State." In Colin I. Bradford, Jr., ed., *Redefining the State in Latin America.* Paris: OECD, 1994.

"Delegative Democracy." *Journal of Democracy* 5, no. 1, 1994. [Chapter 8 in the current book—*Ed.*]

"Do Economists Know Best?" *Journal of Democracy* 6, no. 1, 1995.

"Illusions about Consolidation." *Journal of Democracy* 7, no. 2, April 1996. [Chapter 9 in the current book—*Ed.*]

"Illusions and Conceptual Flaws." *Journal of Democracy* 7, no. 4, October 1996.

"Estado, democratización y globalización: Reflexiones introductorias." Montevideo: Interamerican Development Bank, November 1996.

"Poverty and Inequality in Latin America: Some Political Reflections." In Guillermo O'Donnell and Víctor Tokman, eds., *Poverty and Inequality in Latin America*. Notre Dame, Ind.: University of Notre Dame Press, 1998 [Chapter 10 in the current book—*Ed.*]

"Horizontal Accountability and New Polyarchies." In Andreas Schedler, Larry Diamond, and Mark Plattner, eds., *The Self-Restraining State: Power and Accountability in New Democracies*. Boulder and London: Lynne Rienner Publishers, 1999.

"Polyarchies and the (Un)Rule of Law in Latin America." In Juan Méndez, Guillermo O'Donnell, and Paulo Sérgio Pinheiro, eds., *The (Un)Rule of Law and the Underprivileged in Latin America*. Notre Dame, Ind.: University of Notre Dame Press, 1999.

Index